Praise for *The Psychotherapy Toolbox for Chronic Illness and Chronic Pain*

"As a licensed mental health counselor, I found Debra Burdick's *The Psychotherapy Toolbox for Chronic Illness and Chronic Pain* to be an invaluable, comprehensive guide for clinicians supporting clients living with long-term medical conditions. The book's integration of CBT, ACT, mindfulness, and pain reprocessing therapy offers both depth and practicality. I can immediately use the worksheets and assessments in session. Burdick's approach is compassionate, organized, and deeply grounded in evidence-based care. This resource belongs on the shelf of every therapist who works with clients navigating the emotional and physical challenges of chronic illness or chronic pain."

—Amanda Willse, LMHC

"*The Psychotherapy Toolbox for Chronic Illness and Chronic Pain* is a must-have resource for clinicians that effectively addresses the gap in practical, multifaceted strategies for the complex psychological challenges associated with chronic illness and pain. Its brilliance is showcased in the 77 skills that readily combine several approaches such as ACT, CBT, DBT, MI, and pain reprocessing therapy into this user-friendly tool kit. I strongly recommend Debra Burdick's latest publication; it is truly an essential edition to the clinician's toolbox."

—Bharati Shah Chakraborty, EdD, adjunct professor
and behavioral health clinician

"As a trauma therapist, I appreciate how *The Psychotherapy Toolbox for Chronic Illness and Chronic Pain* goes beyond symptom management to address the full humanity and experience of both client and clinician. Debra Burdick brings empathy, clarity, and structure to an often-overlooked area of mental health care. It's the kind of resource you'll return to again and again for practical interventions and grounded inspiration."

—Julia Israelski, LCSW, PMH-C

"*The Psychotherapy Toolbox for Chronic Illness and Chronic Pain* is a wonderful resource for therapists treating people with chronic illness of any type. It is practical, comprehensive, and very clearly written, addressing the needs of clients and practitioners together. Debra Burdick provides us with a step-by-step guide in helping clients build their own mind-body skills while demonstrating the importance of those skills in the healing process."

—Leo Galland, MD, author of *The Allergy Solution*

"As a physician, my focus is on performing procedures and other treatments for the patient's physical malady. Helpful or not, these actions do not address the patient's response to their disease or how they manage it. Debra Burdick's book, *The Psychotherapy Toolbox for Chronic Illness and Chronic Pain*, helps fill this void by providing clinicians with an excellent scaffolding, appropriate examples, and helpful tools to assist people with management of their condition as well as their responses to their situation. I highly recommend this book to all professionals that care for people with chronic disease states."

—**Paul E. Beebe, MD**, interventional pain management

"*The Psychotherapy Toolbox for Chronic Illness and Chronic Pain* is a fantastic resource. It is well-organized and comprehensive, and at the same time, clear and practical. It is chock-full of excellent information and skills that will help loads of people who suffer from chronic pain and illness."

—**Howard Schubiner, MD**, author of *Unlearn Your Pain* and clinical professor, Michigan State University College of Human Medicine

"*The Psychotherapy Toolbox for Chronic Illness and Chronic Pain* is a must-have for every clinician. The impacts of chronic pain and chronic illness affect more of our clients than we often realize, regardless of our specialty. Debra Burdick provides a wealth of practical, evidence-based skills and provides examples, reflection prompts, and handouts that translate easily into clinical practice. This book provides the tools to empower both therapist and client toward greater resilience and well-being. It's a resource I will return to again and again in my work."

—**Taylor M. Ham, LMFT**, author of *The Health Anxiety Workbook: Practical Exercises to Overcome Your Health Worries*

The Psychotherapy Toolbox for Chronic Illness & Chronic Pain

77 Skills to Support Clients' Physical & Emotional Well-Being

CBT • ACT • Mindfulness • Motivational
Interviewing • DBT • Positive Psychology
• Pain Reprocessing Therapy •
Mind-Body Medicine

Debra Burdick, LCSW

THE PSYCHOTHERAPY TOOLBOX FOR CHRONIC ILLNESS AND CHRONIC PAIN
Copyright © 2026 by Debra Burdick

Published by
PESI Publishing, Inc.
3839 White Ave
Eau Claire, WI 54703

Cover and interior design by Abby Isackson
Editing by Jenessa Jackson

ISBN 9781683738824 (print)
ISBN 9781683738831 (ePUB)
ISBN 9781683738848 (ePDF)

All rights reserved.
Printed in the United States of America.

Reproduction of the worksheets included in this book is highly encouraged for professional use with clients. All pages are copyrighted and permission to reproduce is only granted if the copyright information on each worksheet is included on the copy. Reproduction for all other purposes requires written permission from the author.

The information presented in this book is not intended to substitute for the advice of your medical doctor or your mental health professional. It is published with the understanding that the author is not engaged in rendering any medical or psychological advice. The author disclaims any liability whatsoever for individuals' use of any advice or information presented in the book.

PESI Publishing
pesipublishing.com

Table of Contents

Introduction

An estimated 60 percent of all adults in the US have a chronic illness, with over 40 percent having multiple chronic conditions (Buttorff et al., 2017), and more than 20 percent experience chronic pain (Rikard et al., 2023). A chronic illness is a condition that lasts at least one year and requires ongoing medical attention or limits activities of daily living (or both). Some chronic illnesses are considered incurable but may respond positively to treatment, become well managed, or go into remission. Examples include autoimmune diseases, diabetes, cancer, epilepsy, heart disease, HIV/AIDS, hypothyroidism, multiple sclerosis, neurocognitive disease, and long COVID. Chronic pain is defined as any pain that lasts or comes back for more than three months. Chronic pain isn't just ongoing acute pain, nor is it just pain that lingers. Rather, it's often accompanied by a mix of biological, physical, psychological, and social consequences. These can include a weakened immune system, impaired functioning, depression, decreased energy, and even job loss, all of which add to the burden of the person dealing with it.

In addition, chronic illness and pain inherently cause substantial losses to many aspects of a client's life, including loss of control, loss of function, loss of identity, loss of social contact, and loss of dignity. It is no surprise, therefore, that mental health issues often co-occur and intermingle with chronic medical conditions and pain. To best support our clients, we must address all of these issues, helping them to cope with the significant impact that chronic illness and pain can have on all areas of their life.

The Psychotherapy Toolbox for Chronic Illness and Chronic Pain provides therapists with the skills needed to help clients address all these issues. It is specifically designed to meet the needs of mental health practitioners and other helping professionals who want proven, evidence-based strategies for clients who experience chronic medical illness or pain. These skills are drawn from the fields of mindfulness, cognitive behavioral therapy (CBT), positive psychology, acceptance and commitment therapy (ACT), motivational interviewing, mind-body medicine, pain reprocessing therapy (PRP), and spirituality. They address the reality that each client copes with chronic illness and pain in their own way, and they honor and support self-efficacy by helping clients restore their physical, emotional, and spiritual well-being so they can function more easily throughout their illness or pain.

Within these pages, you'll find over 75 wide-ranging therapy skills, meditations, and affirmations divided into six main sections:

- **Section 1: Therapeutic Issues Specific to Working with Clients with Medical Illness.** These skills are designed to help you address therapist compassion fatigue and burnout, assess and track clients' symptoms, set goals for therapy, learn the interplay between physical and emotional symptoms, navigate options when clients are too ill to attend sessions, and more.

- **Section 2: Mental Health Skills.** You can use the skills in this section to promote greater physical and emotional healing by helping clients become more aware of how their illness is impacted by factors such as stress, thought patterns, and their past. Clients will learn how to shift their mindset, find more helpful thoughts, manage emotions, and grieve losses associated with their illness.

- **Section 3: Behavioral Health Skills.** These skills teach clients how to cope with and shift pain by adopting positive behaviors that promote physical and mental health. This includes eating, sleeping, and moving in a way that nourishes them, as well as resting when they are tired. It also includes strategies for working with the medical community and strengthening the client's social support system.

- **Section 4: Chronic Pain Skills.** This section will guide you to assess whether a client's pain is rooted in lingering physical damage or whether it has become neuroplastic pain—a type of pain that occurs when the brain continues to send out pain signals even though the original injury has resolved. You will also find skills to help the client manage pain and unlearn neuroplastic pain.

- **Section 5: Mind-Body-Spirit Skills.** These skills help clients identify their values, find ways to be of service, tap into the power of their spiritual and religious beliefs, access their intuition, and (when relevant) face their impending death.

- **Section 6: Positive Affirmations.** These positive affirmations reinforce the other skills in the book by providing clients with an opportunity to practice shifting their mindset and stay laser-focused on managing the thoughts, feelings, and behaviors that support their physical and emotional health.

Each skill contains five major components: background information on the skill, an example of the skill in action, an explanation of how to introduce the skill to clients, an opportunity for reflection, and accompanying worksheets or handouts, tailored either toward the clinician or client. I recommend starting with the skills in Section 1, which guide the assessment process, facilitate goal setting, and provide general information to help you adapt your treatment process when working with issues specific to chronic illness or pain. Although the skills in this book are organized in a logical progression, they can be used independently and in any order that makes sense for each particular client. Remember, every client responds to illness and pain in their own way. Use the skills as a starting point and modify them as you see fit for each client to align with your therapeutic approach.

As you progress through the skills, I recommend interspersing affirmations from Section 6 that coordinate with the particular skills. While each affirmation includes a space for client reflection, it's also useful to explore what specific changes the client notices in their life as they incorporate affirmations into their day. There is sound research showing that affirmations can actually change the brain in positive ways (Cascio et al., 2016), so each affirmation is a powerful way to reinforce and consolidate the progress made from incorporating the skills in the rest of the book.

You can find a free PDF of the worksheets and handouts, which you can download and print for your use with clients, at www.pesipubs.com/chronicillnesspain. You can also find the guided audio meditations that accompany some of the skills at www.thebrainlady.com/pesi-meditations.

As you use these skills in your practice, I would love to hear how they have helped your clients deal more effectively with chronic illness or pain. I am grateful to my own clients, who have shown me again and again how these skills can improve their lives.

Therapeutic Issues Specific to Working with Clients with Chronic Medical Illness or Chronic Pain

Skill 1.1 Compassion Fatigue and Burnout

Background: This skill appears first in this book for good reason. It is essential to take care of yourself in order to be able to effectively help your clients. Mental health providers are already at risk for compassion fatigue and burnout, and working with clients who have chronic illness or chronic pain can make this much worse. Because chronic illness and chronic pain are just that—chronic—the issues tend to persist, and therapeutic progress can be slow. This can lead you to experience emotional exhaustion, become detached from your work, and feel a sense of ineffectiveness with your clients. This skill provides a checklist that you can use to recognize and prevent symptoms of compassion fatigue and burnout. It also provides a list of self-care skills that can help to improve it.

The Skill in Action: *Allison had been working with two clients who were particularly challenging. One had cancer and the other had chronic pain. Allison was a very effective, kind, and compassionate helper who loved working with clients, but she noticed that lately she was feeling exhausted and beginning to dread sessions with these clients. She often felt like nothing she said was making any difference. The reality is that she was experiencing secondhand trauma, first when the client with chronic pain told her about the accident that triggered their symptoms, and then when the client with cancer told her about the scary, painful medical procedures they had to endure.*

Allison recognized that she was experiencing some signs of compassion fatigue, so she discussed it in her supervision group and with her personal therapist. When she discussed the progress that each client was making with her group, she realized they had both made significant gains in their ability to manage their illness and pain. She explored options for dealing with her secondhand trauma with her therapist. She also became more mindful of taking time to rest and rejuvenate. She started meditating on a more regular basis, set up a regular massage appointment, and restarted walking daily. She soon started feeling more like herself.

Skill Building: Print out and periodically review Clinician Worksheet 1.1.1: *Compassion Fatigue and Burnout Checklist* to stay on top of how your work with clients may be impacting you. Then review the self-care skills on Clinician Handout 1.1.2 and incorporate as many skills as needed to prevent compassion fatigue and burnout or to repair it if it is present. Use this skill right now and return to it often!

Reflection: Did you discover that you have some symptoms of compassion fatigue and burnout? If yes, how can you use the skills in Clinician Handout 1.1.2 to decrease these symptoms? If no, how can you use the self-care skills to prevent it? Which self-care skills are you already using? Which ones do you want to add to your daily routine? How can you use the symptom checklist and self-care skills to continue monitoring and taking care of yourself?

Compassion Fatigue and Burnout Checklist*

Complete this checklist periodically to notice if you are experiencing symptoms of compassion fatigue or burnout.

- ☐ **Emotional exhaustion.** This goes above and beyond physical exhaustion. You may feel emotionally worn out, drained, depleted, unmotivated, or reluctant to go to work.

- ☐ **Difficulty concentrating** and focusing on tasks. Notice if you are less able to be totally present with clients in session or if you are having trouble focusing or remembering what was previously discussed.

- ☐ **Anxiety and sadness** that may globalize and impact all aspects of your life.

- ☐ **Anger and irritability.** You may notice you have less patience than usual or that you feel annoyed with clients instead of compassionate. This can show up in other areas of your life as well.

- ☐ **Decreased empathy** with the issues your client presents with, especially with issues you would typically empathize with.

- ☐ **Feelings of helplessness and powerlessness.** Be aware if you start to feel that nothing you do or say matters or makes any difference.

- ☐ **Feelings of inadequacy**, especially concerning your work with clients whose chronic illness or pain isn't getting better.

- ☐ **Emotional numbing.** This involves feeling flat, distant, or detached from your emotions and from others. Notice how you are feeling in session.

- ☐ **Physical symptoms** like sleep disturbances, headaches, changes in appetite, and stomach issues.

- ☐ **Lack of motivation.** In burnout, this may include not wanting to go to work.

- ☐ **Loss of pleasure** in activities you once enjoyed. This can also be a sign of depression.

---

* Adapted from Mosunic (n.d.).

- ❑ **Withdrawal from social activities.** Notice if you are less interested in socializing or connecting with others, which often goes alongside losing pleasure in activities you used to enjoy.

- ❑ **Increased sensitivity to trauma.** Notice how you feel when hearing about your clients' trauma. Go within and notice if you are experiencing a heightened stress response.

- ❑ **Fear of the future,** which is also called anticipatory anxiety. Do you feel worried or even panicky about the future? Is the level of your worry unrealistic? Are you having trouble focusing or sleeping? Are you feeling restless or tense?

- ❑ **Questioning the meaning of life.** Do you find yourself wondering what it all means or asking yourself, *Why bother?* Do you feel lost?

Copyright © 2026 Debra Burdick, *The Psychotherapy Toolbox for Chronic Illness and Chronic Pain*. All rights reserved.

Self-Care to Counter Compassion Fatigue and Burnout*

Explore ways you can incorporate self-care into your life to prevent or reduce compassion fatigue and burnout. Print out this list and post it where you can see it regularly to remind you to take care of yourself.

- Set good **boundaries** by looking at your current work-life balance and making changes as needed. Establish working hours and personal time hours. Limit (or better yet, eliminate) after-hours work or phone calls by setting phone hours. Coordinate off-hours coverage. Schedule time off on a regular basis.

- Use **breathing techniques** throughout the day as a quick, effective way to manage stress and anxiety. Use a relaxation breath: Breathe in through your nose to the count of 4 while allowing your belly to expand. Then breathe out through your mouth to the count of 8 and feel your belly contract. This calms the body by activating the parasympathetic nervous system.

- Incorporate **mindfulness** into your day to stay anchored in the present moment and reduce feelings of overwhelm. This can include mindful breathing, meditation, mindful eating, and yoga, all of which can help you feel grounded and build a sense of calm while meeting the challenges of helping your clients.

- Make **self-care** a priority by regularly scheduling time for activities that you enjoy and that rejuvenate you, such as being in nature, pursuing hobbies, or getting a massage. Make a list of these activities and add them to your calendar.

- **Exercise regularly.** Exercise can help you clear your head, improve your mood, and energize you. Pick the form of exercise that you enjoy the most and add it to your calendar. Use Skill 3.8: *Keep Moving* to help you add exercise to your life.

- Make sure you get enough **sleep**. Pay attention to how much sleep you need to feel your best. Experts recommend between 7 to 9 hours per night.

_____

* Adapted from Mosunic (n.d.).

Copyright © 2026 Debra Burdick, *The Psychotherapy Toolbox for Chronic Illness and Chronic Pain*. All rights reserved.

Use good sleep hygiene practices to improve your ability to fall asleep and wake up at the same time each day. See Skill 3.7: *Sleep Hygiene* for guidance on prioritizing sleep.

- Connect with others for **support**. Do not try to do this work alone! Reach out to your professional colleagues, join a relevant support group, participate in a supervision group, and attend personal therapy sessions.

- Decrease sources of **stress**. Step back and make a list of the stressors in your life. Then take action to reduce or eliminate those that you can. See Skill 2.2: *De-Stress* for ideas on lowering your stress load.

- Take time for **self-reflection**. Practice what you teach others. Spend time reflecting inward and processing your own feelings about your work and life. Journal about your day and take time to list things you are grateful for. Notice things you want to change. Become aware of what you need to nurture yourself.

 Copyright © 2026 Debra Burdick, *The Psychotherapy Toolbox for Chronic Illness and Chronic Pain*. All rights reserved.

Skill 1.2 Assessment

Background: A client with a chronic medical illness or chronic pain may present with a variety of mental health symptoms. In fact, their presenting problem is often not chronic illness or chronic pain. Instead, they may present for help with depression, anxiety, anger, frustration, or even substance abuse that stems from their illness or pain. In addition, chronic pain may originate from a traumatic event such as a car accident, physical or sexual assault, or some type of disaster, so clients may present with symptoms of posttraumatic stress disorder (PTSD) as well. Although estimates vary, upward of 35 percent of people with chronic pain also have PTSD (Siqveland et al., 2017). Research has consistently shown a bidirectional relationship between chronic illness and mental health conditions, with each influencing the other (Fiorillo et al., 2023). In addition to your typical mental health assessment, the following assessment can help you determine whether a client has chronic illness or chronic pain and, if so, the extent to which it is impacting their overall mental health and functioning.

The Skill in Action: *Although Andy initially presented for treatment with symptoms of depression, it became clear upon further investigation that his chronic neuropathy in both feet was impacting his ability to function in many areas. For example, it interrupted his sleep, kept him from working on his tree farm (and thus impacted his income), and interfered with his concentration and mood. He also experienced unpleasant cognitive side effects from the medication prescribed for his pain. He didn't realize how much of his depression was stemming from his chronic pain and his many losses related to it. He just knew he needed help with depression. His therapist was able to help him better understand how his symptoms of depression were connected to his pain and then explore options for dealing with the pain, acknowledging and accepting the triggers for depression, and then improving his mood.*

Skill Building: Use the checklists provided in Client Worksheet 1.2.1: *Assessment for Chronic Illness* and Client Worksheet 1.2.2: *Assessment for Chronic Pain* to assess whether a client has chronic illness or chronic pain along with how it impacts their life and mental health. You can either ask your client to fill out the checklists on their own or do it with them. Review their answers as a way to explore how their pain or illness is affecting various aspects of their life and their mental health.

If they report having either a chronic illness or chronic pain, contact their medical providers (with a proper release of information) to better understand what they are dealing with and how it may impact their mental health. Make sure to include a substance abuse assessment if they disclose using drugs or alcohol so you can determine whether they are misusing prescription medications or self-medicating. I also recommend assessing for the presence of illness anxiety disorder and somatic symptom disorder, which are commonly comorbid with chronic illness or chronic pain (American Psychiatric Association, 2022). If chronic pain is present, refer to Skill 4.1: *Assess Pain Type* to determine the appropriate pain management skills for the client's pain type.

Reflection: Ask your client what it was like for them to complete the checklists. Explore whether doing so gave them new insights into how their chronic pain or illness impacts the various areas of their life. What are they having the most difficulty with and what do they feel they need the most help with? Incorporate this information into the findings from your typical mental health assessment. This information can then be used when you are formulating treatment goals in Skill 1.3: *Defining Treatment Goals.*

Assessment for Chronic Illness

Please rate how often these statements are true for you. Use this rating scale:

0................................5................................10

Never   Sometimes   Always

Do you have a chronic illness?

_____ I have been diagnosed with a chronic illness.

_____ I have symptoms of chronic illness that have not been diagnosed.

_____ I have had symptoms of illness for more than a year.

_____ My illness limits my ability to perform activities of daily living.

_____ My illness requires ongoing medical care.

If so, how do you feel about your chronic illness?

_____ I'm not adjusting well to my illness.

_____ I cannot accept my illness.

_____ I worry about my health.

_____ I think about my illness a lot.

_____ I worry that I will never feel better.

_____ I feel angry about being ill.

_____ I feel scared.

_____ I feel depressed.

_____ I am afraid I will die.

_____ I feel stressed.

_____ I feel out of control.

_____ I search for answers online a lot.

Copyright © 2026 Debra Burdick, *The Psychotherapy Toolbox for Chronic Illness and Chronic Pain*. All rights reserved.

_____ I've tried a lot of things to heal.

_____ I don't feel like doing things I used to enjoy.

_____ I'm frustrated.

_____ I want to fix my health.

_____ I feel lost.

_____ I don't feel like myself anymore.

_____ I don't know who I am.

_____ I hate asking for help.

_____ I feel like dying.

How does chronic illness impact your life?

_____ I cannot work anymore.

_____ I can work part time.

_____ My primary love relationship has been negatively impacted.

_____ I cannot enjoy activities like I used to.

_____ I have trouble sleeping.

_____ I don't have my usual energy.

_____ My illness affects how I look.

_____ My concentration has decreased.

_____ I think about my illness a lot.

_____ I have trouble being a good parent.

_____ My friends don't understand.

_____ My friends and family are tired of me talking about my symptoms.

_____ I need help doing things I used to do.

_____ I am having trouble financially.

Copyright © 2026 Debra Burdick, _The Psychotherapy Toolbox for Chronic Illness and Chronic Pain_. All rights reserved.

_____ My sexual pleasure has decreased.

_____ I self-medicate with substances such as drugs or alcohol.

What is your experience with medical providers?

_____ My providers don't take good care of me.

_____ I don't trust my providers.

_____ My health concerns have been dismissed by a medical provider.

_____ I have been told my symptoms are all in my head.

_____ My provider doesn't listen.

_____ My provider doesn't answer my questions.

_____ I have been discounted because of my gender.

_____ My health concerns have been discounted due to my age.

_____ I'm frustrated by how long it takes to get an appointment.

_____ My provider orders too many tests.

_____ My provider gives me medications that have unacceptable side effects.

Copyright © 2026 Debra Burdick, *The Psychotherapy Toolbox for Chronic Illness and Chronic Pain*. All rights reserved.

Assessment for Chronic Pain

Please rate how often these statements are true for you. Use this rating scale:

0..5.........................……….10

Never   Sometimes   Always

Do you have chronic pain?

_____ I have experienced chronic pain for more than 3 months.

_____ I have been diagnosed with chronic pain by a medical provider.

_____ Chronic pain interferes with my ability to function.

_____ My pain started after a traumatic event.

If so, how do you feel about the pain?

_____ I worry about my pain.

_____ I worry that I will never feel better.

_____ I feel angry about being in pain.

_____ I feel scared.

_____ I feel depressed.

_____ I feel stressed.

_____ I am afraid I will die.

_____ I feel guilty.

_____ I don't feel like doing things I used to enjoy.

_____ I'm frustrated.

_____ I feel out of control.

_____ I don't laugh as much as I used to.

_____ I've tried a lot of things to fix my pain.

 Copyright © 2026 Debra Burdick, _The Psychotherapy Toolbox for Chronic Illness and Chronic Pain_. All rights reserved.

_____ I search for solutions online.

_____ I try to push through it.

_____ I feel lost.

_____ I feel like dying.

_____ I don't feel the same way about myself with this pain.

_____ I don't know who I am.

_____ I feel exhausted.

How does chronic pain impact your life?

_____ I cannot work anymore.

_____ I can only work part time.

_____ My primary love relationship has been negatively impacted.

_____ I cannot enjoy activities like I used to.

_____ Pain keeps me awake at night or disturbs my sleep.

_____ I don't have my usual energy.

_____ Pain interferes with my concentration.

_____ I think about my pain a lot.

_____ I have trouble being a good parent.

_____ I don't have much of a social life.

_____ Pain limits my ability to participate in everyday activities.

_____ Pain interferes with my relationships.

_____ Pain interferes with my ability to work.

_____ Pain impacts my income.

_____ Pain impacts my sex life.

_____ I use prescription medications or drugs and alcohol to manage pain.

Copyright © 2026 Debra Burdick, *The Psychotherapy Toolbox for Chronic Illness and Chronic Pain*. All rights reserved.

What is your experience with medical providers?

_____ My providers don't take good care of me.

_____ I don't trust my providers.

_____ My pain concerns have been dismissed by a medical provider.

_____ I have been told my symptoms are all in my head.

_____ My provider doesn't listen.

_____ My health concerns have been discounted because of my gender.

_____ My concerns about my pain have been discounted due to my age.

_____ I'm frustrated by how long it takes to get an appointment.

_____ My provider orders too many tests.

_____ My provider gives me medications that have unacceptable side effects.

 Copyright © 2026 Debra Burdick, _The Psychotherapy Toolbox for Chronic Illness and Chronic Pain_. All rights reserved.

Skill 1.3 Defining Treatment Goals

Background: Defining treatment goals is important for several reasons. First, it allows the client to set intentions for what they'd like to achieve in therapy. Second, it provides clarity and structure for the work to be done in session, as well as a way to monitor progress throughout treatment. Third, most managed care companies require it. With that in mind, this section guides you through the process of defining treatment goals related to chronic illness and chronic pain.

The Skill in Action: *Edie entered therapy when her doctor told her that her pain was now chronic and, despite no evidence of tissue or nerve damage, probably wasn't going to get better. She felt devastated by the thought that the intense pain she experienced 24/7 was going to persist for the rest of her life. She just couldn't believe it!*

At first, Edie wasn't really sure how therapy could help her. With her therapist, she clarified her goals for treatment. First, she wanted to learn to accept the pain and manage the symptoms. This included finding ways to decrease her pain levels and change her relationship with pain. Second, she wanted to determine whether the pain was neuroplastic (i.e., the result of oversensitized pain processing in her brain). Third, she wanted help with her tendency to spend hours on the internet looking up articles about pain and possible treatment options, as this often kept her from being present for her family. And fourth, she wanted help improving her mood and sleep. Edie noticed that she felt a sense of hope after defining her treatment goals. As therapy progressed, her therapist referred to these goals often and kept her on track to achieving them.

Skill Building: To begin, ask the client how they will know whether working with you has helped them. This will assist them in defining their treatment goals and clarifying their expectations for treatment. You can get more specific by asking them to list five to ten goals that they would like to achieve or symptoms they would like to improve. Some clients are extremely tuned in to what they need help with, while others will need help with this task. Refer to Client Handout 1.3: *Sample Treatment Goals for Chronic Illness and Chronic Pain* for examples of treatment goals. Many of these sample goals are correlated with a skill provided in this book. Feel free to use these sample goals as a starting point and adapt them to your client's unique situation.

You can use what you discovered from the assessment checklists in Skill 1.2 when defining a client's treatment goals. For example, if they checked off "I am afraid I will die" on the previous checklists, three goals to address this fear might be (1) explore fear of dying, (2) identify triggers for this fear, and (3) learn three ways to calm fear. Similarly, if they reported "My medical provider doesn't listen," a goal for increasing self-efficacy might be to explore options for representing themselves with their practitioners or for finding a practitioner who listens to them and answers their questions.

Clients with chronic illness or pain often have an overwhelming number of issues to work on, so it is important to help them prioritize their goals and start with those that are within your scope of practice and that will positively impact their lives the most. This will help them stay motivated and moving forward. Keep in mind that goals may change as treatment progresses—and they probably will, especially as a client masters a skill, in which case the goal can be revised to a more advanced goal.

Reflection: How was it helpful for the client to clarify what they hope to improve or achieve in treatment? Did doing so bring up any emotions, such as sadness, frustration, annoyance, or loss? Are their expectations realistic? Encourage them to update these goals periodically as they gain mastery. How does having a list of sample treatment goals help you with this process? What other goals can you add to the sample goals list that will help your clients in the future?

Sample Treatment Goals for Chronic Illness and Chronic Pain

Mental Health Treatment Goals

- Identify my feelings about illness and pain

- Improve my mood

- Decrease anxiety

- Identify and eliminate or limit sources of stress

- Learn relaxation techniques to calm and de-stress

- Identify unhelpful thoughts and "change the channel" to more helpful thoughts (Skill 2.3)

- Identify thought patterns often associated with chronic pain and illness

- Identify losses incurred due to illness or pain

- Identify and process feelings of loss associated with illness and pain

- Find purpose and meaning after losses incurred due to illness or pain

- Identify things that need to change to better manage my pain or illness

- Use visualization exercises to imagine wellness (Skill 3.9)

- Explore options for letting go of thoughts and feelings that no longer serve me

- Improve my ability to be mindful of my emotions

- Identify, explore, and release past traumas

- Identify and reduce behaviors related to any secondary gain that I get from pain or illness, such as getting others to do things I could do myself (Skill 2.10)

- Improve my ability to stay calm during medical tests and procedures

- Incorporate laughter into my day to release stress and pain

Copyright © 2026 Debra Burdick, *The Psychotherapy Toolbox for Chronic Illness and Chronic Pain*. All rights reserved.

- Learn and practice radical acceptance

- Identify the impact of my illness or pain on relationships and explore options for improving relationships

Behavioral Health Treatment Goals

- Improve my ability to work effectively with the medical community

- Explore options for getting an accurate medical diagnosis

- Identify who belongs on my "healing team" and create the team

- Improve my ability to advocate for myself with my medical providers

- Explore alternative treatment options

- Explore options for improving my diet to promote healing

- Improve my ability to get restful sleep

- Explore options for incorporating physical exercise that I am able to do

- Improve my ability to set mindful limits that prevent me from overdoing it

- Do a body scan (or a progressive muscle relaxation or a guided meditation) to promote relaxation and healing

- Explore options for preventing and managing exhaustion

- Identify and replace self-sabotaging behaviors (e.g., doing too much, abusing alcohol, skipping medications, missing medical appointments) with more adaptive behaviors (e.g., asking for help, using my calendar and alarm to remind me to take medications and attend appointments)

- Identify things that need to change (e.g., my work situation, the people I spend time with, doing things I love to do in moderation that I stopped doing)

- Explore options for eliminating substance abuse

Chronic Pain Treatment Goals

- Schedule a medical assessment to rule out tissue or nerve damage as the cause for my pain

- Identify trauma or emotional stress that was present at pain onset

 Copyright © 2026 Debra Burdick, *The Psychotherapy Toolbox for Chronic Illness and Chronic Pain*. All rights reserved.

- **When pain is the result of tissue damage:**

    - Listen to a guided meditation to manage pain

    - Learn and use options to distract myself from pain

    - Do a progressive muscle relaxation for pain

    - Identify thought patterns during pain and explore more helpful alternative thoughts

    - Identify and explore complementary therapies for pain (e.g., neurofeedback, massage, physical therapy)

- **When pain is neuroplastic:**

    - Identify options to change my relationship to pain

    - Explore options to reframe my understanding of the pain as being an oversensitized brain

    - Increase tolerance for pain symptoms

    - Use positive affirmations for neuroplastic pain

    - Use visual imagery to label pain as "just thoughts" or "just sensations"

    - Explore thought patterns associated with pain

    - Identify and explore emotions triggered by pain

    - Use graded exposure to increase tolerance for pain

Mind-Body-Spirit

- Define my reasons to live (Skill 5.3)

- Make a list of things I need help with, who can help, and when I will ask them

- Find a support group for people with my illness

- Find a way to help others

- Write and recite my personal healing prayer every day

- Practice a healing meditation (Skill 5.6)

Copyright © 2026 Debra Burdick, *The Psychotherapy Toolbox for Chronic Illness and Chronic Pain*. All rights reserved.

Skill 1.4 Tracking Progress

Background: Tracking client progress is helpful for several reasons. First, it keeps the therapy focused on the treatment goals you've identified. Second, it provides a way for you and the client to track improvement and monitor symptoms as your work together progresses. Third, it provides a way to assess the effectiveness of treatment and modify treatment as needed. Clients are typically more invested in the treatment when they can see their progress, and they often enjoy watching their ratings improve. This is especially true with chronic illness and pain, where progress may be slower. This skill provides a technique for tracking symptoms and monitoring treatment goals. It will also provide a way to know when the time has come to update treatment goals.

The Skill in Action: *Pam often felt overwhelmed dealing with her heart disease. Between going to doctors' visits, keeping track of her medications, working, cooking healthier meals, and being short of breath, she was often exhausted. Her therapist helped her list and prioritize goals she hoped to achieve in treatment. Pam breathed a sigh of relief once she narrowed her goals down to five things she could focus on to set better limits, even out her energy levels, ask for help with setting up her medications and grocery shopping, and advocate more effectively for herself with her cardiologist. She knew once she met these goals, she could add others from her list.*

Skill Building: Ask clients to rate the severity of each of their symptoms on a scale of 0 to 10 (where 0 is "no problem" and 10 is "the worst it could be"). Depending on the client's level of self-awareness, they may be able to attach a pretty accurate number to each symptom and notice how it changes over time. Seeing their progress inspires hope and motivation for continuing the changes clients are making. List these symptoms in the left-hand column of Client Worksheet 1.4: *Client Symptom Rating Chart*. Each week, ask the client to provide an updated rating of their symptoms. The goal is to lower the rating on each symptom and the overall total as treatment progresses. You can modify goals as symptoms improve and goals are met. A sample worksheet has been provided for you, followed by a blank rating form.

Although most clients find this process easy, a few do not. Some clients may have trouble quantifying their symptoms with a number. They may find it easier to describe the qualitative changes they are noticing. That's okay. If possible, use this information to rate their symptoms yourself. Or skip the numeric rating and keep a log of changes they report. In addition, there may be situations where it is appropriate to ask a significant other, family member, or close friend to help with symptom rating if the client is unable to do so or seems to have a very different view of their symptom levels.

Reflection: Was the client able to rate their symptoms? How accurate do their symptom ratings appear? Would it make sense to ask a family member for their input if the client wants this? How has tracking their symptoms helped the client increase self-awareness and improve their focus on treatment goals? If their symptoms are not improving, how can you change your treatment approach or teach them other skills that are more effective for them?

Sample Worksheet 1.4

Client Symptom Rating Chart

Please rate the severity of each symptom on a scale of 0 to 10 (0 = no problem, 10 = the worst it could be).

Symptom	Date			
	01/05	01/12	01/19	01/26
Depression	10	10	9	8
Fear of medical procedures	10	8	7	5
Hyperfocus on illness	8	8	6	4
Feeling stressed	9	8	9	6
Doing too much	8	8	7	7
Discounted by doctor	9	9	8	6
Anger	7	6	6	4
Eating junk food	10	8	8	3
Impact of trauma	8	8	6	8
Conflict with spouse	8	8	7	8
Total Score	87	81	73	59

Symptom	Date	
	First Date	End Date
Depression	10	8
Fear of medical procedures	10	5
Hyperfocus on illness	8	4
Feeling stressed	9	6
Doing too much	8	7
Discounted by doctor	9	6
Anger	7	4
Eating junk food	10	3
Impact of trauma	8	8
Conflict with spouse	8	8
Total Score	87	59

Copyright © 2026 Debra Burdick, *The Psychotherapy Toolbox for Chronic Illness and Chronic Pain*. All rights reserved.

Client Worksheet 1.4

Client Symptom Rating Chart

Please rate the severity of each symptom on a scale of 0 to 10 (0 = no problem, 10 = the worst it could be).

Symptom	Date										
Total Score											

Symptom	Date	
	First Date	**End Date**
Total Score		

Copyright © 2026 Debra Burdick, *The Psychotherapy Toolbox for Chronic Illness and Chronic Pain*. All rights reserved.

Skill 1.5 Client Self-Advocacy

Background: For clients with chronic illness or chronic pain, self-advocacy involves taking control over their lives and their health care. It includes being assertive with health care providers, stating their preferences, being willing to challenge medical authority, and actively participating in their health care. However, many clients with chronic illness and pain have difficulty advocating for themselves, as their ability to speak up for themselves diminishes when they don't feel well or don't have the energy to do so. This skill provides a checklist for clients to rate their ability to advocate for themselves and helps them practice writing "I" statements they can use to represent themselves at home, at work, and when interacting with medical providers.

The Skill in Action: *Elaine had fibromyalgia and sometimes felt so ill she needed to stay upstairs in bed for several hours or more. She felt angry and neglected when her husband wouldn't come up to check on her or see if she needed anything. She was often thirsty or hungry or simply wanted some company. She was eventually able to tell her husband, "When I am upstairs in bed and in too much pain to go downstairs, I would really appreciate it if you would come up and check on me at least once per hour." Her husband responded warmly, "Oh, of course I can do that. I'd assumed you wanted to be alone left alone like I do when I feel ill." Problem solved!*

Skill Building: Explain to your client why it is important for them to self-advocate when they are ill or in pain. Ask them to use Client Worksheet 1.5.1: *Self-Advocacy* to rate the extent to which they feel they can speak up for themselves and to identify what areas might need improvement. Explain that the preferred way to self-advocate is to use "I" statements, as shown in the checklist. Then present them with Client Worksheet 1.5.2: *Advocate for Myself* and ask them to identify some things they want or need on the worksheet. Once they have done so, ask them to pick something they listed and write exactly how they will advocate for themselves, including what they need help with, who they will ask, and what they will say to that person. Refer to Skill 3.1: *Working with the Medical Community* for specific way clients can advocate for themselves with the medical community.

Reflection: Explore what areas, if any, in which the client has trouble with self-advocacy. Discuss how the client was able to advocate for themselves in a new way and how doing so worked out for them. In what other areas does the client need to improve when it comes to self-advocacy? How has improved self-advocacy impacted their experience with illness or pain?

Self-Advocacy

Self-advocacy is being able to communicate your needs, ask for what you want, and represent yourself. Rate how true each statement is for you using a scale of 0 to 10, where 0 = never true and 10 = always true.

_____ I feel comfortable asking for what I want.

_____ I am not afraid to ask for help.

_____ I tell my medical provider what I need help with.

_____ I get my needs met.

_____ I can problem-solve.

_____ I can research my illness and treatment options.

_____ I make decisions about what treatment options I want.

_____ I speak up for myself in awkward situations.

_____ I am comfortable making my own decisions.

_____ I feel confident asking people such as my spouse and my doctor for what I want.

_____ I feel comfortable telling my doctor about unpleasant side effects of treatment or medications.

_____ I can make eye contact when asking for what I need.

_____ I know my rights as a patient.

_____ I can choose another medical provider if my current one doesn't listen to me.

_____ I use "I" statements to ask for what I need or want.

 Copyright © 2026 Debra Burdick, *The Psychotherapy Toolbox for Chronic Illness and Chronic Pain*. All rights reserved.

Advocate for Myself

Use this worksheet to practice coming up with "I" statements that you can use to get your needs met at home, at work, or with health care providers. To begin, identify some of your needs, wants, likes, or dislikes:

1. I need help with _____.

2. I want you to _____.

3. I choose _____.

4. I need _____.

5. I like _____.

6. I don't like _____.

7. I want _____.

Now pick something you listed and write down exactly how you will advocate for yourself, including what you need help with, who you will ask, what you will say, and when you will approach them. Remember to use "I" statements. Here are some examples to help you get started:

- *Example 1:* "I need help with mopping the floor because doing so hurts too much. I will ask my spouse for help with this and maybe we can get a cleaning person. I will ask them tonight."

- *Example 2:* "I don't like taking this medication because it makes me ache all over. I would like to try a different medication that treats the same issue without this side effect. I will call my doctor's office tomorrow and explain this."

_____

_____

_____

_____

_____

_____

Copyright © 2026 Debra Burdick, *The Psychotherapy Toolbox for Chronic Illness and Chronic Pain*. All rights reserved.

Skill 1.6 The Interplay Between Mental and Physical Illness

Background: Mental and physical illnesses are inextricably intertwined, with numerous studies showing that physical health contributes to mental health and vice versa (Luo et al., 2020). Although it is not within your scope of practice as a therapist to diagnose or treat medical illness, it is necessary to be aware of two important issues: (1) how a client's mental health can influence their ability to successfully deal with medical illness and (2) how the process of dealing with a medical illness can cause a variety of mental health symptoms, especially depression, anxiety, panic attacks, and anger. Therefore, when a mental health issue co-occurs with, or is caused by, a medical illness, it is imperative to help the client with the mental health issue. This skill helps you understand how various mental health diagnoses impact how clients deal with chronic illness or pain.

The Skill in Action: *Lily was having trouble managing her adult-onset diabetes. She had been diagnosed with attention-deficit/hyperactivity disorder (ADHD) years before, and she often forgot to take her insulin as scheduled and ate foods that increased her blood sugar, despite knowing the risks of doing so. Her therapist helped her explore how her symptoms of ADHD were interfering with her ability to take her medications on time, and they set up alarms to remind her to take them. They also looked at her difficulty managing her food intake to help regulate her blood sugar. To help Lily make better food choices, they decided she could post an image of a stop light in the kitchen to remind her to stop and think before eating foods that increased her blood sugar. This was an ongoing issue for Lily, and she had to confront the fact that her ADHD made it more difficult to manage her illness.*

Skill Building: Use Clinician Handout 1.6: *Mental Health Impact on Illness* to review the mental health symptoms that commonly co-occur with medical illness as well as options for addressing them. Work with your client to identify and address how their mental health issues may be impacting their medical illness.

Reflection: Discuss how the client is currently managing their medical illness. Explore what is working for them and what is not. Discuss options for managing their illness that might be more effective for them. Pay attention to the ways their illness is challenging their very sense of self and the ways these challenges show up in how they feel and behave. Use this information to formulate a deeper understanding of the challenges the illness is causing your client and incorporate these factors into your treatment plan.

Mental Health Impact on Illness

Depression

- **Commonly Seen:** Feeling overwhelmed by the illness, negative thinking, catastrophizing, hopelessness, extreme fatigue, difficulty finding motivation for self-care and treatment compliance. Often difficult to distinguish whether the client has underlying depression or if their illness is causing the depression (or perhaps vice versa).

- **Therapy Suggestions:** Help the client recognize negative thoughts and find realistic thoughts that feel better. Explore how illness impacts their depression and how their depression may be impacting their ability to deal with medical illness. Explore situational triggers for depression related to their journey through illness. Discuss losses and grief caused by their illness. Ask the client to double-check with their prescriber that medications prescribed for their illness do not have side effects that contribute to depression.

Anxiety

- **Commonly Seen:** Constant worry about their illness, fear of the unknown, sense of impending danger, difficulty concentrating, trouble sleeping, catastrophizing.

- **Therapy Suggestions:** Discuss triggers for their anxiety. Teach mindfulness and relaxation skills. Help them "change the channel" on anxious thoughts and find thoughts that feel safe and calm. Teach thought defusion techniques to create distance from their worry. Discuss worst-case scenarios of what might happen with their illness and explore options for dealing with the reality. Encourage them to ask their medical provider if any of their medications might be contributing to their anxiety.

Panic Attacks

- **Commonly Seen:** Abrupt episodes of intense fear or discomfort, fear of the unknown concerning the course of their illness or their treatment, fear of upcoming medical tests or procedures that may trigger panic attacks and claustrophobia, fear of dying. Often experience trouble breathing, difficulty staying calm, racing or pounding heart, dizziness, derealization, and sweaty palms.

Copyright © 2026 Debra Burdick, *The Psychotherapy Toolbox for Chronic Illness and Chronic Pain*. All rights reserved.

- **Therapy Suggestions:** Explore triggers for panic attacks. Teach grounding techniques to help the client stay present in the moment. Use mindfulness techniques to shift attention away from their panicky thoughts. Help them practice relaxation breathing and prepare for situations that may cause panic.

Attention-Deficit/Hyperactivity Disorder (ADHD)

- **Commonly Seen:** Trouble concentrating, distractibility during office visits, tendency to miss important information, inability to take medications on schedule due to forgetfulness, tendency to lose things, disorganization, missed appointments, impulsive decisions that affect their illness.

- **Therapy Suggestions:** Help the client identify how their ADHD symptoms may be impacting their ability to take care of their illness. Discuss options for organizing where needed, such as medication schedules and medical appointments. Help them set alarms on their phone to remind them of important tasks. Explore options for asking a loved one to accompany them to doctor visits.

Illness Anxiety Disorder

- **Commonly Seen:** Excessive concern about their health and body, as well as vague pain, gastrointestinal, cardiac, and respiratory complaints. May experience benefits from the attention they receive for their complaints and may be resistant to psychotherapy.

- **Therapy Suggestions:** Teach skills that help them be mindful of thoughts and that help them replace unhelpful thoughts with helpful, realistic thoughts. May benefit from supportive group therapy that focuses on stress reduction and education in coping with chronic illness.

Borderline Personality Disorder

- **Commonly Seen:** Suicide attempts, emergency room visits, splitting the medical staff (e.g., manipulating providers by complaining to one about what another one did), a pattern of denial, feelings of depression, dependency, rage, and non-compliance with medical treatment. Conflict between the wish for boundless care and the threat of abandonment. Desire to be rescued, hope for a magical cure, fantasies about being fought over by service providers.

 Copyright © 2026 Debra Burdick, *The Psychotherapy Toolbox for Chronic Illness and Chronic Pain*. All rights reserved.

- **Therapy Suggestions:** Set firm limits, be supportive, avoid an assault on their needed defenses, focus on current issues related to illness, provide a growth-supporting environment. Use skills from dialectical behavior therapy (Linehan, 2014).

Obsessive-Compulsive Disorder

- **Commonly Seen:** Rigidity, indecision, tendency to constantly seek out more and more information about the illness, as well as frustration and anxiety with changes in routine. The loss of control that is so inherent in chronic illness is their biggest threat.

- **Therapy Suggestions:** Allow and encourage maximum participation in their own medical care. Give detailed information and instructions. Teach skills to help them calm their anxiety and improve their self-awareness.

Narcissistic Personality Disorder

- **Commonly Seen:** Grandiosity and inflated sense of self. They may feel illness, pain, or treatment is a threat to their self-image that is based on autonomy and perfection. May subject themselves to unnecessary risk by insisting on treatments that may or may not be necessary.

- **Therapy Suggestions:** Support their self-esteem and help rebuild a sense of mastery and control that chronic illness or pain interferes with. Help them identify and replace unhelpful and grandiose thoughts and behaviors that interfere with managing their illness.

Paranoid Personality Disorder

- **Commonly Seen:** Pervasive mistrust and suspiciousness of others. Illness may be seen as a feared attack. May scrutinize physicians' questions for hidden meanings and motives. May mistrust providers and treatment.

- **Therapy Suggestions:** Maintain interpersonal distance and respect their viewpoint while gently supporting treatment necessary for their care that they may view with suspicion. Support self-advocacy and self-control.

Schizoid Personality Disorder

- **Commonly Seen:** Aloofness, detachment, denial, and withdrawal. Illness may be seen as an intrusion and threat to fragile stability.

Copyright © 2026 Debra Burdick, *The Psychotherapy Toolbox for Chronic Illness and Chronic Pain*. All rights reserved.

- **Therapy Suggestions:** Respect privacy and emotional distance while helping them comply with medical and psychological care. Help them improve their self-awareness and explore how their personality style may interfere with getting medical care.

Copyright © 2026 Debra Burdick, *The Psychotherapy Toolbox for Chronic Illness and Chronic Pain*. All rights reserved.

Skill 1.7 When Clients Are Too Ill to Attend Session

Background: When clients have chronic illness or chronic pain, there will undoubtedly be times when they are feeling too ill to attend their therapy appointments. It is therefore a good idea to plan for this up front—at the beginning of treatment—and make accommodations when necessary. This skill provides guidance on how to proactively discuss this possibility with clients, explore options for telehealth, and explain your late cancellation or no-show policy.

The Skill in Action: *Jill signed up for a therapy group that focused on helping people with chronic illness. She was missing almost half of the sessions, either because she was having a bad day and felt more ill than usual or, often, because her ride to the sessions canceled at the last minute. Her therapist explored options for her to schedule a medical cab since her ride was quite unreliable. Then they worked together to get Jill set up with telehealth sessions where she could see and hear the other group members and vice versa. After these changes, Jill rarely missed a session and made good progress on her treatment goals.*

Skill Building: Use Clinician Handout 1.7: *Ingredients for No-Show or Late Cancellation Policy* to think about what you want to do if your client cancels late or no-shows when they are ill. Will you charge them a late cancellation or no-show fee? How many times will you do this? Make sure your policy is clear and in writing and review it with your client during the first session or even when they make their first appointment. In addition, discuss options for telehealth so they don't have to leave the house when they are under the weather. You want to make it as easy as possible for them to attend sessions even when they are having a bad day. This will help treatment to be consistent and move forward. If they are very ill, explore how long they expect to be unable to attend so you can arrange your schedule accordingly.

Reflection: How has pre-planning and reviewing your no-show or late cancellation policy helped with client attendance? Has telehealth worked out for those clients who need it the most? How has telehealth impacted treatment?

Ingredients for No-Show or Late Cancellation Policy

Be sure you have a no-show and late cancellation policy in writing that the client signs when they begin treatment. Consider including the following elements.

- List the frequency and type of sessions.

- List their copay or full fee if insurance doesn't pay.

- List your policy for late cancellation (e.g., requiring 24 hours' notice).

- List the late cancellation fee and how you will collect it (e.g., charging their credit card).

- List how clients should notify you when they need to cancel (e.g., email, text, voicemail).

- List the number of free cancellations you will accept (if any).

- List your policy about rescheduling in the same week.

- List what clients should do if they are running late.

- List options and directions for telehealth if the client unexpectedly cannot attend in person.

36   Copyright © 2026 Debra Burdick, *The Psychotherapy Toolbox for Chronic Illness and Chronic Pain*. All rights reserved.

Skill 1.8 Addressing Bias: Gender, Sexual Orientation, Race, Age

Background: Implicit biases are attitudes we hold about race, ethnicity, age, ability, gender, sexual orientation, or other characteristics that operate outside our conscious awareness. When a health care provider holds an implicit bias toward their clients, it can influence their judgment and unintentionally contribute to discriminatory behavior that impacts the quality of care. This can include dismissing symptoms, not ordering diagnostic tests, not prescribing medication, or assuming that a client's symptoms are all in their head. This skill helps clients recognize and address these types of biases when dealing with chronic illness or pain.

The Skill in Action: *Emily had just turned 65. She was the type to avoid doctors if she could, as she never wanted to be seen as a hypochondriac. But this time was different. Her chest had been feeling tight for weeks, and she would experience a strange ache that would flare up whenever she exerted herself. She'd finally given in to her family's pleas and booked an appointment, hoping her doctor would take her concerns seriously. As she told the doctor about the pressure—describing how it wasn't quite pain but was still unsettling, and how it made her feel worn out and breathless—he furrowed his brow and then offered a thin-lipped smile. "It's probably just stress, maybe some acid reflux," he said, his tone casual, as if she'd asked about a nagging cough.*

She mentioned her family's heart history and how a male cousin of hers had experienced similar symptoms. But the doctor seemed almost amused. "Oh, well, you're a woman. Men's heart issues tend to present differently," he said, as if that should settle it. Then he added the real kicker: "You're getting up there in age. Bodies don't bounce back the way they used to." There it was. He never even offered her the tests she knew they'd have scheduled for a man—a treadmill test, maybe an ECG, something beyond a dismissive suggestion to "eat better and get some exercise."

Emily left feeling the familiar frustration many women have faced: being brushed off and left to wonder if she was making a big deal out of nothing. She told her therapist that she knew her body better than that and, with her therapist's encouragement, sought a second opinion. Emily learned that her instincts had been right all along—she had a silent, serious heart issue.

Skill Building: Use Client Handout 1.8 to explore with your client how biases related to age, gender, sexual orientation, and race can impact not only treatment and diagnosis, but also the trust between a client and their provider. If your client feels like their medical provider demonstrates any of these biases, encourage them to advocate for themselves, bring a family member or friend to appointments, or use the hospital health advocates to speak on their behalf.

If your client feels like their medical provider is discounting their concerns because of their marginalized identity, encourage them to ask the provider what tests or treatments would be recommended if the client were part of the more privileged group instead—for example, "How would you treat these same symptoms in a younger person?" If the client is a member of the LGBTQIA+ community, encourage them to find a practitioner who offers inclusive services and care, as many providers lack the knowledge and experience to provide appropriate care for this community. In all cases, explore options for finding a provider that is less biased to ensure the client receives the best treatment.

Reflection: Has the client experienced bias related to age, gender, sexual orientation, race, or another category? How did they feel when it happened to them? How did the bias impact the quality of their treatment? What did they do to address it and make sure they got the treatment they needed? Did they find a provider who treated them without these biases?

Bias Related to Gender, Sexual Orientation, Age, or Race

Research consistently shows that biases related to gender, sexual orientation, race, age, and other categories affect health care delivery and health outcomes. Here are some key findings:

1. **Gender and sexual orientation:** Women often experience delays in diagnosis and treatment, particularly for conditions like heart disease. Women with heart symptoms are also given fewer diagnostic tests and less medication than men (Al Hamid et al., 2024). What's more, heart attacks in women are more likely to be misdiagnosed compared to men, leading to higher mortality rates. Research also shows that women's pain reports are sometimes dismissed or labeled as "emotional" rather than clinical symptoms (Samulowitz et al., 2018). Relatedly, patients who are part of the LGBTQIA+ community face delayed or substandard care, mistreatment, inequitable policies and practices, and little or no inclusion in health outreach or education. They may face discrimination or prejudice and often delay seeking treatment (National LGBTQIA+ Health Education Center, 2016).

2. **Race:** Members of racial and ethnic minority groups face systemic biases that impact their access to and quality of care. Research shows unequal health care across various indicators, including diabetes care, mental health care, maternal health care, preventive vaccination, end-of-life care, cardiology care, and pain management (Hamed et al., 2022). For example, Black patients are less likely to receive adequate pain management due to incorrect assumptions about biological differences in pain perception between Black and White individuals, leading to under-treatment (Hoffman et al., 2016).

3. **Age:** Ageism in health care can affect the duration, frequency, and appropriateness of the treatment that a client receives. It can impact the type of diagnostic or screening tests a provider is willing to order, as well as the scope of treatments they are willing to provide. This can lead to worse mental health outcomes, such as depression, as well as adverse physical health outcomes, such as delayed diagnosis or shorter life expectancy. In fact, one meta-analysis conducted across 45 countries found evidence that age bias is present in health care settings 96 percent of the time (Greenwood, 2020).

Copyright © 2026 Debra Burdick, *The Psychotherapy Toolbox for Chronic Illness and Chronic Pain*. All rights reserved.

Skill 1.9 Choosing Medical Treatment Options

Background: Clients with chronic illness or chronic pain often face difficult decisions when choosing the best medical treatment. There are so many treatment options available, ranging from conservative options such as lifestyle changes and diet choices to more aggressive, invasive options such as surgery. In addition, there are alternative medical options available as well as traditional medical options. Choosing the best treatment option can be confusing and overwhelming. Some clients simply do whatever their doctor tells them without gathering information or considering other possibilities, which might preclude learning about more effective options. This skill provides guidance on helping clients explore their options, advocate for themselves, and choose what they feel is the best option for their situation.

The Skill in Action: *Rhonda was dealing with a myriad of mysterious and debilitating symptoms, and it was two years before she was finally diagnosed with amyotrophic lateral sclerosis (ALS). At one point in her diagnostic journey, a scan discovered a rare tumor in her lung. The first thoracic surgeon she consulted stated that before he could remove the tumor, Rhonda needed a procedure to reduce its size, and he referred her to two other doctors thousands of miles away (one in Florida and one in Germany). Before traveling, she consulted another surgeon who practiced at a major medical center in New York City, which was much closer to home, who said he treated hundreds of tumors like hers every year. He removed the tumor within a few weeks. Rhonda was very thankful that she got a second opinion when choosing a treatment option and became more proactive when dealing with her symptoms that were eventually diagnosed as ALS.*

Skill Building: Review Client Handout 1.9: *Choosing Medical Treatment Options* with your client and use it as a guide to explore what treatment options are best for them. The first step is to encourage your client to talk with their doctor about options that may be available to them. It's important they see a doctor who specializes in their illness, as doctors tend to be experts in their own field and might not always consider other options that might be helpful. In addition, with illnesses that are difficult to diagnose, chronic, or even life threatening, it is important to get a second and maybe a third opinion. Misdiagnoses are common and can lead to unnecessary suffering and even death.

You can also guide the client to look online at research studies concerning the treatment options for their illness. Perhaps you could do it with them in session to advise them which places to look for reliable information. Look for studies published in major journals—the National Library of Medicine is a good starting point (https://www.ncbi.nlm.nih.gov). In addition, explore how well specific treatment options align with the client's religious or cultural background as well as their values and beliefs. For example, some religions prohibit certain types of medical intervention.

Finally, make sure they consider treatments with the best outcome and fewest side effects, and that they also consider recovery time and prognosis. For example, some people who are in their older years who have had a recurrence of cancer choose to forgo another round of treatment, preferring to avoid the side effects and poor quality of life, and instead make peace with dying.

Reflection: Has the client been offered treatment options that make sense to them? Have they explored at least several options? Was their doctor willing to discuss the client's questions about these various options? How well has the client been able to advocate for themselves and get the information needed to make an informed decision? Does the client feel confident about the treatment option they eventually chose?

Choosing Medical Treatment Options

Ask your doctor about the treatment option(s) they recommend.

- Why do they recommend these particular options?

- What do they expect the outcome to be?

- What does the research show the outcome is likely to be?

- What are the side effects?

- How long is the recovery time?

- What is their experience with each option?

- What success have they had with each option?

- What challenges has each option presented?

- Are there other tests that should be done?

- Do you need to be referred to a specialist for your illness?

- What other options are there?

Consider how each treatment option fits in with your:

- Religious or spiritual beliefs

- Cultural background

- Lifestyle

- Stage of life

- Quality of life

Get a second or perhaps a third opinion.

- This allows you to confirm your diagnosis.

- It gives you confidence that you are doing the right thing.

 Copyright © 2026 Debra Burdick, *The Psychotherapy Toolbox for Chronic Illness and Chronic Pain*. All rights reserved.

- Different medical experts recommend different treatments based on their expertise.

- There may be a treatment option your current doctor isn't familiar with.

- It allows you to gather new information and insights.

- It ensures you have explored all the options.

Visit a major health center that specializes in your illness.

- This allows you to gain access to the most recent and advanced treatment options.

- Doctors may have a higher level of expertise and experience with your illness.

Learn about treatment options.

- Search online for treatment options offered for your illness, making sure to access results published in major medical journals.

- Ask others who have the same illness what worked for them.

- Talk with your doctor about what you discover from your information-gathering.

Skill 1.10 Mindfully Compassionate Language

Background: The language you use when working with clients with chronic illness or pain is very important. Clients often hear statements from friends, family, and the medical community that is unintentionally hurtful or discouraging. This can make them feel misunderstood, more alone, not good enough, or like they are a failure or not trying hard enough. On the other hand, language that is compassionate can help them feel understood, less alone, validated, and more hopeful. It is associated with better coping abilities, improved health outcomes, and overall enhanced well-being. This skill provides guidance on being mindful in session about using language that shows compassion to the client, validates the client's experience, and helps them feel heard and understood.

The Skill in Action: *Fatima experienced several autoimmune disorders that were difficult to diagnose, mimicked other disorders, and caused a variety of debilitating symptoms, such as chronic fatigue and whole-body aches. One doctor told her she had these symptoms because she was a woman and that she should just get used to them. Another doctor who accurately diagnosed her told her that she shouldn't be upset, since the illness wasn't that bad because nobody had died from it. A friend even told Fatima that she didn't believe she was sick because she always looked fine. This steady stream of comments made Fatima feel hopeless, stigmatized, disbelieved, misunderstood, and often like a failure—which made her symptoms feel even worse. Her therapist was dismayed to hear all the damaging language that Fatima had been exposed to. By mindfully choosing more compassionate language, the therapist helped Fatima feel understood and validated when it came to her feelings and her experience with chronic illness, and she began to feel more optimistic regarding her overall well-being as well. Throughout treatment, Fatima learned how to recognize damaging language and reject it or rewrite it in her mind. In turn, she was better able to manage her illness and live a good life in spite of it.*

Skill Building: Use Clinician Handout 1.10 to become more mindful of compassionate versus hurtful language when working with clients with chronic illness or pain. Then incorporate the more compassionate statements in session with your clients to more effectively validate and support them. Explore instances where clients were exposed to damaging language from others and discuss how it impacted their health and well-being (or perhaps even how it changed how they managed their symptoms). Pay particular attention to times when invalidating language has made clients feel less-than—like they are a failure, not good enough, or not trying hard enough.

Reflection: How has your awareness of hurtful language often heard by those with chronic illness or pain increased? How has this awareness changed the language you use with clients when discussing their experiences with chronic illness or pain? How has your understanding of the power of language changed? Was the client able to remember any instances where they heard hurtful language? What impact did that language have on how they felt about or managed their illness or pain? How did exploring the impact of hurtful language help the client undo its damage and help them feel validated and supported?

Mindfully Compassionate Language

Language can have a powerful impact on clients with chronic illness or pain and influence their health, well-being, overall outlook, and more. Review the compassionate statements listed here and incorporate them into your work with clients. Then study the examples of potentially hurtful language and consider how to replace them with more compassionate statements. Ask the client if they have ever heard these types of statements and, if so, what the circumstances were and how it made them feel.

Examples of Compassionate Language

- What can I do to help?

- That sounds so painful.

- Are you okay?

- I'm listening.

- Do you need to talk?

- How can I support you best?

- I'm here to help.

- I can only imagine how you must feel.

- I care about you.

- I'm here for you.

- Tell me more about it.

- What do you need right now?

Replacing Potentially Hurtful Language with Compassionate Language

- **You don't look sick.** Just because a person "doesn't look sick" doesn't mean they feel well. Many symptoms are invisible. This statement discounts their inner reality based on how they look. Replace it with "I know you don't feel well, but how do you manage to look great anyway?"

Copyright © 2026 Debra Burdick, *The Psychotherapy Toolbox for Chronic Illness and Chronic Pain*. All rights reserved.

- **We've all been there.** This minimizes the person's experience, which is totally unique to them. Replace it with "Have you ever had to deal with something like this before?"

- **We all have something like that.** Everyone is different, and this statement discounts the client's personal experience. Replace with "Do you know anyone else who is going through what you are?" or "Have you ever gone through this before?"

- **I know how you feel.** It's hard to know how they feel unless they tell you. Replace it with "How are you feeling?" or "I can only imagine how you feel."

- **You seem fine most of the time.** This discounts their difficult experience of chronic illness or pain. Replace it with "How do you manage to function so well despite being so ill or in such pain?" or "How does illness or pain impact your life overall?"

- **I wouldn't want to take that medicine long-term.** This can make them feel judged and less-than because they take medicine that you would not. Replace it with "How has that medicine helped you? Have you had any side effects that make it difficult to tolerate?"

- **Have you tried _____?** Clients with chronic illness or pain have typically tried a lot of treatments, some of which have helped and others of which have not. Although you may be trying to explore other options that might help, this question can imply that you don't think they have tried hard enough yet. Replace it with "What have you tried? What has worked the best for you?" or "Are there other options you are considering?"

- **It could be worse.** This invalidates the client's experience and insinuates that they shouldn't be concerned about their illness or pain because it's not as bad as it could be. Replace it with "How is this different from other difficult things you have dealt with?" or "Are there times when you feel better or worse?"

- **Everything is meant to be.** This invalidates the client's illness or pain, as if they were just meant to have it and there is nothing they can do to help themselves. Replace it with "That sounds so painful/frustrating/unfair."

- **You're too young (or old, etc.) to have that.** Clients of all ages experience illness or pain, and this statement can make them feel like a failure for having something they "shouldn't" have at their age. Replace it with "How are you dealing with your illness or pain?"

 Copyright © 2026 Debra Burdick, *The Psychotherapy Toolbox for Chronic Illness and Chronic Pain*. All rights reserved.

- **That happened to my friend and they healed.** Depending on where the client is in their journey with illness or pain, this can cause a variety of reactions. It can be dangerous for those who have not accepted that their illness is chronic and maybe incurable, and it can make them feel like a failure because they have not healed. It may also offer false hope. Replace it with "Have you heard of anyone else with symptoms like yours? How are they doing?"

- **It's not that bad.** This totally discounts and judges their experience. Replace it with "How bad is this illness or pain making you feel or impacting your life?" or "Have you had to deal with anything else like this before?"

Copyright © 2026 Debra Burdick, *The Psychotherapy Toolbox for Chronic Illness and Chronic Pain*. All rights reserved.

Mental Health Skills

Skill 2.1 Set Intentions That Reflect Goals

Background: Setting an intention is the first step in accomplishing anything. An intention can be defined as something you plan or aim to do. In contrast to goals, which are focused on future outcomes you want to achieve, intentions are focused on the present moment. For example, a client with chronic pain who has the goal to increase their ability to manage pain may set intentions that involve changing the channel when they notice their pain, doing a progressive relaxation meditation every day to calm their mind and body, and using skills to learn to accept their pain. Clients who set intentions such as these are much more likely to achieve their treatment goals than those who do not. This skill introduces the concept of setting an intention to clients. It helps them focus on what thoughts and actions support their ability to successfully deal with chronic illness and pain.

The Skill in Action: *Ben had been chronically ill with type 2 diabetes for a few years when he started therapy. His presenting problem was that he was very anxious because his blood sugar was not well-regulated, leaving him often feeling scared and out of control. With the help of his therapist, he set a goal to reduce his anxiety. He then set an intention to use skills to replace worry thoughts with calmer, realistic thoughts, as well as another intention to speak with his diabetes specialist about new ways to get his blood sugar under control. With these changes, he gradually became more able to calm his worry. He also tried a new exercise, medication, and eating schedule that began to get his blood sugar under better control.*

Skill Building: Use Client Handout 2.1 to help clients understand what an intention is, understand the benefits of setting an intention, and create their own unique intentions. Guide them to choose realistic intentions that align with their treatment goals. Encourage your client to write down their intentions on a sticky note and post it where they can see it daily to help them stay focused.

Reflection: In what ways does defining an intention keep your client focused? How does it help them make progress toward achieving their goals? What obstacles have interfered with your client's ability to set intentions before, and how can you help them overcome these obstacles? Notice how the process of setting an intention, focusing on it, and bringing one's attention back to it when distracted is the basic process of mindfulness.

Set Your Intention

- An **intention** is something that you plan to do in the present moment to help you achieve a goal, whereas a goal is something you hope to accomplish in the future.

- **Refer to your treatment goals** to help you define your intentions.

- **Benefits of setting your intention:** People who set an intention have a higher success rate of achieving their goals.

- **Choose positive intentions** that help you feel better and that help you think and behave in ways that support your goals.

- **For each treatment goal, create an intention or several intentions** that support it. For example, if your goal is to improve your mood, an intention might be to notice and replace negative thoughts with positive thoughts. Or if your main goal is to support your body's health, an intention might be to avoid sugary or fatty foods and to eat a balanced diet.

- **Be specific when defining your intention.** An example of a specific intention that supports the goal of de-stressing might be "I intend to pay attention to my mind and body and notice when I feel stressed." A second, supportive intention might be "I will listen to a progressive relaxation meditation every day to calm my mind and body." Or if your goal is to find a specialist for your illness, an intention might be to ask your current doctor for a referral or to search online and call for an appointment.

- **Write your intentions on a sticky note and post it** where you can see it regularly. Or put it on your smartphone screen so you see it every time you use your phone.

- **Read each intention out loud several times a day,** especially before you go to bed and when you start your day each morning.

- **Be mindful** of your intention throughout the day. It is normal to get distracted, but as soon as you notice that you are not focusing on your intention (or you are thinking or behaving in ways that do not support your intention), simply refocus your attention and get back on track. This gets easier with practice.

- **Update your intentions** as you achieve and create new goals.

Copyright © 2026 Debra Burdick, *The Psychotherapy Toolbox for Chronic Illness and Chronic Pain*. All rights reserved.

Skill 2.2 De-Stress

Background: Stress and how you respond to it can negatively impact the health of your mind and body. In fact, studies show that stress contributes to most chronic illnesses, including diabetes, cardiovascular and heart disease, cancer, and neurodegenerative diseases like Alzheimer's (Liu et al., 2017; Mariotti, 2015). Conversely, being chronically ill or in chronic pain is inherently stressful, which adds to the overall stress load. Because stress and illness are so intertwined, it is critically important to address the stress in a client's life as well as their response to stress. This skill helps clients identify their stressors, reduce or eliminate stressors when possible, and lower their stress response.

The Skill in Action: *Mary had an enormous load of stress on her plate. Not only did she have many responsibilities at home and at work, but her chronic neck pain was now adding even more stress, as she felt ill every day and had to fit in numerous doctors' visits for tests and treatments. When her therapist reflected back to her about how much stress she was carrying, she burst into tears. Together, they made a list of Mary's five biggest stressors, which allowed Mary to realize that she needed to delegate more at work and get some help at home. She also learned to tune into her body and discovered that her neck became tense and she got severe headaches when she was stressed. She knew that was not helping her neck pain improve. After she delegated and got a cleaning crew at home, she started taking better care of herself and gradually learned to relax her body. She reported feeling a huge sense of relief and noticed her neck pain was slowly improving.*

Skill Building: Use Client Handout 2.2: *De-Stress* to help your client identify the top five stressors that may be negatively affecting their health, and ask them to identify which of these stressors they can change, avoid, or eliminate. For example, if a major stressor is their job, work with them to figure out how they can modify their current work situation or find a new job that is less stressful. Or if a major stressor is their illness, teach them how to tune into their body so they can notice any connection between their stress levels and their symptoms or pain levels. For example, does feeling stressed exacerbate the symptoms of their illness or make their pain more intense?

For any stressors that the client cannot eliminate or reduce, discuss therapeutic options they can use to turn down the stress response and calm their mind and body. This includes using options provided in this book, such as Skill 3.10: *Progressive Muscle Relaxation* and Skill 3.11: *Body Scan*.

Reflection: Ask your client what role they think stress plays in their chronic illness or pain. Explore how de-stressing helps their physical health as well as their mental health. Discuss options for periodically tuning into their stress level and using skills to calm their response. What practice works best for them to de-stress? How have they been able to reduce or eliminate stressors? What ongoing stress must they deal with?

De-Stress

1. **Be mindful of what stresses you.**

   - Make a list of five things that stress you, numbered from most to least stressful.

   - Circle any stressors that you can change, reduce, or eliminate. Write down steps to accomplish this, focusing on the biggest stressor first. Include a time frame for completing the changes.

   - Identify areas where you can ask for help and delegate whenever possible.

2. **Notice how you respond to those stressors you cannot change.**

   - Turn your attention inward and notice how your body responds when you feel stressed.

   - Where does stress show up in your body?

   - How does stress impact your chronic illness or pain?

   - How does your illness or pain impact your stress level?

3. **Calm your mind and body and turn down your stress response.**

   - Breathe in through your nose to the count of 4. Exhale slowly through your mouth like you are blowing a bubble to the count of 8. Repeat three times.

   - Take your pulse and notice how it slows as you breathe and calm.

   - Reframe a stressful situation that you cannot change. For example, if pain is making it difficult to walk, you can take care of yourself by sitting periodically and using that time to rest or meditate. You can also make a list of people you can ask for help when pain gets in the way.

   - Make a list of everything you are grateful for.

   - Use the other skills in this book, such as Skill 3.10: *Progressive Muscle Relaxation*, Skill 3.11: *Body Scan*, Skill 3.5: *Set Mindful Limits*, and Skill 4.A.4: *Mindfulness for Pain Management*.

Copyright © 2026 Debra Burdick, *The Psychotherapy Toolbox for Chronic Illness and Chronic Pain*. All rights reserved.

Skill 2.3 Change the Channel

Background: When we are feeling ill or in pain, it is not unusual for us to feel depressed, anxious, fearful, angry, guilty, or hopeless—and it is often easy to become completely focused on our illness or pain. When clients constantly do this, their symptoms tend to worsen, increasing the negative impact on their quality of life. This skill uses a mixture of CBT, ACT, and motivational interviewing techniques to help clients change or defuse unhelpful thoughts that are getting in their way of feeling better. Clients can use it whenever they are in physical or emotional pain, or when they notice themselves getting stuck in negative or worry thoughts.

The Skill in Action: *Julie had been ill with a collection of symptoms that the medical community found mysterious and hard to diagnose. As the illness continued, she became depressed and very worried that she would have to spend the rest of her life with these symptoms. She noticed that she was often thinking about how bad she felt, constantly looking up her symptoms on the internet, and worrying so much she couldn't fall asleep. She realized that the more she focused on her symptoms, the worse she felt.*

At her therapist's suggestion, she learned to "change the channel" in her mind whenever she found herself thinking negative or unhelpful thoughts about her symptoms. In these moments, she pretended to reach into her pocket for an imaginary remote control and "changed the channel" to something that felt better, like a channel with her grandchildren's faces on it or a channel with a beautiful, peaceful sunset. The first few days, Julie set an alarm to remind her to do this practice three times each day, after which it became automatic. She noticed that when she tuned into her body, she usually felt considerably better after watching the more helpful channel. She gradually began to notice that her automatic thoughts were more positive, she felt less bothered by her symptoms, and she was enjoying her life more even though her symptoms had not yet resolved.

Skill Building: Use Client Worksheet 2.3 to guide clients in learning this skill. Explain that what they are thinking about is the "channel" they are watching. Encourage them to tune in throughout the day and notice what channel they tend to watch in their mind. Is it the fear channel when they worry about their illness? Is it the anger channel when they think about the awful reaction they had to a medication prescribed by their doctor?

Then guide them to think about three "channels" in their mind they would enjoy watching instead. These channels should represent positive, helpful things to them, such as peace, happiness, self-care, health, well-being, fun, safety, calm, or contentment. Ask them to decide what shows they would put on each of their channels. They can write down these channels and accompanying shows on the worksheet.

To get into the habit of "changing the channel," you might suggest they set an alarm to remind them to pause and tune into their thoughts throughout the day. Explain that when they notice they are watching a channel that doesn't feel good, they can pretend to reach into their pocket and pull out an imaginary remote control that changes the channel to something more helpful. You can also remind them to post the completed worksheet where they can see it to remember their chosen channels and shows.

Reflection: Which of the client's chosen channels help them feel the best? Would it be helpful to create more channels like these? Were there any channels that made them feel worse? If so, see if the client can identify the reasons they thought this channel would feel good in the first place. For now, they can replace this channel with one that feels better, but encourage them to periodically go back to it and see if things have shifted enough for it to be the helpful channel they thought it would be. As the client continues practicing this skill, do they notice any shifts in their automatic thought patterns? Are they focusing less on their illness or pain? Is their mood more positive, more often? Are they more able to notice unhelpful thoughts and replace them with helpful thoughts? Have they noticed any changes in their symptoms, either physically or emotionally?

Change the Channel

Did you know that you can choose what you want to think about? That's right! And since you can only have one thought at a time, it's important to make sure it's one that feels good.

Imagine that what you are thinking about is like watching a TV channel. What you are thinking about is the channel you are watching now.

Take a moment to reflect inward and notice what you are thinking about right now. Are your thoughts calm, happy, sad, worried, angry, or something else? Are you thinking about your illness? Are you focused on pain? If you notice mostly unhelpful or feel-bad channels in your mind, such as the illness, worry, anger, or sadness channel, think about what three channels would feel better to watch instead. For example, these might be happy, peaceful, relaxed, safe, wellness, self-care, or feel-good channels. Be specific and write them down here.

1. _____

2. _____

3. _____

Now choose three different shows you could put on each of your channels that feel good to you. These are shows that make you smile, make you feel loved, trigger feelings of gratitude, or remind you of times when you felt better. Some examples might be petting your cat or dog, swimming, dancing, playing sports, playing your favorite game, or spending time with a family member. It could also be your favorite music or band, a warm bath, a massage, your favorite food, a hobby, a peaceful place (like the mountains, a forest, or a lake), or whatever else feels good to you. An example is provided for you first:

Calm Channel

Show 1: Gentle ocean waves

Show 2: Getting a massage

Show 3: Watching the sunset

 Copyright © 2026 Debra Burdick, *The Psychotherapy Toolbox for Chronic Illness and Chronic Pain.* All rights reserved.

Channel 1: _____

Show 1:_____

Show 2:_____

Show 3:_____

Channel 2: _____

Show 1:_____

Show 2:_____

Show 3:_____

Channel 3: _____

Show 1:_____

Show 2:_____

Show 3:_____

Now that you have chosen your channels and shows, place this list where you will see it every day so you can remember to periodically tune into what you are thinking about. Set an alarm to remind you to do this three times a day for the first three days. Whenever the alarm goes off, tune into your thoughts, and if you notice that your thoughts are negative or unhelpful, pretend that you are picking up an imaginary remote control and using it to "change the channel" to one of your feel-good channels. Imagine that you are watching one of your chosen shows on this channel. Do you feel better watching this channel?

Use this process anytime you find yourself getting stuck in negative or unhelpful thoughts. Notice what changes you experience in your thought patterns or your symptoms of illness or pain.

Copyright © 2026 Debra Burdick, *The Psychotherapy Toolbox for Chronic Illness and Chronic Pain*. All rights reserved.

Skill 2.4 Dealing with Loss

Background: Clients with chronic illness or pain often experience significant losses in many areas of their life, such as loss of privacy, loss of bodily functions, and loss of autonomy and identity. These losses can be devastating and impact their very sense of self. They can also continue to be present over extended periods of time and change or increase over time. This skill helps clients identify their losses as well as their feelings about these losses and then take steps to more effectively accept and cope with their new reality and live a good life despite illness or pain.

The Skill in Action: *Jayne woke up after open heart surgery to discover that she was suddenly 100 percent blind. Her complete vision loss was apparently caused by an unexpected loss of blood to her brain during the surgery. She couldn't even see any light. This monumental loss started a journey of self-discovery, recovery, and transformation. After recovering from heart surgery, she spent several months in a rehabilitation center that specialized in teaching clients the skills needed to live without eyesight. During this time, she often felt helpless, hopeless, enraged, depressed, scared, frustrated, and devastated. After working with a therapist, Jayne was gradually able to accept her blindness and focus on learning how to function without eyesight. She incorporated gadgets that helped her tell time, use the phone, and listen to books on tape. She regained confidence in the different areas of her life, including dating a former friend who loved her so much that her blindness didn't matter to him. Realizing that she wanted to be of service to others, she trained to become a suicide hotline counselor, which she could do without eyesight. Her life was never the same as before her loss, but she found ways to live a good life despite her blindness.*

Skill Building: Use Client Worksheet 2.4.1 to help the client identify the losses they may have experienced due to their chronic illness or pain. This allows both you and the client to get a fuller understanding of how the client is being affected and to identify areas in which the client needs the most assistance. Since this step often triggers sadness and tears, use Client Worksheet 2.4.2 to help the client identify and understand their emotions surrounding these losses. Finally, use Client Handout 2.4.3 to help the client accept what is and thrive despite the losses caused by illness and pain.

Reflection: How much illness and pain-related loss is the client experiencing? What feelings were triggered by this exercise? Was the client able to practice radical acceptance by acknowledging reality as it is, even if they don't like it? Does the client believe they can thrive despite illness and pain? What anchor did they choose in Client Worksheet 2.4.3 to stay grounded when they experience difficult emotions? What steps have they taken toward living a good life despite illness and pain? What obstacles have blocked their progress?

Types of Loss from Chronic Illness and Pain

These are losses commonly experienced by those who are chronically ill or have chronic pain. Check off all that apply to you.

❏ **Function:** Inability to do things you normally do, such as walk, concentrate, take a shower, work, play with your kids, read, cook, or speak.

❏ **Sense of identity:** The definition of yourself and who you are is lost as your life transforms from wellness to illness and pain. This changes as your roles, functioning, and relationships change.

❏ **Control:** Difficulty being in charge of your own life. Feeling out of control as loss of bodily function, illness or pain, medical appointments, treatments, and home therapy take over.

❏ **Role:** Changes in your roles can include no longer being able to work or work full-time, do household chores, do parenting activities, drive, or do other things you used to do independently.

❏ **Relationships:** Inability to participate in romantic, parental, friend, or work relationships as usual. Changes occur in family dynamics due to your illness or pain. Children may feel fearful of losing you or resentful that they need to fill in for you or care for you. Spouses and partners may feel abandoned or helpless.

❏ **Body image:** Changes in appearance due to illness or treatments, such as loss of hair, loss of muscle strength, scars from surgery, disfigurement, or changes in weight.

❏ **Beloved activities:** Inability to participate in activities you enjoy, such as exercise, hobbies, sports, children's activities, social outings, and parties.

❏ **Dignity:** Being treated like you aren't a person during tests and treatments. For example, feeling disfigured and humiliated when technicians joke and talk like you aren't there while marking radiation boundaries on your body.

❏ **Privacy:** Loss of privacy during medical tests or treatments as parts of your body that are considered private are poked and prodded; answering personal questions or sharing a room in the hospital or emergency room.

❏ **Financial stability:** Loss of income due to medical expenses or reduced ability to work.

Copyright © 2026 Debra Burdick, *The Psychotherapy Toolbox for Chronic Illness and Chronic Pain*. All rights reserved.

Common Feelings About Chronic Illness and Chronic Pain

These are common feelings that people experience in response to chronic illness or pain. Check off all that you have experienced.

- ❏ **Depression and grief:** Sadness, despair, hopelessness, sleep disturbance, crying, withdrawal, fatigue, loss of pleasure, poor concentration, negative thinking.

- ❏ **Fear and anxiety:** Fear of the unknown, fear of what's next with the illness or pain, fear of dying. Anxiety about symptoms or pain as well as medical tests or treatments.

- ❏ **Anger and rage:** Anger about why this illness or pain has happened to you, as well as frustration or helplessness for being deprived of life as you knew it.

- ❏ **Resentment:** Feeling resentful when others can do things you cannot. Resenting others who get well when you don't.

- ❏ **Shame:** Feeling ashamed of being ill or of the limits your illness places on you.

- ❏ **Failure:** Feeling like a failure when nothing you do improves your illness or pain.

- ❏ **Hopelessness:** Feeling like nothing is working and nothing will.

- ❏ **Helplessness:** Feeling out of control and unable to help yourself.

- ❏ **Other:** _____

Copyright © 2026 Debra Burdick, *The Psychotherapy Toolbox for Chronic Illness and Chronic Pain*. All rights reserved.

Steps Toward Transformation

Follow these steps to practice accepting your current reality and thrive despite the losses you have experienced as a result of chronic illness or pain.

1. Identify the losses caused by chronic illness or pain (Client Worksheet 2.4.1).

2. Identify options for dealing with these types of losses.

   a. Identify and process the feelings associated with your loss (Client Worksheet 2.4.2). Allow yourself the time and space to sit with these feelings.

   b. Practice radical acceptance (Skill 2.8).

   c. Practice shifting difficult emotions to more positive, helpful ones. This can include the following skills:

      i. *Mindfulness of Emotions* (Skill 2.7)

      ii. *Reframing Thoughts* (Skill 2.6)

      iii. *Change the Channel* (Skill 2.3)

   d. Stay grounded when you are experiencing difficult emotions.

      i. To do so, choose an anchor to keep you present in the moment, such as a small stone in your pocket.

      ii. Touch this anchor object as you focus on your breathing to bring you back to the here and now.

   e. Find purpose and meaning in life despite your chronic illness or pain.

      i. Start by identifying your values (Skill 5.1). Make a list of what matters most to you.

      ii. Then explore how you can incorporate values-driven actions into your everyday life.

Copyright © 2026 Debra Burdick, *The Psychotherapy Toolbox for Chronic Illness and Chronic Pain*. All rights reserved.

Skill 2.5 Identify and Motivate Change

Background: In order to successfully manage chronic illness and pain, clients must often make significant changes in many areas of their lives, such as changing their eating, work, and sleep habits. It even requires them to shift their mindset, turning their focus away from "why me?" thoughts and toward more helpful and positive coping thoughts. Unfortunately, many clients are resistant in the face of change, even when they know that the change would benefit them. This skill uses techniques from motivational interviewing (Miller & Rollnick, 2023) to help clients explore what is getting in the way of change and to create a plan for making this change happen.

The Skill in Action: *Jason was diagnosed with heart disease several years before he sought help from a therapist. Although he was very conscientious about taking his prescription medications, he was very resistant to and unsuccessful at losing weight per his doctor's recommendations. His extra weight increased his risk for further coronary artery disease and made it more difficult to exercise without being short of breath. Jason was also very particular about his food choices and had a limited number of foods that he liked. He was rigid and inflexible about trying new foods and rarely did so. In therapy, Jason listed his weight as something he needed to change. He acknowledged that this would require him to change his diet significantly. When he explored his resistance to doing so, he remembered that his father and brother were quite abusive to him when he was young, and he deliberately chose not to eat foods that they liked. Thus began a lifelong habit of avoiding and disliking certain foods; in fact, he disliked most foods designated as heart healthy and loved those that were not. With the help of his therapist, Jason was able to explore this resistance so he could feel more in charge of his diet and make steady, incremental changes that would make a difference in his health condition.*

Skill Building: Use Client Worksheet 2.5.1: *Sample Changes* to help clients explore the possibilities for changes that might be helpful to them, followed by Client Worksheet 2.5.2: *What Needs to Change?* to help them identify actions they can take that support their well-being. If clients are having trouble with this, add in the motivational interviewing techniques summarized in Clinician Handout 2.5.3: *Motivating Change*, which are intended to help clients explore and resolve any ambivalence. During this process, make sure the client understands that you want what is best for them and that you and they are equal partners in this process. Be sure to honor the client's expertise about what is best for them and help them preserve their autonomy.

Reflection: Was the client able to identify any positive changes they need to make? Were they able to start by focusing on one change? Were they able to process what gets in their way of making change? Have they previously been successful at making a change? If they exhibited ambivalence about change, how did they respond to the motivational interviewing prompts? Were they able to take charge of making change? What patterns of ambivalence or resistance did they discover during this process?

Sample Changes

Check off any changes you can commit to making that would help you better manage your chronic illness or pain.

❒ I will change my mindset to a more positive outlook. This may include noticing negative thoughts when I think about my illness or pain and replacing them with more helpful and reality-based thoughts.

❒ I will change how I speak up and represent myself at the doctor's office.

❒ I will set better limits to protect my energy and my health.

❒ I will change how I manage my pain and find new ways that work better.

❒ I will meditate more often.

❒ I will change how I talk to my spouse and children and get better about letting them know what I need from them.

❒ I will no longer be reluctant to ask for help.

❒ I will rest more often and not feel guilty when I rest.

❒ I will find new things that I can enjoy within the limits of my illness and pain.

❒ I will change my diet to include only food and drink choices that support my health.

❒ I will change my sleep habits to get better sleep.

❒ I will change how often I reach out to my friends.

❒ I will change how often I exercise and find options to keep moving that fit with my illness and pain.

❒ I will find a way to be of service to others.

❒ I will create a healing team that includes people such as my doctor, spouse, children, and nutritionist.

❒ I will change my work situation and find a less toxic work environment.

Copyright © 2026 Debra Burdick, *The Psychotherapy Toolbox for Chronic Illness and Chronic Pain*. All rights reserved.

❏ I will find ways to improve my mood by tuning into my feelings and thoughts, doing activities that help me feel better, and connecting with my friends more often.

❏ Other: _____

 Copyright © 2026 Debra Burdick, *The Psychotherapy Toolbox for Chronic Illness and Chronic Pain*. All rights reserved.

What Needs to Change?

Make a list of changes you have already made since your chronic illness or pain started. What helped you make the change? What changes were you forced to make? Which ones did you make purposefully? How did you feel after making the change?

_____

_____

_____

_____

Make a list of things that you still need to change for you to successfully manage your illness or pain, feel better, or maybe even improve your symptoms.

_____

_____

_____

_____

What changes do you resist and keep putting off? How can you motivate yourself to make these?

_____

_____

_____

_____

Once you've identified changes you still need to make, circle those that you can do starting today and number them in order of priority. If there are certain changes you need help with, make sure to identify on the list who you will ask for help. Post this list where you can see it every day, and check off any changes as you complete them. Notice how you feel when you have made a positive change that is on your list.

Copyright © 2026 Debra Burdick, *The Psychotherapy Toolbox for Chronic Illness and Chronic Pain*. All rights reserved.

Motivating Change

- **Engage** with the client by empathizing, accepting, affirming, and asking open-ended questions (the basic process of therapeutic engagement!).

  ° "What is it like to be chronically ill?"

  ° "It sounds like your chronic illness affects almost everything about your life."

  ° "It seems like it must be tough to deal with."

  ° "You've clearly tried a lot of things. It looks like you have managed pretty well to deal with the medical community."

- **Focus** on an agreed-upon goal.

  ° Ask the client what change(s) they think might be helpful to them. For example, "What do you struggle with the most that would make a big difference in your life if you changed it?" For example, improving sleep hygiene might significantly improve fatigue and mood if the client currently doesn't have a regular sleep schedule.

  ° Use Client Worksheets 2.5.1 and 2.5.2 to help them choose a goal.

  ° Agree to focus on one change at a time. For example, if the client says, "I know I need to eat a healthier diet and I probably could if I put my mind to it," then the focus will be on eating a healthier diet.

- **Evoke** "change talk" by asking open-ended questions, reflecting on the client's statements, and summarizing what the client says.

  ° "Change talk" is any statement the client makes that supports change. For example, you might say, "You said you need to eat a healthier diet. What are the reasons you think you need to eat a healthier diet? Have you ever eaten a healthy diet before?" In response, the client might say, "I think it will help me feel better. Last time I avoided gluten and dairy and ate only organic fruits and vegetables, I had more energy and my stomach didn't bother me."

 Copyright © 2026 Debra Burdick, *The Psychotherapy Toolbox for Chronic Illness and Chronic Pain*. All rights reserved.

- Reflect on the client's statement. For example, you might say, "So you know that a healthier diet would help you feel better and you are just looking for ways to be successful."

- Help the client **plan** what steps they will take next.

  - Continuing with the previous example, you might say, "So you have eaten a healthier diet before and think you can again if you put your mind to it. What do you think you will do next to add healthier options to your diet?"

Copyright © 2026 Debra Burdick, *The Psychotherapy Toolbox for Chronic Illness and Chronic Pain*. All rights reserved.

Skill 2.6 Reframing Thoughts

Background: When clients are ill or in pain, it is natural for them to get caught up in a stream of negative automatic thoughts such as "I feel so bad today," "I hate feeling this way," "What if I don't get better?" "I'm afraid of pain/being ill," "I need to fix it," "I'm going to die," or "I will never feel better." These unhelpful thoughts can rule the content of a client's mind and prevent them from living a full life despite illness or pain. This skill helps clients become more aware of their negative thought patterns and teaches them how to find thoughts that are more realistic, believable, and helpful. It combines cognitive restructuring, reframing, and thought defusion.

The Skill in Action: *Alice had been dealing with back pain for over a year, which doctors had been unable to explain. She had tried everything and anything to relieve her pain, but she still felt stressed and tense all the time. It was difficult to live her life because she spent much of her time thinking about the pain, worrying about it, and trying to fix it. With the help of her therapist, she began to tune in and notice any self-defeating thoughts she was having throughout the day, like "I'm afraid I will be in pain for the rest of my life." She then learned to replace these thoughts with more calming thoughts that turned down her stress response, like "I am safe. I have recovered from pain before in my life. I trust that I will live a good life with or without pain. I will enjoy my family today." By simply shifting her thoughts, she noticed that she felt less stressed and that her pain even lessened a bit. Since Alice also had a tendency to go online to try to find treatments to fix her pain, she decided to limit her online searches to one per day. Instead, she took a deep breath, remembered when she felt well, and looked at photos of her family. With these changes, she began to feel like pain was no longer overtaking her life.*

Skill Building: Use Client Handout 2.6.1: *Common Thought Patterns During Illness and Pain* to help clients become more aware of the cognitive distortions behind their thought patterns, followed by Client Handout 2.6.2: *Reframing Thoughts* to teach them how to replace any negative or unhelpful thoughts with thoughts that are realistic and move them forward. Instruct clients to use these handouts to periodically tune into their thoughts and notice the types of thoughts they are having. Whenever they are having a negative thought (e.g., "My health will never be the same"), have them practice replacing it with a more helpful or realistic thought (e.g., "I am taking control of my health and have found a medical professional that I trust to help me"). Encourage them to notice how they feel before and after using this type of reframing.

Reflection: What types of cognitive distortions did your client notice? Did learning about these thought types help them understand their own thought patterns? How did cognitive reframing change how they felt? Did the client begin to feel like they had more control over their thoughts and therefore their feelings?

Common Thought Patterns
During Illness or Pain

- **Focusing on the negative:** Constantly paying attention to the negatives of illness or pain and noticing how symptoms have changed for the worse, often to the exclusion of noticing more positive things in life.

    ° *Example:* Always thinking about how bad you feel or how many things you can no longer do, and ignoring how good it feels when your friends visit or that your pain has been getting a little better.

- **Discounting the positive:** Ignoring or dismissing the positive aspects of life when you have illness or pain.

    ° *Example:* Thinking about how bad you feel and ignoring the fact that your symptoms are better today, or that the weather is beautiful, or that your partner made your favorite lunch for you.

- **Catastrophizing:** Viewing and thinking about illness and pain as worse than it really is; perceiving a setback as the end of the world.

    ° *Example:* Thinking that a new pain or symptom necessarily means you are getting drastically worse or will die soon.

- **Figuring it out:** Constantly thinking about your illness or pain and searching for answers to understand it and make it go away.

    ° *Example:* Spending huge amounts of time searching the internet, looking up your symptoms and potential treatments, always looking for another way to heal.

- **Trying to fix it:** Spending a lot of time (and often money) thinking about how to heal your illness or reduce pain and what treatments to try.

    ° *Example:* Having difficulty accepting your illness or letting it be. Trying everything and anything no matter the cost.

- **Fortune telling:** Predicting the worst possible outcome for your illness, pain, or treatments.

    ° *Example:* "I just got diagnosed with cancer, so I'm doing to die."

Copyright © 2026 Debra Burdick, *The Psychotherapy Toolbox for Chronic Illness and Chronic Pain*. All rights reserved.

- **Fighting it:** Thinking about how to fight illness or pain, push through it, or overcome it.

  ° *Example:* Never resting, becoming exhausted, trying to do too much, pretending you aren't ill or in pain.

- **Always/never thinking:** Thinking in extremes with words like *always*, *never*, *every time*, *everything*, *everyone*, and *no one*. Seeing everything as "all good" or "all bad."

  ° *Example:* "I *always* get negative side effects from medication" or "Doctors *never* listen to me."

- **Mind reading:** Believing you know what others are thinking even when they haven't told you.

  ° *Example:* "Oh, no! My doctor looks upset. He must have bad news for me."

- **Jumping to conclusions:** Making assumptions before you have all of the evidence.

  ° *Example:* Assuming you need surgery when you read an MRI report about your back before discussing it with your doctor.

- **Minimization:** Downplaying the importance of certain events; this might involve minimizing a symptom, not following through with a treatment, or ignoring a doctor's recommendations.

  ° *Example:* Ignoring your pain, not telling your doctor about it, and telling your doctor everything is fine when it is not so.

Copyright © 2026 Debra Burdick, *The Psychotherapy Toolbox for Chronic Illness and Chronic Pain*. All rights reserved.

Reframing Thoughts

Thought	Thought Type	Reframe the Thought
I will never feel better.	Always/never thinking	I don't know that. I've been ill and then felt better.
My pain is so bad.	Focusing on the negative	I'm in pain, but I loved talking with my son today.
I must get everything done.	Fighting it	I can rest and ask for help.
I need to fix my illness.	Fixing it	I will do what I can to get better but also relax and let my body heal.
I have a disease, so I'm going to die.	Fortune telling	There is no way to know that. I will focus on being present today.
My test results must mean something awful.	Jumping to conclusions	I don't really know what they mean until my doctor explains them to me.
I'll figure out how to heal if I just keep trying.	Figuring it out	Trying to figure it out all the time exhausts me. I'll relax and ask my doctor how to get better.
Nothing is going right.	Discounting the positive	Even though today is hard, my bloodwork showed improvement.
This test result means I'll need surgery.	Catastrophizing	I don't know that. I'll ask the doctor.
Oh no! The doctor looked worried when she reviewed my test result.	Mind reading	I'll relax. Maybe she was frustrated with the computer, not my test result.
I won't call my doctor. This stomach pain will go away.	Minimization	I will take this pain seriously and call the doctor.

Copyright © 2026 Debra Burdick, *The Psychotherapy Toolbox for Chronic Illness and Chronic Pain*. All rights reserved.

Skill 2.7 Mindfulness of Emotions

Background: When clients are chronically ill or in chronic pain, they will undoubtedly experience a variety of emotions, such as worry, fear, anger, resentment, guilt, and sadness. By becoming more mindful of their emotions, they can increase their emotional self-regulation and resiliency, which is so critical when dealing with chronic illness or pain. This skill provides a simple process for being mindful of emotions, identifying the emotion without judging, and examining the present moment of the feeling without getting pulled into the past or future. It also helps the client become aware of any connection between their emotions and their illness or pain.

The Skill in Action: *Andrea had been diagnosed with fibromyalgia about six months before contacting a therapist. She was a very skilled research biologist, but she was often extremely stressed, and her anger bordered on rage at times. This was making it difficult for her to focus on work and competently do her job. With the help of her therapist, Andrea started learning how to identify signs that anger was escalating in her body (e.g., a racing heartbeat, muscle tension in her neck, and feeling hot), as well as what situations her anger was usually tied to (e.g., when her pain and brain fog interfered with her concentration, or when her boss gave her more work when she already felt overloaded). She also began noticing that her anger caused her pain levels to increase, making her feel even worse than before. This self-awareness helped her realize how important it was to learn to de-stress. Eventually, with lots of practice, she was able to lower her stress levels, after which her anger and pain levels seemed lower and more stable.*

Skill Building: Use Client Handout 2.7: *Mindful Awareness of Emotions* to help clients explore the three basic components of an emotion: (1) psychological or cognitive appraisal (the story behind the emotion); (2) physical response (how the emotion manifests in the body); and (3) our subjective experience of the emotion (how it feels to us internally). Then work with them to understand the process of nonjudgmentally observing and describing their emotions without trying to change them. Since emotions are often carried in the body, and even more so during illness or pain, you want to help the client notice if there is any connection between their physical symptoms and their emotions. Encourage your client to journal about their experiences whenever they practice mindfully observing their emotions, as journaling is a great way to consolidate what they are learning about the relationship between their emotions and their illness or pain.

Reflection: Ask your client what it was like to focus on their emotions as an observer. Were they able to identify and name the emotion? Where did it show up in their body? What thoughts triggered the emotion? What was their story behind the feeling? What did they notice about the connection between their emotions and their physical illness or pain? What have they learned from being more mindful of their emotions and journaling about their experience?

Mindful Awareness of Emotions

All emotions have three components:

1. **Psychological or cognitive appraisal:** This involves how you interpret your emotions or think about the situation. The thoughts or stories that accompany an emotion often pull your attention toward the past or the future, leading you to lose focus on the present moment. For example, you may feel overly upset about a new scar from surgery because you were teased about your appearance during adolescence or because you worry about finding a partner in the future.

2. **Physical sensations:** This involves how the emotion manifests in your body. All emotions have some physical component. For example, you may experience a stomachache, a pounding heart, tense shoulders, or a feeling of heat across your face.

3. **Subjective experience:** This involves how you feel the emotion internally in your mind. This can be subtle or quite obvious, as people experience emotions in different ways. For example, you may feel irritated, stressed, content, worried, or calm.

To start becoming more aware of your emotions, follow these steps:

1. The first step is to tune in and notice what you are feeling in a given moment. Simply notice the feeling without judging it or trying to change it. Identify the feeling by giving it a name.

2. Next, spend a moment exploring where this emotion is showing up in your body. For example, do you notice that your stomach hurts when you are anxious? Does your neck hurt when you are feeling stressed? Does your chest feel tight when you are angry? Have you noticed this feeling in your body before? Did you associate it with an emotion?

3. Notice if there is a connection between this feeling and your symptoms of illness or pain. For example, does your pain increase when you feel stressed? Do certain symptoms increase when you are worried, fearful, angry, or frustrated? Does changing or calming your emotion change your symptoms or pain?

Copyright © 2026 Debra Burdick, *The Psychotherapy Toolbox for Chronic Illness and Chronic Pain.* All rights reserved.

4. Reflect on what led to this emotion. What triggered it? Is this a feeling you have felt before? If so, what was going on back then that triggered this emotion? How is this past experience impacting your emotions today? How often do you feel this way?

5. Practice this periodically, especially when you are noticing a strong emotion.

 Copyright © 2026 Debra Burdick, *The Psychotherapy Toolbox for Chronic Illness and Chronic Pain*. All rights reserved.

Skill 2.8 Accepting What Is

Background: When a client with chronic illness or pain has trouble accepting the reality of their situation, they may become trapped in sadness, anger, and other painful emotions. This can cause them to behave in ways that make things worse. According to the principles of radical acceptance (Linehan, 2014), clients first need to accept their current situation if they want to make a change that reduces suffering. For example, if a client refuses to accept that their illness is causing exhaustion, then they will not be inclined to limit activity and rest when they are tired. In contrast, by accepting that they are exhausted, they can make a more effective change that helps their circumstances (e.g., taking a nap or delegating tasks). While they don't have to like that they are easily exhausted, they can acknowledge that this is reality and choose a more effective path forward. This skill provides a process for clients to practice radically accepting their illness or pain.

The Skill in Action: *David started therapy after he was diagnosed with chronic obstructive pulmonary disease (COPD), which left him short of breath, wheezing, coughing, and fatigued. He was being treated by a renowned lung specialist but still couldn't believe his diagnosis and was stuck in feelings of depression and anger. In therapy, he practiced how to radically accept both his diagnosis and his feelings about this diagnosis by tuning into his emotions and practicing letting them be. Then he practiced acknowledging that his diagnosis was accurate even though he didn't like it. It took a few weeks of practice before David felt like he could actually accept the reality of his illness and stop fighting against it, but once he did, he was able to better face his daily symptoms and more effectively handle his treatments. For example, his depression eased as he learned more about COPD and agreed to try recommended treatments, which were very helpful at managing his symptoms.*

Skill Building: Introduce the concept of radical acceptance and explain how it can reduce the emotional suffering surrounding the current situation with illness or pain. Use Client Handout 2.8: *Radical Acceptance* to walk clients through the steps of radically accepting their current situation. Encourage them to begin practicing this skill in less emotionally charged situations (e.g., radically accepting when the grocery store is out of their favorite ice cream flavor), as this will make it easier to practice radical acceptance during more difficult situations related to their chronic illness or pain.

Reflection: What emotions arose for the client as they practiced accepting the reality of their difficult situation? What resistance did they experience when they tried to practice this skill? How did accepting "what is" change how they felt? Were they better able to tolerate the distress caused by their pain or illness? Did they experience a sense of relief? Were they able to accept their situation even though they didn't like it?

Radical Acceptance

Radical acceptance involves accepting reality *as it is* instead of focusing on what you wish it could be or feel it should be. Here are the steps to practicing radical acceptance.

1. Identify what is difficult about your current situation with regard to your chronic illness or pain. For example: "I don't have enough energy to do everything I used to do, but I keep trying to do it all."

2. Stay in the present moment and pay attention to the emotions you are experiencing as you think about the situation. Allow emotions such as disappointment, sadness, or grief to surface, simply noticing these emotions without trying to change them or push them away. Let them be.

3. Similarly, tune into your body's sensations as you think about what you need to accept. Notice any tension, tightness, or pain you feel in your body and just let it be.

4. Then remind yourself that in order to change something you first have to accept it as it is. For example, if you are too tired, then you need to accept that you are tired. Once you accept that you are tired, then you can rest. Set an intention to stop fighting the reality of your situation and let go of the need to control the situation.

5. Then take some time to practice accepting your situation (and your emotions about it) for what it is with your mind, heart, and body. To do so, inhale through your nose to the count of four and exhale through your mouth as if you are blowing a bubble to the count of eight. Then repeat out loud, "It is what it is. I may not like it, but I can accept it."

6. Remember that life can be worth living even when it is painful.

Copyright © 2026 Debra Burdick, *The Psychotherapy Toolbox for Chronic Illness and Chronic Pain*. All rights reserved.

Skill 2.9 Release the Past

Background: Numerous studies show a relationship between a history of trauma (especially childhood trauma) and chronic illness and chronic pain (e.g., Felitti et al., 1998; Karimov-Zwienenberg et al., 2024). Trauma may contribute to mental and physical illness as the body continues to deal with the effects of being in survival mode long after the event occurred (van der Kolk, 2014). For example, an overlap has been found for those with fibromyalgia and those with anxiety, depression, and PTSD (Schubiner, 2022). Research supports the theory that letting go of suppressed emotions can be beneficial to the physical body. Many survivors of cancer who experienced radical remission expressed a belief that illness is a blockage on the physical, emotional, or spiritual level of our beings and that releasing the blockage by letting go of the past can positively impact health (Turner, 2014).

Although treating trauma per se is beyond the scope of this book, it is important to remember how past traumas or intense emotional experiences may still be impacting the client with chronic illness or pain. This skill provides a summary of the basics of trauma-informed therapy. Additionally, it provides options for helping clients identify past incidents of trauma or intense emotions, explore any connection between trauma and their illness or pain, and then let go and release the past.

The Skill in Action: *Jacob had a long history of chronic back pain. The medical community repeatedly told him there was no unhealed tissue or structural damage left over from a car accident he was involved in during his teens, so they could not identify any source of pain. When he felt stressed, his back pain always increased. His therapist helped him explore his current feelings about the long-ago car accident, and Jacob realized he hadn't processed his feelings after it happened. He remembered that he had felt helpless, extremely scared, and embarrassed when the accident occurred, and he noticed that he often felt that way when he was stressed as well. His therapist helped him set an intention to let go of the car accident and the feelings it evoked. He laughed when he realized that after the accident, he had become a student crosswalk monitor to help kids stay safe and then a police officer who often worked in traffic control. As a result, he could see the good that came out of his accident.*

Jacob tried a variety of options to let go of the impact the accident had on his present life. He felt like the options that worked the best for him were seeing the good that came from it, joining a yoga class that helped him get in touch with and love his body, visualizing the accident but changing the ending so he didn't get hurt, writing the story of his accident and burning it in his fire pit, and repeating a mantra that helped him stay present when he felt stressed ("I am safe and my back is healed"). Gradually, he noticed that his back pain was not as severe or as frequent.

Skill Building: Refer to Clinician Handout 2.9 to review options for assisting clients in letting go of a past traumatic experience and their feelings associated with it. Look back to your assessment (Skill 1.2) to explore past experiences that the client identified as causing intense emotions and that may have been traumatic for them. The most common emotions clients with illness or pain tend to hold on to are stress, fear, regret, shame, guilt, anger, sadness, and resentment. Some of these may be suppressed emotions, which are any emotions they are hanging on to from their past, whether positive or negative, conscious or unconscious. In that case, the client may benefit from deeper work such as hypnotherapy or eye movement desensitization and reprocessing (EMDR). Refer to www.emdria.org for more information and for certification in EMDR. If you do not do trauma work, refer the client to a colleague who specializes in it.

Reflection: Was the client able to identify past experiences that they are still holding on to in the present? Why did they think they were still holding on to those past hurts? Could they identify their feelings? Did they identify any connection between the past event and their current illness or pain? Were they able to identify what might change if they were able to let go? What strength, skill, knowledge, or clarity was the client able to identify? Were they surprised that something good came out of the negative experience? Which of the activities on the options list helped the client the most?

Options for Letting Go of the Past

Traumatic events, or even events that caused intense emotions, have been shown to increase the likelihood of some types of chronic illness or pain. In his book *The Body Keeps the Score*, Dr. Bessel van der Kolk (2014) explains that the body may remain in survival mode long after the event, which causes a strain on the nervous system and may result in chronic illness or pain.

Trauma-informed therapy involves (1) creating a safe place for clients to express their feelings without judgment, (2) teaching clients about stress reactions and managing stress, (3) teaching them emotion regulation skills, (4) practicing cognitive restructuring and thought defusion, (5) helping them shift from a "what's wrong with me" to "what happened to me" perspective, and (6) making meaning of their trauma. Although trauma-informed therapy is beyond the scope of this book, you can use many of the mental health skills in Section 2 for this purpose. In addition, refer to the following guidance to help clients feel safe, process their feelings, explore any connection between the illness or pain and the trauma, and let go of the past and move forward.

First, determine whether the client has experienced past events that were intense or felt traumatic. This entails exploring the client's history and assessing for PTSD, which is typically done during the initial assessment. Any event that caused intense emotions can feel traumatic to a client. If there is unresolved trauma and that is beyond your scope of practice, refer them to a trauma specialist.

If a trauma history is present and you will continue working with the client yourself, keep the following options and recommendations in mind:

- Create a safe place for the client and help them choose one event that still triggers intense feelings, such as stress, fear, regret, anger, shame, guilt, sadness, or resentment. Ask them to gently feel and sit with the feelings this event evokes in the present, reminding themselves that they are safe. Avoid re-traumatizing them. There is no need to ask them to remember or describe the details. Instead, help them practice mindfulness to bring their attention to the present moment instead of the past. Check in with the client often to monitor and assess progress through this challenging process.

  ° Use Worksheet 4.A.2: *Mindfulness of Surroundings* to help them ground themselves in the present moment.

  ° Use Skill 2.7: *Mindfulness of Emotions* to help them tune into how they feel and process their feelings with them in session.

Copyright © 2026 Debra Burdick, *The Psychotherapy Toolbox for Chronic Illness and Chronic Pain*. All rights reserved.

- Use Mindful Affirmation 6.11: *I Am Safe* to help them create safety in the present moment.

- Suggest referring them to a therapist who specializes in EMDR or hypnotherapy to orient trauma back to the past instead of the present.

- Discuss using neurofeedback to calm their overaroused brain and help them reregulate it.

- Ask the client to choose or create their own mantra that helps them rewire automatic negative thoughts about the past event and repeat it silently or aloud. Examples include:

  - I am safe, or I am finding ways to feel safe.

  - I choose to let go of the past or to create space around what happened.

  - I am noticing my surroundings and staying fully present in the moment.

  - I am resilient.

  - I am ready to move forward.

  - My experiences made me who I am, and I am awesome.

- Explore what, if any, connection might exist between the traumatic event and their current illness or pain. For example:

  - Did their physical symptoms start after the event?

  - Did a traumatic accident cause injury related to their pain or illness?

  - Does remembering the event increase symptoms?

  - If they were a victim of abuse or assault, is their illness or pain related to a physical injury or violation they incurred at that time?

- Help them move forward by working with them to consider why they hold on to the past hurts and what would change if they were to let these go.

  - Work with the client to set an intention to let go of what happened in the past. For example: "I intend to bring my attention to the present whenever I notice I am thinking of the past event. Then I will use a mantra for safety and let it go."

Copyright © 2026 Debra Burdick, *The Psychotherapy Toolbox for Chronic Illness and Chronic Pain*. All rights reserved.

- Identify the strength, skill, knowledge, or clarity they have gained from the painful past event. Focusing on these lessons may make it easier to let go.

- Have them practice visualizing a rewritten version of the event with a more positive ending. Help them change the ending to one where they are in charge and the trauma does not occur.

- Encourage them to practice accepting what they cannot change in the past. Use Skill 2.8: *Accepting What Is* to help them practice acceptance and move on.

- Suggest that they write a letter to the person(s) who hurt them and say what they wish they could have said then. They do not need to send it!

- They can also choose to forgive those that hurt them. Help them write a letter of forgiveness explaining that they will never like what the other person(s) did that hurt them, but they have chosen to let go of it now. They can choose whether or not to send the letter.

- Ask the client to list the past traumatic event(s) on paper and destroy the list when they are done as a way to let it go. Perhaps do a small letting-go ceremony around a fire pit and burn what they wrote.

- Explore activities that provide a safe space for the client to let it all out. This can involve expressing their feelings though art, music, dance, or play. Perhaps they can draw an angry picture, write or perform music that speaks to them, dance and act out their emotions through movement, or engage in some playful activities, such as blowing bubbles or playing with a pet. You may also suggest that the client do some bodywork, such as yoga, massage, or cranial sacral therapy, to help them reconnect with their body and feel comfortable being present.

Copyright © 2026 Debra Burdick, *The Psychotherapy Toolbox for Chronic Illness and Chronic Pain*. All rights reserved.

Skill 2.10 Secondary Gain

Background: Clients who are chronically ill or in pain often experience some type of hidden benefit, called secondary gain, due to their symptoms. For example, they may get others to do things for them that they might be capable of doing for themselves, such as cooking or cleaning. Their illness might serve as a great excuse to stay home when they don't want to take part in a difficult family gathering or go to a toxic work environment. They might get out of taking care of others because they are ill, which relieves their guilt. They may use their illness as an excuse for lashing out and taking their anger out on others. In addition, if they are receiving disability benefits due to their chronic illness or pain, they will lose this income if they get well. All of these factors can keep people stuck in illness. This skill provides guidance on helping clients recognize the hidden benefits they may be getting from staying ill.

The Skill in Action: *Maria had severe arthritis that made it difficult to walk. She started asking everyone in her family to do tasks for her around the house and to grocery shop for her. When a new medication improved Maria's pain considerably and she could walk much more easily, she didn't let her family know and continued her pattern of expecting everyone to wait on her. While her family members were glad to help, they often felt annoyed when Maria treated them like servants, especially if she could do something for herself. When Maria's therapist explored her behavior with her, Maria realized that she enjoyed being waited on and was afraid it would stop if she got better. But she knew her family members were not happy with her. Reluctantly, she started doing more things for herself and only asking for help when she really needed it. She noticed she felt better about being able to do things for herself and gained back some strength in her muscles that she had lost when she sat down all day. Her family members were thankful, and their annoyance with her decreased.*

Skill Building: Explain the concept of secondary gain to your client. Use Client Worksheet 2.10 to help them examine what hidden benefits their chronic illness or pain might be providing them, both consciously and subconsciously. For example, are they avoiding a difficult work situation rather than finding ways to improve it or find a better job? Do they expect others to wait on them hand and foot when they could do things for themselves? Look for behaviors that started when their illness or pain was interfering with their day-to-day functioning but have since resolved now that they are feeling better. Discuss what hidden benefits the client would lose if they got well. Remind them that it's often necessary to ask for help, but they must confront the fact that they may need to give up these hidden benefits and find more effective options for dealing with difficult issues in order to get better.

Reflection: What type of hidden benefits does the client gain as a result of their chronic illness or pain? How does the thought of losing these benefits impact the client's ability to manage their illness or get well? What issues does the client avoid addressing? How does this fit with their mental health issues or overall personality?

Secondary Gain

When you are ill or in pain, you undoubtedly need to (and should) ask for help. But it's important to notice any times when you're using your illness or pain to your advantage (e.g., to get out of doing things) rather than dealing with issues that need to be addressed. We call these kinds of hidden benefits "secondary gain." Use this worksheet to think about how you might be using your chronic illness or pain for secondary gain.

To begin, think about whether you use your illness as an excuse to avoid certain responsibilities or get others to complete tasks for you that you could do for yourself. Do you expect special treatment?

_____

_____

_____

Do you keep asking others to do things that you once needed help with (e.g., cooking, cleaning) even though you are well enough now to do them yourself? While it's often necessary to ask for help, be mindful of how you might have developed a pattern of using your illness or pain as an excuse.

_____

_____

_____

Are you reluctant to let others know you are feeling better because doing so would mean losing certain benefits, such as disability income? What types of benefits are you worried about losing?

_____

_____

_____

As you answer these questions, be honest with yourself. You must give up any secondary gain behavior to be well.

Copyright © 2026 Debra Burdick, *The Psychotherapy Toolbox for Chronic Illness and Chronic Pain*. All rights reserved.

Skill 2.11 Relationships

Background: Chronic illness and pain can have a profound impact on a client's relationships, including their relationship with themselves, their love partner, their parents, their children, their siblings, their friends, and their coworkers. Even clients who had good relationship skills prior to becoming ill may have difficulty navigating relationships once they are ill or in pain. For example, they may struggle with communicating, being intimate, taking on certain roles, asking for help, feeling too dependent, feeling misunderstood, and more. This skill helps clients identify changes in their relationships due to their illness or pain and clarifies the areas they need help with.

The Skill in Action: *Sue loved her husband, George, and felt like she had a wonderful marriage. However, when she began to have chronic, unremitting pain, she worried that she was losing her connection with George. She was often irritable and impatient, and she didn't enjoy sex when her pain was so bad. She was having trouble completing tasks around the house, and her performance at work was slipping because her desk chair was aggravating her pain. With the help of a therapist, Sue learned how to better understand and manage her anger, set realistic expectations for herself, and ask for help. Sue was able to talk to her husband and share her concerns about their relationship. Together, they worked out new ways to share intimacy, such as finding more comfortable positions for Sue and exploring how they could meet their needs when Sue's pain was too great for sex. They also developed a code Sue could use to let George know when she was feeling angry or exhausted, and George started to chip in a lot more around the house. Sue explained her pain issue to her boss as well, who got her an ergonomic chair and lowered her work hours by a few hours per week, both of which helped immensely. Finally, Sue talked with her doctor to make sure he knew the level of pain she was dealing with. The doctor seemed to hear her for the first time and explored several new treatment options.*

Skill Building: Use Client Worksheet 2.11.1 to help clients identify how their various relationships have been impacted by their chronic illness or pain. Use the client's answers to brainstorm ways in which they can lessen this impact where possible. For example, if a client's boss doesn't understand why they need to cut back to part time, explore how the client might contact someone in their human resources department (who is familiar with the Americans with Disabilities Act) to explain what they need at work to accommodate their illness or pain. Then use Client Worksheet 2.11.2 to specifically examine the ways in which a client's love relationship has been strained by chronic illness or pain, and brainstorm possible solutions. For example, if their partner is angry because the client can't help out as much as they used to, but the client hasn't been honest with their partner about their illness, explore how the client can open up communication, represent themselves, explain their illness, discuss what they are capable of, and ask for what they need. As you are brainstorming alternatives, make sure to help the client see the situation from their partner's perspective as well.

Reflection: How does the client's chronic illness or pain strain their existing relationship skills? Do they have trouble with similar issues in more than one relationship? What basic relationship skills can you help them learn to address these impacts on their relationships? On the flip side, has their chronic illness or pain had any positive impact on their relationships or their ability to represent themselves?

Client Worksheet 2.11.1

My Relationships

Check off any changes your illness or pain has caused in your relationships.

Love Partner

- ❏ We experience reduced intimacy, closeness, or sexual desire.

- ❏ We don't spend as much time together or engage in shared activities.

- ❏ We have difficulties communicating.

- ❏ My partner is my caregiver, which changes my role from equal partner with them to being dependent on them.

- ❏ I feel guilty about not doing my share.

- ❏ My partner worries about me.

- ❏ My partner experiences loss, too, because I can no longer share activities with them or take care of household chores, and they may not share their feelings about this.

- ❏ My partner often feels ignored.

- ❏ I often feel ignored.

- ❏ My partner treats me like a sick child.

Children

- ❏ I am not able to participate in my children's activities as often.

- ❏ I have difficulty taking care of my children.

- ❏ My children fear losing me.

- ❏ My children get angry that I cannot do things other parents do.

Other Family Members

- ❏ My family members function as caregivers, which changes their role in my life, potentially including a role reversal in that they now care for me when I used to care for them.

Copyright © 2026 Debra Burdick, *The Psychotherapy Toolbox for Chronic Illness and Chronic Pain*. All rights reserved.

☐ My family doesn't understand what I'm dealing with.

☐ My family feels helpless and doesn't know what to do to help.

☐ It is hard to stay connected when my illness prevents me from visiting them or otherwise staying in touch.

Friends

☐ We have difficulty getting together socially.

☐ We have difficulty staying in touch.

☐ My friends have trouble understanding what I'm going through.

☐ I have difficulty relating to my friends' lives from my perspective.

☐ My friends get tired of hearing about my illness or pain.

☐ I often feel left out.

Boss and Coworkers

☐ My boss and coworkers may not understand how my illness impacts my ability to work.

☐ My boss worries that I won't do my share at work.

☐ There are concerns that my illness is impacting my work performance or my ability to keep working.

☐ I am losing my connections with my coworkers, as I have missed a lot of work due to illness or medical appointments.

☐ I am uncertain about my work future because I don't know if my illness will prevent me from continuing or returning to work.

Medical Providers

☐ I find it hard to feel like my providers really know who I am.

☐ I don't get enough time to discuss my issues with them.

☐ I often feel discounted.

☐ My providers feel impatient with my lack of progress.

☐ My providers blame me for my illness or pain.

Copyright © 2026 Debra Burdick, *The Psychotherapy Toolbox for Chronic Illness and Chronic Pain*. All rights reserved.

Love Relationship Skills

Think about the relationship you have with your spouse or love partner, and use this checklist to determine which relationship skills have been negatively affected by your illness or pain ("impacted"), which skills you are still able to use effectively ("good at"), and which skills you need help improving ("need help").

	Impacted	Good At	Need Help
Expressing love	☐	☐	☐
Sharing and discussing feelings	☐	☐	☐
Being honest about our needs	☐	☐	☐
Communicating openly	☐	☐	☐
Treating each other with kindness	☐	☐	☐
Being respectful	☐	☐	☐
Being honest	☐	☐	☐
Trusting each other	☐	☐	☐
Having empathy	☐	☐	☐
Being able to resolve conflict	☐	☐	☐
Seeing things from each other's perspective	☐	☐	☐
Having fun together	☐	☐	☐
Compromising	☐	☐	☐
Being vulnerable and letting each other in	☐	☐	☐
Understanding each other	☐	☐	☐
Listening without blaming or getting defensive	☐	☐	☐
Being intimate	☐	☐	☐
Showing appreciation for each other	☐	☐	☐
Helping each other	☐	☐	☐
Managing emotions	☐	☐	☐
Letting go of past disagreements	☐	☐	☐
Forgiving each other	☐	☐	☐
Spending time together	☐	☐	☐
Keeping promises	☐	☐	☐
Standing up for each other	☐	☐	☐

 Copyright © 2026 Debra Burdick, *The Psychotherapy Toolbox for Chronic Illness and Chronic Pain*. All rights reserved.

Skill 2.12 Mindset and Imagining Wellness

Background: Your mindset is a set of beliefs or attitudes that shape how you make sense of yourself and the world. Your mindset influences how you think, feel, and behave in any given situation. When it comes to chronic illness and pain, mindset has been shown to impact treatment outcomes as well as the ability to make positive change. For example, adopting a growth mindset might consist of believing you can get well or being open to learning new ways to manage your illness or pain. This skill guides clients in adopting a more helpful mindset that moves them toward their healing goals. It also provides a meditation they can use to imagine how they would feel if they were completely well. Every time they practice this meditation, they can send their body a powerful healing message and perhaps adopt a more positive mindset.

The Skill in Action: *Jim was not surprised when he was diagnosed with type 2 diabetes, as his mother had been diagnosed at the same age. He believed there was nothing he could do to manage his out-of-control blood sugar levels, especially since his mother couldn't, so he didn't try. This fixed mindset caused him to engage in behaviors that made his diabetes worse, such as eating foods that spiked his blood sugar and leading a sedentary lifestyle. When Jim explored this fixed mindset with his therapist, he opened to the possibility that perhaps if he exercised, brought his weight into the range recommended to him, and adopted a healthy diet, he could get his blood sugar under control. With this new mindset, he began to focus on his weight by exercising and eating more mindfully. With these changes, he was amazed to discover that he was able to stabilize his blood sugar levels and even reduce his need for medication. He also practiced imagining wellness, which helped him feel better and motivated him to maintain the changes he had made.*

Skill Building: Use Client Worksheet 2.12.1 to help clients understand the difference between a fixed mindset and a growth mindset, including the specific types of mindset statements that ring true for them. Discuss how these statements guide their behavior and, in turn, can help or hinder their ability to manage their illness or pain. Help them explore and reframe any false beliefs that their mindset is based on (see Skill 2.6: *Reframing Thoughts*). Be aware that what medical providers say can powerfully shape a client's mindset. For example, if a doctor adds morphine to a client's IV drip and tells the client they should expect to feel relief, that client is more likely to experience less pain than another client who has morphine added to their IV without their knowledge.

Next, use the brief guided meditation on Client Handout 2.12.2: *Imagine Wellness* to help clients imagine how it would feel to be completely well. A key to success with this skill is to go beyond simply *thinking* about wellness to imagine how it *feels* in their mind and body. The mind is a very powerful healer that can shift a person's physiology. If the client can't remember how they used to feel when they were well, ask them to imagine what they think it would feel like or how they would want to feel. Be prepared to process feelings of sadness and loss for some clients, as the meditation may remind them of the many losses their illness or pain has caused.

Reflection: Does the client have a fixed mindset or a growth mindset? Is their mindset based on any false beliefs? If they have a fixed mindset, how can you help them shift out of it? For example, just because a client's parent died from heart disease does not mean that they will, especially if they choose positive health behaviors. How does imagining wellness help the client shift their mindset?

Mindset

A **fixed mindset** is a belief that you cannot learn, change, or control something in your life. This type of mindset hinders your progress because it prevents you from being flexible, adopting new behaviors to manage your pain or illness, or being open to finding new ways to take care of yourself. Here are some examples of fixed mindset statements. Check off any that apply to you:

❑ Stress is going to kill me.

❑ I'm going to die from _____.

❑ Nothing will help me.

❑ My illness runs in my family, so nothing will help me.

❑ Nothing I try works, so why bother?

❑ I can't change.

❑ I never heal well.

❑ Other: _____

❑ Other: _____

In contrast, a **growth mindset** makes you open to learning new things, helps you be more flexible, and gives you more control of your life. A growth mindset supports your progress because you can take charge of your health, adopt healthy behaviors as you learn new things, and set positive expectations that help motivate you to take the best care of yourself. Here are some examples of growth mindset statements. Check off any that apply to you:

❑ I can control how I respond to stress.

❑ I am in charge of my mind, body, and health.

❑ I am in good hands, so I am confident the treatment will work.

❑ My body is good at healing.

❑ I expect to successfully manage my illness or pain.

❑ I can change.

Copyright © 2026 Debra Burdick, *The Psychotherapy Toolbox for Chronic Illness and Chronic Pain*. All rights reserved.

☐ I know diet and exercise help my health and pain.

☐ I expect to live a long, productive, and enjoyable life.

☐ Other: _____

☐ Other: _____

 Copyright © 2026 Debra Burdick, *The Psychotherapy Toolbox for Chronic Illness and Chronic Pain*. All rights reserved.

Imagine Wellness

You can find the guided audio for this meditation at **www.thebrainlady.com/pesi-meditations**.

Imagination is a powerful way to help your brain remember what being well feels like. Use the following meditation to imagine how you would feel if you were well.

Begin by closing your eyes or relaxing your gaze. Inhale through your nose while you count to four . . . 1, 2, 3, 4 . . . Then exhale through your mouth while pursing your lips to the count of eight . . . 1, 2, 3, 4, 5, 6, 7, 8 . . . And now just breathe normally.

Spend a few moments imagining what it would feel like to be completely well. Perhaps you can remember how it felt in the past when you were completely well and pain free. If not, imagine what it would feel like or how you would like to feel.

(*Pause*)

Tune into your thoughts. If you were well, what would you be thinking about? Would you be thinking about how wonderful it feels to be completely well? Perhaps you would be thinking about how comfortable your mind and body feel. Or maybe you would think about all the things you can do now that you are completely well. Spend a few moments tuning into what you would be thinking when you are completely well.

(*Pause*)

Now notice how your body would feel when you are completely well. Would your body feel healthy, vibrant, comfortable, strong, flexible, or at ease? Tune in and imagine that your body feels that way right now. Feel it!

(*Pause*)

Now pay attention to what emotions you would feel when you are completely well. Would you feel relieved, content, happy, relaxed, free, or perhaps even joyful? Take a few moments to imagine these emotions. Feel them!

(*Pause*)

Spend 20 to 30 seconds three times a day, as well as a full minute at bedtime, imagining you are feeling completely well. Make sure you imagine *feeling* it, not just thinking about it.

Copyright © 2026 Debra Burdick, *The Psychotherapy Toolbox for Chronic Illness and Chronic Pain*. All rights reserved.

Skill 2.13 Let Thoughts Go By on a Lazy River

Background: For many clients, it can become difficult, if not impossible, to stop focusing on symptoms of chronic illness or pain. Their symptoms have a way of grabbing their attention and drawing them in, over and over again, and sometimes continuously. The more they pay attention to their symptoms, the worse they typically get. This skill uses the metaphor of a lazy river to help clients interrupt and replace their constant stream of unhelpful thoughts related to their symptoms of illness or pain.

The Skill in Action: *Sheila had a tumor the size of an orange removed from her brain, which left her with a number of disabling conditions, including emotional reactivity and poor organization. She would become enraged easily, especially when a family member discounted her disability and claimed she was making it all up. She would still be enraged several days later. In therapy, she learned how to use the lazy river technique to practice letting go of angry thoughts. She would picture her family member sitting in a raft and then let the raft flow by without engaging with the angry thought that this family member triggered. After practicing this technique for a while, she decided to imagine a happy, helpful raft floating down the lazy river as well. Whenever that raft floated by, she got in it and went for a ride. This process helped her regulate her anger and gave her some control over her tendency toward reactivity.*

Skill Building: Use the guided meditation on Client Handout 2.13: *Lazy River Meditation* to help clients imagine they are watching rafts float by in a lazy river (or, alternatively, watching leaves floating down a stream). Explain that this process helps them get into the practice of letting illness or pain thoughts float by without engaging in them. Encourage them to practice this guided meditation several times per day whenever they notice that they are focused on symptoms or pain. As they familiarize themselves with the meditation, ask them to notice what negative rafts tend to float by during their day. Encourage them to practice focusing on the positive, healing rafts instead and let the others go by.

Reflection: What thoughts or images did the client see in the unhelpful rafts? Were they able to let those rafts go by? How did they feel as they watched these rafts float down the river without going along for the ride? What did their positive rafts look like? How did it feel to ride the positive raft downstream? How did practicing this guided meditation change their stream of unhelpful thoughts? Did they gain more control of their thoughts? Did it change their experience of illness or pain symptoms?

Lazy River Meditation

You can find the guided audio for this meditation at **www.thebrainlady.com/pesi-meditations**.

Sometimes our minds get really busy and we keep thinking about things that aren't important or that don't feel good, especially during illness or pain. This meditation helps you practice noticing your thoughts and feelings and letting go of them without paying attention to or engaging with them. This practice helps you gain control of your thoughts by dismissing unwanted thoughts and staying focused on the present.

Take a moment to settle into a comfortable position, and either close your eyes or lightly lower your gaze to the floor. Take a few deep breaths in . . . and out . . . in . . . and out . . .

Now imagine you are at a water park watching colorful rafts float by on a lazy river. Take a moment to picture the river with rafts of all different sizes, shapes, and colors flowing by. The goal is to simply notice them and let them float by. Don't get onto the rafts or get "hooked" by them.

As you picture yourself standing beside the river, watching the rafts coming toward you, imagine that your thoughts, wishes, feelings, and bodily sensations are riding in the rafts. Watch them come toward you on the river. You might notice a word or picture on the side of the raft that represents your thoughts or feelings.

As they come closer to you, just watch them come and float by, and then look upstream to see what comes down the river next. Remember, do not get into any of the rafts. Do not pay special attention to any particular raft. Just let them all go by.

Try not to attach to or push away what you notice on the river. Just let it all come and go by.

Keep watching the steady stream of rafts floating by for a few more moments. Notice the rafts and what they are carrying, but just let them float by. If you see any rafts that look unhappy or angry, let those rafts go by.

Now imagine that you see a raft with something happy or fun written on it or that looks positive or pleasing. What do you see? Keep looking for the happy rafts,

Copyright © 2026 Debra Burdick, *The Psychotherapy Toolbox for Chronic Illness and Chronic Pain*. All rights reserved.

and when you find one you like, imagine that you get into that raft and float down the lazy river with the happy thoughts or feelings that go with it.

Keep floating in the happy raft for a little while. Then, when you are ready, gently get out of the raft, leave the lazy river, and come back to the present moment.

 Copyright © 2026 Debra Burdick, *The Psychotherapy Toolbox for Chronic Illness and Chronic Pain*. All rights reserved.

Skill 2.14 Staying Calm During Medical Tests and Procedures

Background: Clients with chronic illness and pain must often undergo medical tests and treatment procedures that can be extremely anxiety provoking. Some may be painful, such as surgery or dental work, while others may cause claustrophobia, such as getting an MRI or having one's head immobilized during radiation treatment. In addition, some clients may have such a strong blood-injection-injury phobia that the thought of getting their blood drawn can cause them to faint. This isn't to mention that they may worry about complications from a procedure or experience intense fear that a test result will be indicative of a serious issue. This skill provides a relaxation meditation that clients can practice before and during medical tests or procedures to calm their fear and anxiety.

The Skill in Action: *Safi was due to have an MRI in a couple of weeks. She knew from past experience that she felt extreme claustrophobia when she had this scan. Plus, she hated the side effects of the anti-anxiety medication that the doctors gave her to make being in the MRI machine more bearable. When she told her therapist she was very worried about the upcoming scan, he walked her through a guided relaxation meditation and gave her an audio recording of it to listen at home every day until the MRI. Once the day of the scan came, she listened to the meditation before and prearranged to have the technician play her meditation on the headphones during the scan. She later described her experience to the therapist: "Every time my attention wandered from my breathing and started to focus on the fact that I was in that tube, I accepted the thought, dismissed it, and returned my attention to counting my exhales. I began to feel a sense of comfort, and instead of feeling confined in a tiny space, I felt like I was snuggled into a safe cocoon. As the MRI machine bombarded me with clicking, tapping, whirring, and popping sounds, I noticed them but then returned my attention to counting my breaths. I was able to float through the rest of the test. I slowly became drowsy and drifted in and out of sleep. I am way less worried about future MRIs or other tests now that I know I can calm myself like this."*

Skill Building: When a client is anxious about an upcoming medical test or procedure, teach them the guided meditation on Client Handout 2.14 to help them turn down their stress response. Encourage them to listen to this meditation several times a day until they can quickly calm their mind and body when they need to. They can then use the meditation before and sometimes even during any medical test or procedure that causes fear, anxiety, or claustrophobia. Explain that it is normal to become distracted while doing this meditation, but as soon as they notice that their mind is drifting, they can gently return their attention to the meditation.

Reflection: Was the client open to listening to the meditation? How did they feel while listening? Were they able to stay focused? Were they able to dismiss distractions and return their attention to the meditation? Have they noticed any change in their anxiety, fear, tension, or stress levels as they continue to practice? How has the meditation helped them during medical tests or procedures?

Staying Calm During Medical Tests and Procedures

You can find the guided audio for this meditation at **www.thebrainlady.com/pesi-meditations**.

Practice the following guided meditation several times a day until you can do it easily and effortlessly. The more you practice it when you aren't experiencing any worry, fear, panic, or claustrophobia, the easier and more effective it will be to use when you are feeling distressed. Then you can use it before—and potentially during—any medical test or procedure that is difficult for you.

To begin, close your eyes and take a deep belly breath, inhaling through your nose to a count of four and then exhaling slowly through your mouth with pursed lips, like you are blowing a huge bubble, to a count of eight. Continue to breathe this way while you imagine that you are inhaling peace, comfort, and relaxation . . . and exhaling stress, worry, and tension.

Now breathe normally while observing the feeling of your breath. Start counting each time you exhale. When you've counted four breaths, start over and count another set of four. If you become distracted, that's okay. Just bring your attention back to counting. Keep doing this for several minutes.

Every time your attention wanders from your breath and starts to focus on the fact that you're having a medical test or procedure, acknowledge the thought and then return your attention to counting your exhales. Notice your heart rate as it slows down to a normal pace. Notice how your shoulders, face, and legs feel as they begin to relax. Become aware of the moisture in your mouth. Tune into a sense of comfort, and imagine you feel like you're snuggled into a safe cocoon.

Now imagine that you are floating gently and effortlessly on a soft cushion in a pool or calm lake. Imagine the feel of the water—the gentle waves flowing around you. Picture the blue sky, the beautiful clouds, and the sparkling water. Visualize the peaceful scene around you and listen to the sounds of the birds. You're far away as you float through the rest of the test or procedure. Whenever your attention comes back to the room, acknowledge where you are, that all is proceeding according to plan, and then take a few more relaxation breaths and return your attention to your imagined peaceful place until the procedure is complete.

 Copyright © 2026 Debra Burdick, *The Psychotherapy Toolbox for Chronic Illness and Chronic Pain*. All rights reserved.

Skill 2.15 Laugh

Background: Norman Cousins (1979) demonstrated the power of laughter in his classic book *Anatomy of an Illness*, where he described how people can take charge of their own health by using humor to boost their body's capacity for healing. Not only does laughter result in the release of endorphins (which are natural "feel-good" hormones that can boost mood and relieve pain), but laughter can induce several physiological changes to the body that reduce stress, such as decreased blood pressure and increased oxygen intake. It can also rewire the brain in positive ways. Although laughter can be healing, most of us don't do it often enough, especially during illness or pain. This skill reminds clients to practice laughing out loud on a regular basis.

The Skill in Action: *Joanna felt miserable. She had just been diagnosed with cancer and started chemotherapy a few weeks ago. She was experiencing severe side effects from the treatment, and all she could think about was how awful she felt. When Joanna's therapist suggested she try laughing, she thought her therapist was crazy. How could she possibly laugh when she felt so ill? But she trusted her therapist and gave it a try in session by simply starting to laugh for no reason at all. At first, she just made sounds like she was laughing. But as she did so, she laughed harder and harder as the sound of her laughter made her laugh even more. Soon, she was genuinely laughing. She noticed a feeling of release and relief after laughing in session. This prompted her to start noticing opportunities for humor around her, like when the chemotherapy nurse joked with her during infusion sessions or when her neighbor laughed about the landscaper's outfit with her while driving her to her treatments. Joanna also loved watching funny cat videos online. All of this helped her to feel more relaxed, joyful, and connected to others. She no longer thought her therapist was crazy!*

Skill Building: Explore the benefits of laughter with the client. Since it may be difficult for clients who are dealing with chronic illness or pain to even consider laughing, let them know that you are not discounting their experience. Rather, you are encouraging them to allow themselves to laugh despite how bad they may feel at the moment. Some clients will have an easier time with this than others. To remind them of the benefits of laughter, it can help to ask them to remember a time when they laughed out loud. Ask them to really tune into this experience and remember how good it felt.

Then use Client Handout 2.15 to encourage them to set an intention to notice funny things around them every day. Ask them what things make them smile or laugh out loud. Perhaps it's a grandchild's funny words as they learn to talk, a favorite sitcom, a pet, or funny videos on social media. Explore how they can find more laughter in their life, and discuss when and how they can practice laughing out loud every day. Laugh with them right now. Simply laugh. Now laugh again and just keep laughing. Go for a true belly laugh.

Reflection: Was the client open to laughing? Did they feel silly? Do they already laugh a lot? How does setting an intention to laugh help them laugh more often? How does deliberately laughing out loud for no particular reason feel to them? Do they notice feeling less pain or feel safer after they laugh?

Laugh

Laughter can be healing. That's right! When you laugh, your body releases "feel-good" hormones known as endorphins, which have been found to boost mood and decrease pain. Laughter can even turn down the danger signals that pain and illness may send to your brain and help you feel calm and safe.

Here are some ways to start incorporating more laughter into your day:

- Notice funny things around you! This can include:

  ° The funny antics of a child or pet

  ° A joke

  ° A comedy show

  ° A pun or word play

  ° A funny video on social media

- Remember a previous time when you laughed out loud. Bring the experience to mind and see if you chuckle out loud or smile as you think about it again.

- Just start laughing for no reason at all. Go ahead and do it now—laugh! Keep laughing until it's hard to stop.

Notice any changes in how you feel now that you have laughed. For example, do you feel lighter? More relaxed? Less focused on your pain or illness?

 Copyright © 2026 Debra Burdick, *The Psychotherapy Toolbox for Chronic Illness and Chronic Pain*. All rights reserved.

Behavioral Health Skills

Skill 3.1 Working with the Medical Community

Background: As helpful and essential as the medical community is, clients often find it challenging and frustrating to work with medical providers. First, it can be difficult to get an appointment with their desired provider in a timely manner, as wait times often exceed many months. Even follow-up appointments can be equally tough to schedule at times. Second, many clients find it hard to discuss their symptoms and feel like their concerns aren't taken seriously. Some providers don't seem to want to answer the client's questions at all, and depending on a provider's area of expertise, some will be better than others at explaining diagnoses as well as the treatments for them. This skill helps clients explore options for taking control of their health care, representing themselves with their medical providers, and preparing for office visits and asking questions.

The Skill in Action: *Antwone had been monitoring a heart-related condition for a few years. After his latest angiogram, his doctor recommended bypass surgery to open up several major clogged arteries, and he referred Antwone to a heart surgeon. Before his appointment with the heart surgeon, Antwone reviewed the results of his angiogram and took time to educate himself about his condition, the bypass surgery, and its associated risks and prognosis. Since he didn't understand some of the information he'd read, he wrote down questions he wanted to ask the surgeon. At his appointment, he followed up on these questions and asked the provider how many of these surgeries he had performed and what the outcomes were. Antwone felt like the provider was reluctant to answer his questions, ignored some of them, and seemed irritated by the rest.*

Antwone felt like he should get a second opinion, so he found a highly respected heart surgeon at a major medical center nearby and got an appointment right away. He again asked the same questions to this new provider, who readily answered his questions and made him feel like they were a team. Antwone felt much more comfortable with and reassured by this provider, so he decided to have her do the bypass surgery. His surgery and recovery went well, and he continued asking questions throughout the process, which the provider was happy to answer.

Skill Building: Explain to clients that it is important for them to take control of their health care so they can receive the best possible care. Explore areas where they have been successful at advocating for themselves and what areas need improvement. Discuss the process of making an appointment, and encourage clients to ask to be put on a waiting list if the wait is long and to consider calling a different provider to find an appointment that will be sooner.

Use Client Handout 3.1 to explain the importance of preparing for their medical appointment in advance. Explain that the more questions a patient asks their medical provider, the better their treatment outcome is likely to be. Therefore, they should review any of their prior bloodwork or medical results and highlight what has changed so they can ask the provider about it. Encourage them to look online for reputable articles that discuss their symptoms and treatment options. The more informed they are, the better questions they can ask, and the better care they will receive.

In addition, discuss the importance of finding providers that welcome their questions and are willing to discuss their health concerns with them. Some providers are more open to questions than others, so clients may need to search for a new provider who is more willing to communicate and answer their questions. Some people even interview multiple prospective medical providers to make sure they are a good fit, so that is an option for your client as well.

Reflection: In what areas was the client already able to effectively self-advocate and in what areas did they need help? How did doing some research ahead of their visit prepare them and help them get the best treatment? What types of questions seemed to help the client the most? Was their provider willing to answer their questions and help them understand the answers and feel reassured? Were they able to find another provider if their current one didn't readily answer their questions?

Working with the Medical Community

The following steps can help you take control of your health care, better represent yourself with providers, and prepare for office visits.

- Search online to learn about your symptoms, their possible causes, diagnosis, treatment options, and prognosis and make a list of questions to ask your doctor.

- Look at your test results when they are posted and look up what they mean online so you can ask educated questions when you see your provider. Although you want to educate yourself to the best of your ability, be careful not to jump to conclusions or predict the worst before talking with your provider.

  ° If you don't understand the medical jargon or the test results, add that to your list of questions.

  ° Be aware there is a lot of misinformation online, so visit trusted websites such as your provider's website, national medical associations, WebMD, the Cleveland Clinic, or the Mayo Clinic. You can also look up research articles listed on the National Library of Medicine (https://pubmed.ncbi .nlm.nih.gov).

- At your office visit:

  ° State why you are there, including your chief complaint. Describe your symptoms, what makes them worse or better, and your pain level. Explain how your current pain level compares with previous experiences of pain, as well as the results of what you've tried already.

  ° Present the results of previous testing and be specific about what you need help with.

  ° Share your medical and family history with the provider.

  ° Bring a list of your medications and dosages, and explain what you take them for and how they help.

 Copyright © 2026 Debra Burdick, *The Psychotherapy Toolbox for Chronic Illness and Chronic Pain*. All rights reserved.

- Why you should ask questions:

  ° Research shows that if you ask lots of questions, you may have a better treatment outcome.

  ° You can become an active participant in your treatment versus a passive recipient.

  ° You can safeguard yourself against medical errors and oversights.

  ° Asking specific questions helps providers explore wider treatment options.

  ° It allows you to increase your understanding of your condition and treatment options.

- Types of questions to prepare before your office visit and to ask your provider:

  ° Who: Who will I meet with today? Who will be my main provider? Who will be involved in my care? Who will coordinate my treatment with the various providers involved in my care? Will I see a doctor, nurse practitioner, physician's assistant, nurse, medical assistant, or technician?

  ° What: What is my tentative and final diagnosis? What is my prognosis? Will my condition improve? What tests do I need? What are the best tests for my condition? What treatment options are there? What treatment do you recommend? What medications do you recommend? What side effects does this treatment or medication have and how can I manage them? Does this medication interact with other medications I take? What other treatment options are there? What is your opinion of this information I found on the internet? How many times have you done this treatment procedure? What results or complications have you had?

  ° Why: Why do you recommend this medication or treatment rather than another option? Why do you want me to try this first? Why don't you want me to schedule more in-depth testing yet? Why do you think you can help me? Why is this option better than an alternative medicine approach? Why is your recommendation different from my previous provider's?

Copyright © 2026 Debra Burdick, *The Psychotherapy Toolbox for Chronic Illness and Chronic Pain*. All rights reserved.

- When: When should I get the tests or treatment? How often do I need the treatments? How long should I take the medication? When can I expect to see improvements from the medication or the treatment? When is my next office visit? How often should I see the provider?

- Where: Where do I see my provider? Where do I get the recommended tests or treatment procedures? Are there multiple offices within easy driving distance?

- How: How do I take the medication? How do I get the recommended treatment? How do I prepare for the medical test or treatment procedure? How do I make sure my insurance will cover this? How do I make sure all my providers have access to my test results?

- If you feel your provider discounts your concerns, doesn't listen to you, or doesn't answer your questions, let them know what you want, and if they don't improve, consider finding another provider.

 Copyright © 2026 Debra Burdick, *The Psychotherapy Toolbox for Chronic Illness and Chronic Pain*. All rights reserved.

Skill 3.2 Get an Accurate Diagnosis

Background: In order to get proper treatment, clients must first get an accurate diagnosis. This can be a multi-step process and is often fraught with frustration because symptoms may be hard to identify, the root cause may be difficult to determine, there may be overlapping health conditions, the symptoms may be intermittent, and appointments and testing may not be available. Also, different medical providers may disagree on what the diagnosis is. This skill helps clients take control of their health and guides them through the process of getting an accurate diagnosis.

The Skill in Action: *Ray began seeing a therapist after his wife, Katy, started having trouble with her memory. Both Ray and Katy's friends had been noticing some disturbing changes. For example, she often forgot about recent events, including activities they had done together, and would ask a question that had just been answered moments before. She seemed more anxious than usual while at the same time being more outgoing and less inhibited. At the urging of Ray's therapist, Ray took Katy to see her primary care provider, who didn't seem concerned and attributed these changes to normal aging. However, as several months went by, Katy's condition continued to deteriorate. For example, she would leave for walks and get lost, and she often became combative with her husband in thinking he was her brother.*

Ray finally demanded a referral to a neurologist who specialized in treating dementia and Alzheimer's disease. Katy had an MRI and a PET scan, which ruled out bleeding disorders and tumors and confirmed the presence of amyloid proteins and tau (also known as plaques and tangles). After about two years of gradual decline and numerous interactions with a variety of medical providers, Katy was diagnosed with Alzheimer's disease. Ray had to make the heartbreaking decision to place Katy in a memory care unit when it became too difficult for him to care for her at home. This was a journey through hell for Ray, as he lost his wife as he knew her while advocating for her with the medical community until an accurate diagnosis was found.

Skill Building: Explain to clients that getting an accurate diagnosis can often involve consulting with an array of medical providers as well as having a number of diagnostic tests. Sometimes, this can be a multi-step process that is often frustrating, time-consuming, and frightening. Use Client Handout 3.2 to guide clients in how they can best represent themselves throughout this process. Remind them that they must take control of their health by asking questions and doing their own research so they can learn about possible diagnoses for their symptoms (see Skill 3.1: *Working with the Medical Community*). At the same time, caution them not to jump to conclusions before consulting with the provider. In addition, remind your client that in order to get an accurate diagnosis (and, in turn, proper treatment), they may need to visit a major medical center that specializes in their symptoms. When they receive a diagnosis, they should make sure this diagnosis makes sense to them so they can trust that their provider fully understands their symptoms, and they can have faith in treatment recommendations. It is also possible that they will need to get a second—or maybe even a third or fourth—opinion.

Reflection: Was the client able to use these prompts to take control of their health and represent themselves? If so, how did they feel about this new way of approaching their health care? What was the most frustrating part of this process? Did they feel like the diagnosis they were given made sense to them? Did they feel confident in the provider? If they sought another opinion, what led them to do so?

Get an Accurate Diagnosis

In order to get the proper treatment, you must have an accurate diagnosis, and in order to get an accurate diagnosis, you must provide as much information as possible to the provider.

- Consult with a provider who specializes in your symptoms. These specialists will have the most up-to-date experience in diagnosing as well as treating your illness or pain.

- If you have had difficulty getting a diagnosis, visit a major medical center that treats your condition, even if it requires you to travel. Major medical centers are typically on the cutting edge of medical diagnosis and treatment and may have more experience with your specific illness or pain. If travel is too expensive, look into the possibility of doing a telehealth visit.

- Write down every symptom (even if they seem unrelated) and bring the list to your appointment. Describe your symptoms, and be specific about when they occur, when they started, and what has helped. Don't jump to conclusions about your diagnosis. Let the expert diagnose you.

- Share your medical and family history with the provider. This helps them make informed assessments and determine whether you may have a genetic predisposition to certain diseases.

- Bring a list of your medications (or the actual pill bottles). Discuss what they treat and how they help.

- So you don't forget the questions you want to ask, write them down and bring the list of questions to your appointment.

- Get the recommended tests to confirm or rule out a diagnosis. Ask the provider what the test will show and why it should be done. Use it to gather as much information as possible to ensure an accurate diagnosis.

- Make sure the diagnosis makes sense to you. If not, ask for more explanations until you feel it is accurate.

- Get a second, third, or maybe even a fourth opinion if needed. Various providers will have different expertise. Consult as many as you feel you need to make sure you feel that your symptoms are understood and that you have an accurate diagnosis.

Copyright © 2026 Debra Burdick, *The Psychotherapy Toolbox for Chronic Illness and Chronic Pain*. All rights reserved.

Skill 3.3 Create a Healing Team

Background: A healing team is a group of trusted individuals who work together to support the client in their journey through chronic illness or pain. This can include medical providers, alternative healers, mental health clinicians, religious or spiritual guides, family members, friends, colleagues, and pets. It can even include elements of nature that a client finds healing, such as a garden, park, or beach. Since clients with chronic illness and pain can often feel alone and isolated in their experience, it can be a powerful skill for them to have a list of supporters who can help them navigate their symptoms, grief, trauma, or other challenges. This skill discusses the benefits of a healing team and guides the client in creating theirs.

The Skill in Action: *Hank suffered a brain aneurysm followed by a stroke, which required him to have two brain surgeries in two days. This started a long and arduous road to recovery. His motor skills, his ability to walk or use one hand, his eyesight, his memory, and his problem-solving skills were all impacted. Through continuous rehabilitation, he eventually regained his ability to walk, and his cognitive function improved to the point that he was able to work part time with the help of a job coach. During this time, his healing team consisted of his wife of many years, children, primary care provider, neurologist, neurosurgeon, physiatrist, physical therapist, massage therapist, psychotherapist, neurotherapist, ophthalmologist, disability job coach, best friend, former military buddies, two past employees, minister, close neighbors, beloved dog, and even his vegetable garden. He depended on this healing team for many different things, and they were instrumental in helping him stay motivated and gradually regain functioning.*

Skill Building: Explain the concept of a healing team to the client, and use Client Worksheet 3.3 to guide them in making a list of who belongs on their team. This should consist of people (or pets) who know the client well, who have their best interests at heart, and who they trust implicitly. Remind them to select the very best to be on their healing team. Ask the client to think about what they need to heal and how each member of their team specifically contributes to their recovery. Guide them to list their healing team members, including each member's role and contact information. They should be prepared to add additional members as the need arises and to let certain members go as they progress and their needs change.

Reflection: Does the client already have a healing team? If not, were they able to compile a list of team members who could help them on the road to recovery? What did they think about creating a healing team? What benefits did they think the healing team would provide? Did they ask anyone to be a team member who declined?

Create a Healing Team

Your personal healing team is designed to support you on your journey through chronic illness or pain. Team members can come from various sources and might include medical providers, mental health clinicians, alternative healers, religious or spiritual guides, family members, friends, colleagues, and pets. You can even include aspects of nature that support your healing, like a garden, park, or beach.

Make a list of who belongs on your healing team, including what specific role they play in your recovery and their contact information. For example:

- Your spouse's role might be to serve as your love and life partner, caregiver, sounding board, and medical advocate.

- Your therapist's role might be to help you regulate your emotions and teach you skills to deal with your illness or pain.

- Your primary care physician's role might be to coordinate your care with specialists.

- Your specialist's role might be to help you get an accurate diagnosis and the best treatment.

- Your pastor's role might be to tap into your religious or spiritual beliefs to gain emotional strength and resilience.

- Your friends' roles might be to keep you socially connected, be there when you need emotional support, laugh or cry with you, and drive you to appointments.

- Your pet's role might be to comfort you, love you unconditionally, and make you smile.

- Your garden's role might be to ground you and keep you in touch with the healing power of nature.

Allow only those who are honest, helpful, validating, encouraging, knowledgeable, and inspiring to be on your team. List them in the table on the next page.

Copyright © 2026 Debra Burdick, *The Psychotherapy Toolbox for Chronic Illness and Chronic Pain*. All rights reserved.

Team Member	Role	Contact Info

Once you've created your list, reach out to each member of the team and be clear about what you need from them and how they support your well-being. Your healing team can be a relatively informal group, or you can invite members and even introduce them to each other when appropriate, depending on what you need. It helps to let each member know you consider them part of your healing team and be specific about how they can help you. Be ready to add new members and remove members as your needs change.

 Copyright © 2026 Debra Burdick, *The Psychotherapy Toolbox for Chronic Illness and Chronic Pain*. All rights reserved.

Skill 3.4 Manage Fatigue

Background: Clients with chronic illness or pain often experience fatigue and even exhaustion. Fatigue can be a symptom of their illness or pain, as well as a result of all they must do to manage their illness or pain, such as physical therapy, doctor's appointments, and medication management. After all, their responsibilities don't magically disappear when they are ill or in pain. However, when clients just keep going and don't rest, not only do their symptoms not improve, but they will likely worsen. This can create a vicious cycle of extreme ups and downs in both their energy and symptoms. This skill helps clients tune into their bodies and manage their fatigue.

The Skill in Action: *Deb had been diagnosed with chronic fatigue syndrome and was exhausted most of the time. After working with a therapist, she made several changes that helped even out her energy. First, she reduced her work hours to part time, which allowed her to rest periodically during the day. Second, she realized that she was particularly tired around 5:00 p.m. every day, so she took 20 minutes around that time to lie down and listen to a guided meditation. Third, she had been attending all of her daughter's numerous soccer practices, leaving her feeling totally wiped out by the time she got home around 7:00 p.m. She talked with her daughter and husband and worked out a plan to attend the games but not the practices. She also realized that she became more exhausted when she tried to clean the house, so she broke the cleaning into smaller blocks and just did a little at a time. She also hired a cleaning crew to take care of the tasks that were too difficult for her. Deb still experienced constant fatigue from her illness, but she began to feel more in control of it and reluctantly accepted that she needed to rest when she was tired.*

Skill Building: Explore the level of fatigue the client experiences. For example, are they always tired or does their fatigue fluctuate? Are they tired when they overextend themselves, tired when they don't sleep well, too tired to get out of bed, too tired to go to work, or tired after certain activities? Ask them to use Client Worksheet 3.4.1 to keep track of their energy levels throughout the day so they can notice what makes their fatigue worse and what makes it better. As you review the log, notice how much sleep they get on a regular basis and ask what their sleep quality is like. Refer to Skill 3.7: *Sleep Hygiene* to help them establish healthy sleep habits if poor sleep is contributing to their fatigue. In addition, make sure to explore whether they push themselves to get things done even when they are feeling exhausted. Explain that if they instead tune into their energy levels (using Client Worksheet 3.4.1) and match their energy output to the energy they have at the moment, they may find that their symptoms remain more stable and they feel less fatigued.

Use Client Handout 3.4.2 to brainstorm small steps the client can take to manage and prevent fatigue. If they are staying in bed all day, explore whether this is necessary due to their symptoms or if they are having trouble motivating themselves to get up because they don't feel well. Discuss the benefits of getting up, stretching, moving as much as possible, and focusing on a task that is doable for them.

If the client tends to push themselves too hard, encourage them to write "I will rest when I am tired" on a sticky note and post it where they can see it to remind them to do so.

Reflection: Has fatigue been a big factor for the client? What makes it worse? What lessens it? Does the client get enough sleep? Are they trying to do too much despite feeling exhausted? How can they pace themselves? Has the client been able to ask for help and, if not, what gets in their way? Did anything change after the client tracked their energy levels and took steps to pace themselves and to rest?

Daily Energy Log

Use this log to keep track of your energy levels throughout the day, making sure to note what you were doing at the time.

Time of Day	Energy Level (0 = no energy at all, 10 = tons of energy)	Activity
6 a.m.		
7 a.m.		
8 a.m.		
9 a.m.		
10 a.m.		
11 a.m.		
12 p.m.		
1 p.m.		
2 p.m.		
3 p.m.		
4 p.m.		
5 p.m.		
6 p.m.		
7 p.m.		
8 p.m.		
9 p.m.		
10 p.m.		
11 p.m.		
12 a.m.		

Copyright © 2026 Debra Burdick, *The Psychotherapy Toolbox for Chronic Illness and Chronic Pain*. All rights reserved.

How to Manage Fatigue During Illness or Pain

The following small steps can help you better manage and prevent fatigue throughout the day. Above all, listen to your body and rest when you are tired!

Plan Your Day	**Rest**
• Set easy goals to begin with. • Prioritize activities and do the most important first. • Break activities and events into small pieces. • Pace yourself to prevent overdoing at any one time. • Let things go if you are too tired.	• Rest between activities, and only do what you feel able to do. • Rest up ahead of events that you must participate in. • Set an alarm to remind yourself to take a break, stretch, and drink some water at least once per hour. • Periodically tune into your energy, and when it is low or waning, take a break. • Repeat aloud, "I will rest when I am tired."
Ask for Help	**Avoid Staying in Bed All Day**
• Identify things you need help with. • Ask family, friends, or coworkers to help when needed. • Hire help for things that exhaust you, such as cleaning your home or tending the yard.	• Get up or sit up as much as possible. • Set a sleep schedule and stick to it (see Skill 3.7).
Exercise (Within Your Limitations)	**Adapt Your Responsibilities as Needed**
• Walk, even if it's with a walking aid. • Stretch. This can be done in bed or sitting or standing. • Do aerobics. There are great chair exercise videos online if you have difficulty standing or walking.	• Sit instead of stand when possible, such as during meal prep. • Spread out chores by doing a little at a time, or get help. • Consolidate chores into fewer trips. For example, make one trip upstairs (instead of many) by leaving items at the bottom of the stairs and taking them up all at once. • Reduce your work hours or take a leave of absence or disability leave.

 Copyright © 2026 Debra Burdick, *The Psychotherapy Toolbox for Chronic Illness and Chronic Pain*. All rights reserved.

Skill 3.5 Set Mindful Limits

Background: It can be difficult for clients to accept that their chronic illness or pain puts limits on what they are able to accomplish. For example, they may not be able to work full-time or at all, they may need help with chores or cleaning, and they may not be able to volunteer or attend their child's sports events. In these instances, it's important for clients to step back and look at what they can reasonably expect of themselves while they are ill or in pain. For example, instead of doing the housework, they can perhaps ask their family for help or hire a cleaning crew. This skill helps clients tune into how their illness or pain is impacted when they do too much and helps them set mindful limits that support their health.

The Skill in Action: *Louisa had chronic pain throughout her muscles and joints, and she felt exhausted all the time. However, she was a task-oriented person and insisted on doing everything herself despite the pain. For example, one day she got so tired of looking at her dirty kitchen floor that she got down on her knees to scrub it. Everything hurt while she was doing it, but she was determined to get it clean. For the next week, she was unable to get out of bed except for bathroom trips and to make herself a snack. Her pain and exhaustion were through the roof. Louisa's therapist explored how scrubbing the floor had severely increased her pain and exhaustion. Together, they brainstormed how Louisa could have had her floor cleaned without doing it herself. She talked with her adult children, and they readily agreed to help her with things she needed done around the house. They encouraged her to ask for help whenever she needed it and to set better limits on what she tried to do herself.*

Skill Building: To begin, explore why it's important for the client to step back and look at what they can reasonably expect of themselves while they are ill or in pain. Discuss how it works better for them to reduce their load and rest when they are tired, rather than overdoing it and then relapsing into exhaustion and increased pain for the next few days. With that in mind, encourage the client to spend some time thinking about how they can set healthy limits on what they try to do. Using Client Worksheet 3.5, have them write down all the items on their weekly to-do list and then identify how they will set mindful limits for each item that impacts their pain or symptoms. Have them write down how they will stop, reduce, or delegate things that others could do or that are not totally necessary. For example, perhaps they can ask their teen to make dinner twice a week and their husband to grocery shop, rather than doing it themselves. Perhaps they can work fewer hours, resign from a time-consuming volunteer committee, or limit what they agree to bring to family gatherings. What can they give up for now? What can they delegate? What can they ask for help doing? Note that this exercise is likely to bring up feelings of loss, frustration, anger, and guilt about not being able to do everything they are used to doing, so make sure to spend time processing this with the client.

Reflection: What limits has chronic illness or pain placed on the client? How do they feel about these limits? Did they feel guilty or like a failure? Are they able to see the connection between doing too much and their symptoms? Were they able to accept the need to set limits? How has setting better limits improved their health? How did they feel about asking for help? Were they able to find people to delegate to or to ask for help? What things did they want to keep doing?

Set Mindful Limits

Use this worksheet to help you set reasonable limits on your to-do list so you can avoid feeling exhausted, stressed, or increased pain. List any activities that you currently do (e.g., cleaning, volunteering), then describe how you will set mindful limits to reduce, stop, change, ask for help with, or delegate those activities that exhaust you or flare your symptoms (e.g., ask your family to help with chores or hire a cleaning crew, reduce your volunteer work from daily to weekly).

Current Activity	How to Set Mindful Limits

Copyright © 2026 Debra Burdick, *The Psychotherapy Toolbox for Chronic Illness and Chronic Pain*. All rights reserved.

Skill 3.6 Eat to Support Health

Background: Food is a form of natural medicine that can either help or hurt a client's health. In fact, nutrition has been identified as a key lifestyle factor that plays a role in pain management (Elma et al., 2022). By making simple dietary changes, clients can mitigate the effects of chronic inflammation in the body, such as cardiovascular disease, cancer, diabetes mellitus, chronic kidney disease, liver disease, autoimmune diseases, neurodegenerative disorders, and more. This skill introduces a food diary to help clients be more mindful about what they eat and understand the connection between food and their health, including information about anti-inflammatory foods.

The Skill in Action: *Allison had fibromyalgia and often felt like she had been run over by a truck. Her whole body ached, her brain was often foggy, and she often had diarrhea for days on end without being able to figure out what was causing it. With her therapist's encouragement, Allison started keeping a food diary, which allowed her to identify that milk was one culprit causing her symptoms. She eventually sought out an allergist, who tested her blood for food allergies (RAST test) and found that she was highly allergic to more than 50 foods! When she removed these offending foods from her diet, she started feeling better, but she lost a significant amount of weight given the very small variety of foods she was able to eat.*

This led Allison to consult with an integrative medicine specialist, who did some testing that showed her intestinal wall was too permeable and that food was being absorbed before being properly broken down, thereby essentially poisoning her. He called this "leaky gut" and explained that it might be the root cause of her fibromyalgia symptoms. He further added that this may have been the result of past antibiotic use that had caused severe intestinal pain. He helped Allison gradually heal her intestinal wall using an anti-inflammatory diet, a variety of dietary supplements, and digestive enzymes. She was slowly able to add back a variety of foods, although not all. She gradually gained back the weight she had lost until she was in the recommended weight range for her height. This healing journey took over 15 years and caused Allison to learn a huge amount about how foods can positively or negatively impact symptoms of illness and pain.

Skill Building: Explain to the client that chronic inflammation has been identified as a contributing factor in many common chronic illnesses and pain. Use Client Handout 3.6.1 to explain the major dietary sources of chronic inflammation, and explore what the client is eating that may be causing inflammation. In addition, some clients have food sensitivities or food allergies that can flare symptoms and pain. Although the client may already have a good sense of what foods exacerbate their symptoms, the most common culprits are peanuts, tree nuts, milk, eggs, wheat, soy, fish, and shellfish. Artificial sweeteners can trigger symptoms of migraines and pain as well. To help the client begin exploring the connection between their current eating habits and pain symptoms, ask them to track their food intake using the food diary on Client Worksheet 3.6.2. A sample food diary is provided first. Note that it may take up to three days for a reaction to occur after eating a food.

If you find a suspected food culprit (and there may be more than one), encourage the client to work with an allergist or a nutritionist to consider an elimination diet, where they eliminate all forms of that food from their diet for seven days. It may take a few days for the symptoms to ease, but if this is a problem food, the symptoms should gradually decrease. After eliminating the food for seven days, they can reintroduce it in small amounts and eat increasingly larger servings to see if symptoms worsen. If there is no change in symptoms, they can add the food back into their diet. Since elimination diets can be challenging, it is important they work with a nutritionist to ensure that they do not become unnecessarily restrictive. At a minimum, encourage clients to make sure they stay hydrated, limit sugar and unhealthy fats, and eat lots of plant-based foods. Explain that they can choose organic foods to avoid toxins such as pesticides, hormones, antibiotics, and food additives.

Finally, encourage the client to ask their medical provider to test for possible vitamin and mineral deficiencies that are often present in chronic pain and many chronic illnesses. These include the B vitamins (especially B-12 and B-6), vitamin D, calcium, magnesium, zinc, omega-3 fatty acids, amino acids, copper, vitamin E, and folic acid.

Reflection: How has food played a role in the client's illness or pain? Was the client open to making changes in their food choices? What has gotten in the way of eating healthier? How can they adapt their diet if they are very picky and substitute healthy choices that they like? Did they identify any food allergies or sensitivities? How has becoming mindful of the connection between food and health helped them make better food choices? How has making changes in their diet changed their symptoms?

Sources of Chronic Inflammation

Inflammation has been found to contribute to chronic illness and pain. There are foods that can fight inflammation in the body, as well as foods that can make it worse. This handout provides you with several examples so you can make more informed dietary choices for your chronic illness or pain.

Inflammatory Foods		
Sweets: sugar, soda, candy, cereals, snacks, cake	Refined grains: white rice, white bread, pasta	Foods high in omega-6 fatty acids: fried foods, vegetable oils, fast food, baked goods, pastries
Foods high in salt: snacks, chips, packaged foods, frozen meals, canned foods	Foods high in saturated fat: butter, whole milk, cheese	Red and processed meat: bacon, beef, cured meats, hot dogs, deli meat

Anti-Inflammatory Foods		
Fruits and vegetables: berries, apples, grapes, cherries, tomatoes, avocados, broccoli, peppers, mushrooms, leafy greens	Whole grains, nuts, and seeds: chia seeds, flaxseed, walnuts, whole grain rice, whole wheat flour	Foods high in omega-3 fatty acids: extra virgin olive oil, fatty fish (e.g., salmon), meat and dairy from grass-fed animals
Unsweetened green tea and black coffee	Herbs and spices: turmeric, ginger, mint	Dark chocolate and cocoa

Low zinc or magnesium blood levels can contribute to inflammation as well. You can increase these in your diet as follows:

Dietary Sources of Magnesium	Dietary Sources of Zinc
Pumpkin seeds, almonds, cashew, black beans, spinach, Swiss chard, avocado, dark chocolate	Meat, shellfish, seeds, nuts, dairy, eggs, whole grains

Obesity is another source of chronic inflammation, so be mindful of this and consult your health care providers as needed.

 Copyright © 2026 Debra Burdick, *The Psychotherapy Toolbox for Chronic Illness and Chronic Pain*. All rights reserved.

Food Diary

Use this log to track the connection between your food intake and your symptoms of illness or pain. Label the columns with the top five symptoms that bother you, and use the following scale to rate your symptoms:

0 = no problem, 1 = a little problem, 2 = mild problem, 3 = moderate problem, 4 = major problem, 5 = very severe problem

After a day or two, see if there are any patterns where your ratings go up or down within three to four hours of eating certain foods or within 24 hours of eating certain foods.

Date	Time	Food/Drink	Symptom				
			Pain	GI Distress	Brain Fog	Fatigue	Poor Sleep
1/28	9 a.m.	1 egg, orange juice, milk, white toast with butter	0 1 2 ③ 4 5	0 1 ② 3 4 5	0 1 2 ③ 4 5	0 1 2 ③ 4 5	0 1 2 ③ 4 5
	11 a.m.	2 candy bars	0 1 2 3 ④ 5	0 1 2 3 ④ 5	0 1 2 3 ④ 5	0 1 2 3 ④ 5	⓪ 1 2 3 4 5
	12:30 p.m.	White bread, tuna, mayo, water, banana	0 1 2 3 ④ 5	⓪ 1 2 3 4 5	0 1 2 3 ④ 5	0 1 2 3 ④ 5	⓪ 1 2 3 4 5
	3:30 p.m.	Twizzlers, soda	0 1 2 3 4 ⑤	⓪ 1 2 3 4 5	0 1 2 3 4 ⑤	0 1 2 3 4 ⑤	⓪ 1 2 3 4 5
	6:00 p.m.	Flounder with lemon, broccoli, sweet potato with butter	0 1 2 3 4 ⑤	0 1 2 3 ④ 5	0 1 2 3 ④ 5	0 1 2 3 4 ⑤	⓪ 1 2 3 4 5
	7:30 p.m.	Chocolate chip cookies	0 1 2 ③ 4 5	0 1 ② 3 4 5	0 1 ② 3 4 5	0 1 2 ③ 4 5	⓪ 1 2 3 4 5

In this example, pain, GI distress, brain fog, and fatigue increase shortly after eating either white bread or sugar and improve several hours later. If this pattern continues, it may help to eliminate foods with gluten or that are high in sugar or refined grains to see if symptoms improve.

Copyright © 2026 Debra Burdick, *The Psychotherapy Toolbox for Chronic Illness and Chronic Pain*. All rights reserved.

Food Diary

Use this log to track the connection between your food intake and your symptoms of illness or pain. Label the columns with the top five symptoms that bother you, and use the following scale to rate your symptoms:

0 = no problem, 1 = a little problem, 2 = mild problem, 3 = moderate problem, 4 = major problem, 5 = very severe problem

After a day or two, see if there are any patterns where your ratings go up or down within three to four hours of eating certain foods or within 24 hours of eating certain foods.

Date	Time	Food/Drink	Symptom				
			0 1 2 3 4 5	0 1 2 3 4 5	0 1 2 3 4 5	0 1 2 3 4 5	0 1 2 3 4 5
			0 1 2 3 4 5	0 1 2 3 4 5	0 1 2 3 4 5	0 1 2 3 4 5	0 1 2 3 4 5
			0 1 2 3 4 5	0 1 2 3 4 5	0 1 2 3 4 5	0 1 2 3 4 5	0 1 2 3 4 5
			0 1 2 3 4 5	0 1 2 3 4 5	0 1 2 3 4 5	0 1 2 3 4 5	0 1 2 3 4 5
			0 1 2 3 4 5	0 1 2 3 4 5	0 1 2 3 4 5	0 1 2 3 4 5	0 1 2 3 4 5
			0 1 2 3 4 5	0 1 2 3 4 5	0 1 2 3 4 5	0 1 2 3 4 5	0 1 2 3 4 5

 Copyright © 2026 Debra Burdick, *The Psychotherapy Toolbox for Chronic Illness and Chronic Pain*. All rights reserved.

Skill 3.7 Sleep Hygiene

Background: Like food, sleep is a form of medicine. The body and mind need sleep to stay healthy, especially when dealing with chronic illness or pain. The problem is that not only can difficulty sleeping worsen pain and illness, but the reverse is also true in that illness and pain can contribute to poor sleep. This often keeps clients trapped in a vicious cycle. In conjunction with this skill, I recommend assessing your client for symptoms of sleep-wake disorders, such as insomnia, and referring them to their primary care physician for narcolepsy, or having them assessed by a sleep medicine specialist for breathing-related disorders such as sleep apnea. This skill guides clients to be mindful of their sleep habits and explore options for improving their sleep hygiene.

The Skill in Action: *Holly often felt groggy and would fall asleep whenever she sat quietly during the day. She never felt rested after waking up and had difficulty falling asleep at night. Given that she had been diagnosed with type 2 diabetes, she spoke to her endocrinologist about her constant fatigue, wondering if it was related to her condition. However, after closely monitoring her blood sugar, it became clear that Holly's fatigue didn't seem connected, as she felt exhausted all the time. She decided to work with her therapist to improve her sleep habits, which involved reducing the temperature of her sleep environment, stopping work at least an hour before bed, and no longer doing work in the bedroom. They also figured out that Holly felt her best with eight hours of sleep, so she started setting an alarm to remind her to get ready for bed, ensuring she had enough time for a full night's rest. Since Holly often struggled to fall asleep because she worried about her diabetes, her therapist suggested she listen to a guided relaxation or sleep meditation at bedtime. After implementing all these changes, Holly gradually noticed she was far less tired during the day.*

Skill Building: Encourage your client to start thinking about sleep as a form of medicine and to make getting a good night's sleep a top priority. Use Client Worksheet 3.7.1 to help them be as specific as possible about what time they get in bed, fall asleep, wake up, and get out of bed, as well as how they feel upon waking and how sleepy or restless they are during the day. If they are unsure about how much time they are actually sleeping, they might benefit from using a fitness tracker that monitors movement and heart rate to estimate how long they are asleep at night. Some popular devices are Vital, Amazfit, Fitbit, and Apple watches. Although these don't actually measure sleep like an EEG does, they can give clients a better idea of how long they are asleep. A word of caution: If a client becomes so focused on the tracker that it interferes with their ability to sleep, it may be doing more harm than good, so if that happens, recommend that they try sleeping without it.

Use the log in Client Worksheet 3.7.2 to track how much sleep the client needs to feel their best. They can then set a sleep schedule to accommodate the ideal amount for them. Most adults need seven to nine hours of sleep per night, but everyone is different. Sleep is very habitual, so encourage them to follow the same sleep and wake schedule every day, even on the weekends. Keep in mind that sleeping too much can make clients feel as bad as sleeping too little. In addition, some clients with chronic illness or pain may spend much of the day in bed, which can be counterproductive for sleep as well as contribute to loss of bone and muscle mass. If this is the case for your client, explore whether their illness is so severe that they cannot get out of bed or even sit up. If they are able, encourage them to sit up or get out of bed and stay awake as much as possible during the day.

Finally, use Client Handout 3.7.3 to teach clients the basics of good sleep hygiene. If the client snores or if making these recommended changes does not improve their daytime fatigue, encourage them to get a sleep study to rule out sleep apnea. For those whose chronic lack of sleep is severe, encourage them to consult a holistic provider for natural sleep aids or a medical provider for prescription sleep medication with the fewest long-term side effects or risk of addiction. If pain interferes with sleep, encourage them to speak to their doctor about options for pain management.

Reflection: Based on your assessment, does the client have a sleep issue that is impacting (or impacted by) their illness or pain? If there are signs of a sleep disorder or sleep apnea, are they willing to consult with a sleep specialist? Was the client able to create a schedule that allows them to go to bed and wake up at the same time each day? If not, what is getting in their way? Were they able to identify things they could change in the bedroom to make it more sleep friendly? Did they experience any positive changes to their illness or pain symptoms after improving their sleep hygiene?

Are You Sleeping?

Do you feel sleepy throughout the day? Do you fall asleep at work, while reading, or while riding in the car? Do you have trouble concentrating? Are you cranky and grumpy, easily annoyed, and quickly frustrated? Do you have trouble motivating yourself to do things? These can all be signs that you are tired.

Answer the following questions to start getting a better idea about your sleep habits and how they may be contributing to your fatigue.

1. What time do you go to bed? _____

2. What time do you fall asleep? _____

3. How many times do you wake up during the night? _____

4. How long does it take before you fall back to sleep? _____

5. What time do you wake up in the morning? _____

6. What time do you get out of bed? _____

7. How tired are you when you wake (0 = fully rested, 10 = exhausted)? _____

8. Are you a restless sleeper (think about how your blankets look in the a.m.)? Yes ___ No ___

9. How tired are you during the day (0 = not at all tired, 10 = extremely tired)? _____

10. Have you ever noticed or been told you that you snore? Yes ___ No ___

Copyright © 2026 Debra Burdick, *The Psychotherapy Toolbox for Chronic Illness and Chronic Pain*. All rights reserved.

Client Worksheet 3.7.2

Get the Sleep You Need

To figure out your sleep needs, use this log to track your sleep for two weeks. This will allow you to figure out how many hours of sleep you need per night to feel your best.

Date	Bedtime	Wake Time	Hours Slept	How Tired? (0 = fully rested, 10 = exhausted)

Based on your findings, how many hours of sleep do you need to feel your best?

_____

Now let's figure out your ideal bedtime to make sure you get this many hours of sleep per night. To do so, subtract the number of hours of sleep you need from the time you need to get up in the morning. For example, if you need 9 hours of sleep, and you need to get up at 6:30 a.m. for work, your ideal bedtime is 9:30 p.m.

Wake time   Hours of sleep   Ideal bedtime

_____   –   _____   =   _____

Now you can start planning ahead to go to bed at an hour that allows you to maximize your sleep needs.

    Copyright © 2026 Debra Burdick, *The Psychotherapy Toolbox for Chronic Illness and Chronic Pain*. All rights reserved.

Sleep Hygiene Tips

Sleep is a form of medicine that is essential for your health. Use the following sleep hygiene tips to ensure you are getting the best sleep possible.

- Use your bedroom for sleep and nothing else (except sex). That means removing any TV, computers, tablets, phones, games, projects, or crafts from the room.

- Make the bedroom peaceful, clean, organized, and not cluttered, as it's hard to sleep in chaos.

- Get a comfortable, supportive bed.

- Keep the bedroom cool and dark.

    ° Set the temperature somewhere between 65 to 68 degrees at night.

    ° Use a sound machine to block outside noise.

    ° Darken the room with room darkening shades.

    ° Remove, turn around, or cover lights from electronics such as clocks.

- Go to sleep and get up at the same time every day. Set an alarm to go to bed to avoid staying up too late.

- Avoid screens, sugar, caffeine, and activating shows or books before bedtime. Use blue light blocking glasses in the evening if you do use a screen.

- Exercise during the day.

- If worry keeps you awake, schedule a "worry time" each day at least two hours before bed.

- Wind down at bedtime by reading a book, listening to relaxing music, or listening to a guided meditation.

- If medications interfere with sleep, talk with your prescriber about a different medication option or dosing schedule that does not interfere with sleep.

- Consult a sleep specialist to rule out sleep apnea or get natural sleep aids if needed.

Copyright © 2026 Debra Burdick, *The Psychotherapy Toolbox for Chronic Illness and Chronic Pain*. All rights reserved.

Skill 3.8 Keep Moving

Background: The human body is meant to move, and even though illness or pain may limit a client's ability to stay active, it's still important to move as much as possible within those limits. Moving helps clients maintain muscle strength, flexibility, and general conditioning. It can also reduce stress and improve mood, pain, and sleep. This skill helps clients recognize the value of exercise and explore ways to incorporate physical activity that's appropriate for their condition.

The Skill in Action: *David used to exercise regularly. But ever since his chronic back pain began, he had virtually stopped exercising, as he was afraid to move in ways that made it hurt. Over time, he felt weaker and less stable. He also noticed his mood had worsened. David wanted to start moving his body again, so he worked with his therapist to brainstorm options for adding physical activity back into his schedule. He also began attending physical therapy, where he learned some strengthening and stretching exercises he could do without increasing his back pain. In fact, he noticed his pain was decreasing slowly as he regained flexibility and strength. Eventually, David was able to incorporate aerobic exercise back into his schedule, which improved his mood significantly. Although he had to be careful not to flare up his back pain, he discovered that he could exercise more than he thought and that doing so carefully actually helped his pain.*

Skill Building: Discuss with clients the myriad benefits of moving their body, including flexibility, muscle strength, circulation, mood, sleep, pain, immune function, weight control, and so much more! Explore whether the client is exercising and, if not, what prevents them from doing so. Then use Client Handout 3.8 to explore what types of exercise they are capable of doing and that they enjoy. Make sure to consider potential modifications as well. For example, if they cannot practice yoga on the floor, perhaps they can do it sitting in a chair. There are numerous excellent chair yoga videos online, as well as apps, that provide a low-impact, full-body workout. Similarly, if the client can't walk for 10 minutes, perhaps they can walk for one minute. If needed, they can use a cane or walker to help them balance. If they can't walk at all, perhaps they can stretch and move their arms, legs, neck, and shoulders while sitting or lying down. Just help them figure out how they can *move*!

The goal is to encourage clients to incorporate movement in their life and make a commitment to moving every day. Remind them to start slowly and gradually increase the intensity and duration of the activity as their illness allows. Caution them not to overdo it or push themselves too fast. They should also always check with their doctor before starting a new exercise routine and consider enlisting the help of a physical therapist or personal trainer to design exercises tailored to the limits of their illness or pain.

Reflection: Was the client already exercising? If not, what was preventing them? Were they afraid that moving would create pain? Could they see the benefits of adding movement into their life? Were they able to identify any exercise they could do and enjoy? Were they able to address their fear of exercise and find movements that didn't hurt? Did they notice any connection between exercise and their mood? How did exercise impact their illness or pain?

Types of Exercise

Moving your body any way you are able is essential to staying conditioned. Not only does it help with weight and strength, but it also improves mood, sleep, flexibility, and pain. The goal is to start as small as you can tolerate and gradually increase the intensity and duration of the exercise as you are able. Aim for at least 30 minutes of exercise 3–4 times per week, even if it's simply stretching, taking a walk, or doing chair exercises. Use this handout to brainstorm how you will incorporate exercise into your daily life. Place a reminder on your calendar for the exercise you choose. Be sure to talk with your doctor before starting any new exercise practice and be mindful not to overdo it.

Stretching

- Stretching can improve flexibility, reduce stiffness, and increase range of motion.

- Warm up by walking in place or pumping your arms while sitting or standing for 3–5 minutes.

- Stretch various muscle groups and hold each stretch for 20 seconds before releasing it. Repeat each stretch 2–3 times.

Walking

- Walking is a low-impact exercise that can help with aerobic conditioning, heart and joint health, and mood.

- Wear shoes with good support.

- Start slowly and then increase the pace and distance when possible.

Flowing Movements

- Both yoga and tai chi combine deep breathing, flowing movements, gentle poses, and meditation. They increase flexibility, balance, and range of motion while also reducing stress.

- Look online for free videos or apps, or check out classes offered at a local gym, recreation center, or senior center.

Copyright © 2026 Debra Burdick, *The Psychotherapy Toolbox for Chronic Illness and Chronic Pain*. All rights reserved.

Water Exercises

- Water helps support body weight by minimizing gravity, making it a great low-impact exercise.

- Water exercise promotes flexibility, range of motion, strength, and aerobic conditioning. This can include swimming, water aerobics, and other gentle water exercises.

Strength Training

- Strength training can make your muscles stronger while reducing pain and stiffness.

- Use free weights like dumbbells, hand weights, or kettlebells, picking a weight that is right for you.

- Do resistance training using a machine or resistance band.

Cycling

- Cycling is a low-impact, non-weight bearing form of exercise that improves muscle strength and cardiovascular function.

- Ride your bike outdoors to get fresh air as well as exercise.

- You can also ride a stationary bike indoors, which is a safe way to get your joints moving and improve cardiovascular fitness.

Pilates

- Pilates is a low-impact activity that can increase flexibility for enhanced joint health.

- Many poses activate core muscles and improve balance.

- Look for a certified trainer online or at a local gym, recreation center, or senior center.

Other Low-Stress Physical Activities

- Chair exercises are a great way to improve mobility, balance, and posture without the risk of falling. Look online for free videos or apps.

- Engage in light gardening. Perhaps create raised beds to avoid bending over.

 Copyright © 2026 Debra Burdick, *The Psychotherapy Toolbox for Chronic Illness and Chronic Pain*. All rights reserved.

Skill 3.9 Remembered Wellness

Background: "Remembered wellness" is what happens when you allow the body and mind to recover its memory of wholeness and completeness, of innate order, balance, harmony, and flow. It is about remembering a time when you felt well and bringing that experience to mind. Importantly, the human body reacts to imagination and visualization as it would to an actual event, so it doesn't know the difference between imagined wellness and real wellness. In fact, one study showed that people who spent time imagining they were exercising actually got stronger without exercising (Ranganathan et al., 2004)! This skill enlists the power of "remembered wellness" through a guided meditation that taps into the power of the mind's imagination. By having clients recall a time when they felt healthy, they can create a sense of wellness in the present, supporting their healing journey.

The Skill in Action: *Janie had been chronically ill with two autoimmune diseases for two years. She struggled to live a good life due to feeling ill every day. Her therapist introduced her to the concept of "remembered wellness" and shared a meditation that led Janie through the process of remembering a time when she was well. She cried when she first tried to remember feeling well because she could hardly remember what that felt like. She processed her feelings with her therapist and then tried again. The second time she was able to remember what it felt like to have plenty of energy, to feel strong and vital. She remembered being able to easily walk for miles and to ride her bicycle. She remembered having a feeling of well-being most of the time. When she was done with the meditation, she noticed that she felt a little better. She continued to listen to the meditation every day and repeatedly pictured her body healthy the way it used to be. She wasn't sure, but she thought that she was feeling a bit better every day.*

Skill Building: Explain the theory of "remembered wellness" to the client and discuss how they can recreate and manifest a feeling of wellness in their body by simply remembering a time when they felt well. Use the guided meditation in Client Handout 3.9 to walk them through this process. If they cannot remember feeling well, encourage them to imagine what it would feel like. Some clients become quite emotional during this meditation, since it may remind them of the losses they have experienced due to their illness or pain, so make sure to set aside time to process and acknowledge these feelings before gradually shifting back to remembering or imagining wellness. Encourage your client to use this skill whenever they want to improve their current physical or emotional health, especially when dealing with chronic illness or pain.

Reflection: How did the client experience this meditation? Were they able to remember a time when they felt well? How did they feel in the past compared to how they feel now? What felt different about their life then versus now? Which of these feelings from the past can they carry with them in the present? What did they notice about their current feelings when they completed the meditation? Did the meditation trigger feelings of loss?

Remember Wellness Meditation

You can find the guided audio for this meditation at **www.thebrainlady.com/pesi-meditations**.

During illness or pain, it can be difficult to remember a time when you felt well. This meditation uses the power of your imagination to think back to a time when you felt wholly and completely well—with no painful or uncomfortable symptoms—so that you can bring along this "remembered wellness" into the present day.

Take a deep, relaxing breath, and as you exhale, close your eyes or soften your gaze and focus your attention within. As you do so, let go of all thoughts about today and quiet your mind.

Now spend a moment remembering a time when you felt well—really well and pain free. Think back to before you were ill or in pain. Let your unconscious mind choose a time in your life, no matter how brief it was, when you felt really good. Even if you had unpleasant things going on at the same time, just retrieve the memory of when you felt really well. Be selective and choose only the memories of when you felt the best.

Take your time to remember that point in your life. Remember how you felt then. Your muscles are in peak condition. Your body is in excellent health. Your thoughts are happy. Your mood is content, blissful, and peaceful. Use whatever words best describe that state for you.

Breathe that memory in now. Let it amplify. Remember it. Feel it. Let it flow through you. Now imagine you feel an inner wave of joy. Go ahead and smile. Truly enjoy the memory as it spreads throughout your mind and body.

Notice how, for the moment, your brain doesn't know the difference between then and now. Imagine bringing that feeling from when the memory occurred to right now. Almost like a copy and paste from then to now. Every cell, every muscle, every neuron, every fiber of your brain and body is remembering. As you remember wellness, notice how it starts to spread throughout your mind and body. You are remembering and experiencing that peak state right now, physically, emotionally, spiritually, and intellectually.

 Copyright © 2026 Debra Burdick, *The Psychotherapy Toolbox for Chronic Illness and Chronic Pain*. All rights reserved.

Let your body feel, right now, that peak wellness. Your memory is guiding your brain to function now like it did when you were well. Immerse yourself in this state of wellness.

You might like to imagine a color that represents this incredible wellness. What color would you choose? The color anchors the feeling. Imagine that color now.

Remember that your body knows how to heal. We've all fallen down and scraped ourselves, or cut ourselves shaving, and then healed. Begin to notice every day all the ways your body shows you it knows how to heal, when you are eating, breathing, urinating, sweating, sleeping, or laughing. Notice that there's a certain a way you breathe that is all part of that healing process. Allow every adjustment that is part of this peak health. Find a place to be grateful for the way things are now, while at the same time being thankful that your body remembers wellness.

Ask yourself for a word or phrase that represents your peak wellness. You can use this anytime you need to remember and invoke wellness. This could be a simple phrase such as "I am well." Repeat it silently now.

When you are ready, let yourself gradually come back to the room and slowly open your eyes. Bring your remembered wellness with you. Know that the remembered wellness starts a process that continues throughout the day, night, weeks, months, and on into your future. As you return to the present, be aware that your remembered wellness has been activated and is now operating in the present.

Copyright © 2026 Debra Burdick, *The Psychotherapy Toolbox for Chronic Illness and Chronic Pain*. All rights reserved.

Skill 3.10 Progressive Muscle Relaxation

Background: Progressive muscle relaxation is the process of gradually tensing and releasing different muscle groups throughout the body. This practice was first introduced by Dr. Edmund Jacobson (1929), who discovered that tightening a muscle and holding tension for 7 to 10 seconds and then releasing it allowed the muscle to relax. This technique can be extremely helpful to calm the mind and body, especially for clients who hold tension in the body or who experience tension that is triggered by pain. This skill provides a script and an audio recording clients can use to relax the mind and body.

The Skill in Action: *Jody was a busy lady. She often had more to do than she could possibly get done and felt stressed as a result. When her therapist asked her to tune into her body during periods of stress, Jody noticed that her muscles were tense, her neck hurt, and she often had a headache. To help relieve this stress, Jody's therapist taught her a progressive muscle relaxation technique and encouraged her to practice every day. The skill only took a few minutes to practice, Jody could do it on the go, and her whole body felt less tense every time she did it. She also noticed her neck wasn't hurting as much and her headache went away every time she practiced. After doing progressive muscle relaxation every day for a week, Jody realized she wasn't getting as tense, almost like the practice helped her push a reset button on her stress response.*

Skill Building: Refer to Client Handout 3.10 to guide clients through a progressive muscle relaxation script. Throughout the practice, they should hold each muscle group for 7 seconds and then release it for 10 seconds before moving on to the next muscle group. Explain that the result may be a feeling of physical relaxation and decreased pain, as well as an overall decrease in their stress response. Ask them to tune into their body before doing the practice and again after to notice what, if anything, has changed. Once they familiarize themselves with the skill in session, encourage them to practice it daily, perhaps setting a reminder on their phone so they do it at the same time each day. Some clients may benefit from doing it at bedtime to improve sleep.

Reflection: What did your client experience while doing the progressive muscle relaxation? Were they able to notice the difference between a tense muscle and a relaxed muscle? Did they feel more relaxed at the end of the meditation? How did they handle any distracting thoughts that came up during the practice? Did they experience any particular emotions during the exercise? In what ways does practicing this technique help them?

Progressive Muscle Relaxation

You can find the guided audio for this meditation at **www.thebrainlady.com/pesi-meditations**.

Progressive muscle relaxation is a simple and effective way to relax your body and decrease pain. To begin, find a comfortable position and take three deep belly breaths, exhaling slowly each time. As you exhale, imagine that the tension throughout your body is beginning to flow away.

Start by tightening the muscles in your forehead by raising your eyebrows as far as you can. Hold for 7 seconds . . . and then relax for 10. Imagine your forehead muscles becoming smooth and limp as they relax.

Now tighten the muscles around your eyes by clenching your eyelids tightly shut. Hold for 7 seconds . . . and then relax for 10. Imagine sensations of deep relaxation spreading all around your eyes.

Next, tighten your jaw by opening your mouth so wide that you stretch the muscles around the hinges of your jaw. Hold for 7 seconds . . . and then relax for 10. Let your lips part and allow your jaw to hang loose.

Move your attention to the back of your neck and tighten the muscles here by pulling your head way back, as if you were going to touch your head to your back (be gentle with this muscle group to avoid injury). Focus only on tensing the muscles in your neck. Hold for 7 seconds . . . and then relax for 10. Since this area is often especially tight, it's good to do the tighten-relax cycle twice.

Take a few deep breaths and tune into the weight of your head resting on your shoulders. Then tighten your shoulders by raising them up as if they were going to touch your ears. Hold for 7 seconds . . . and then relax for 10. Imagine this weight releasing as you let the tension go.

Now tighten the muscles around your shoulder blades by pushing your shoulder blades back as if you were going to touch them together. Hold the tension in your shoulder blades for 7 seconds . . . and then relax for 10. Since this area is often especially tight, repeat the tighten-relax sequence twice.

Moving down to the muscles in your arms, clench your fists and tighten your biceps by drawing your forearms up toward your shoulders, as if you are "making

Copyright © 2026 Debra Burdick, *The Psychotherapy Toolbox for Chronic Illness and Chronic Pain*. All rights reserved.

a muscle" with both arms. Hold for 7 seconds . . . and then relax for 10. Notice how much lighter your arms feel as you release.

Now tighten your triceps—the muscles on the undersides of your upper arms—by extending your arms out straight and locking your elbows. Hold for 7 seconds . . . and then relax for 10.

Next, tighten the muscles in your chest by taking in a deep breath and holding it. Hold for 7 seconds . . . and then relax for 10. Imagine any excess tension in your chest flowing away with the exhalation.

Then tighten your stomach muscles by sucking your stomach in and holding it in. Hold for 7 seconds . . . and then relax for 10. Imagine a wave of relaxation spreading through your abdomen.

Tighten your lower back by arching it up. Hold for 7 seconds . . . and then relax for 10.

Tighten your buttocks by pulling them together and squeezing as hard as you can. Hold for 7 seconds . . . and then relax for 10. Imagine the muscles in your hips going loose and limp.

Squeeze the muscles in your thighs all the way down to your knees. You will probably have to tighten your hips along with your thighs, since the thigh muscles attach at the pelvis. Hold for 7 seconds . . . and then relax for 10. Feel your thigh muscles smoothing out and relaxing completely.

Tighten your calf muscles by pulling your toes toward you (flexing carefully to avoid cramps). Hold for 7 seconds . . . and then relax for 10.

Finally, tighten your feet by curling your toes downward. Hold for 7 seconds . . . and then relax for 10.

Now imagine a wave of relaxation slowly spreading throughout your body, starting at your head and gradually penetrating every muscle group all the way down to your toes.

 Copyright © 2026 Debra Burdick, *The Psychotherapy Toolbox for Chronic Illness and Chronic Pain*. All rights reserved.

Skill 3.11 Body Scan

Background: The body scan is a simple technique that involves focusing your full attention on each part of the body, noticing whatever sensations arise, accepting them, and sending kind and compassionate thoughts to each area of the body. Through regular practice, this skill can help clients enter deep states of relaxation, accept their body as it is, and work more effectively with feelings of physical discomfort and pain. Not only does the body scan have physical and emotional calming benefits, but it also helps clients become more mindful of the ways in which the body is impacted by stress and anxiety. This skill guides the client through a body scan meditation.

The Skill in Action: *Miguel found himself getting very angry and resentful with the limits his illness was placing on every aspect of his life. He struggled with chronic back pain, which prevented him from playing sports with his kids, standing or sitting for any length of time, and even working full-time. Whenever he felt stressed or tense, his back screamed at him. His therapist encouraged him to practice a body scan to help him become more aware of his bodily sensations and break the cycle of tension. At first, he was skeptical and wondered what good it could do. But after trying it in session and practicing it every day at home, he noticed that he was actually beginning to relax. In fact, he realized he hadn't felt this relaxed in a long time. His body felt like it was letting go of all the tension it had been carrying. His mind started calming more as well, and he noticed he wasn't getting angry as often. Miguel started doing a quick body scan whenever he wanted to push the reset button on his stress response. He even tried it while he was standing in line at the store or sitting down at work, or whenever he had a few minutes of stillness.*

Skill Building: Explain to clients the benefits of doing a body scan, and read through Client Handout 3.11 to walk them through this practice. As they do the meditation, they should tune into how each part of their body feels, just noticing what's there without trying to change it. Since emotions almost always have a physical component that shows up in the body, encourage the client to pay attention to what emotions may show up as tension or discomfort in various parts of their body. With practice, they will be able to use these physical sensations as a key to their emotions. For example, do they get a stomachache when they are nervous or worried? Do they get a stiff or sore neck when they feel stressed? Encourage them to practice the body scan slowly every day for a few days. Once they feel comfortable doing it, they can also do a quick body scan whenever they are feeling stressed out.

If they become uncomfortable or emotional at any point during the practice, ask them if they want to continue or to stop. Be aware that if the client has experienced physical or sexual abuse, they may remember deeply buried feelings or thoughts when they focus on certain parts of their body. Let them know they can stop at any time or skip that area, and encourage them to try again another time as they become more comfortable with the practice. If they need to stop, process what came up for them, helping them integrate the past memory with the safety of this moment.

Reflection: How did your client feel during and after the body scan? What did they notice about their body? Were they able to stay focused? Did they fall asleep? Did they become more relaxed or more agitated? What was it like for them to simply observe and accept their sensations? Did any thoughts or emotions arise when they focused on specific areas of their body?

Body Scan

You can find the guided audio for this meditation at **www.thebrainlady.com/pesi-meditations**.

This body scan meditation will help you become more mindful of your bodily sensations and reduce tension that you are holding in your body. It is a great antidote to stress, as it quickly gets you out of your head.

Begin by settling into a comfortable position, either lying down on your back or sitting quietly in a chair. Close your eyes or lightly lower your gaze, and begin to breathe in slowly through your nose to a count of four . . . 1, 2, 3, 4 . . . and then breathe out through your mouth, pursing your lips like you are blowing a huge bubble, to a count of eight . . . 1, 2, 3, 4, 5, 6, 7, 8. Now just breathe normally.

Bring your attention to your left foot. Just notice the sensations in this foot, including your toes, your heel, the bottom of your foot, and the top. Notice what it feels like. Then move up to your left ankle. Notice how your left ankle feels. Pay attention to whatever sensations are there. Is any pain there? Does it feel hot or cold? Does it feel light or heavy? Accept the sensations as you become aware of them.

Then pay attention to your left leg, starting at the bottom and slowly moving up to your knees and thighs, all the way to your hips. Notice whether your left leg feels tight or relaxed, warm or cold, light or heavy. Send loving, compassionate thoughts to your left leg, starting from your foot and moving up to the top of your thigh. Thoughts like "I appreciate you. I know it must be hard sometimes to constantly support my body and carry my weight."

Now pay attention to your right foot. Just notice the sensations in this foot, including your toes, your heel, the bottom of your foot, and the top. Notice what it feels like. Then move up to your right ankle. Notice how your right ankle feels. Pay attention to whatever sensations are there. Is any pain there? Does it feel hot or cold? Does it feel light or heavy? Accept the sensations as you become aware of them.

Then pay attention to your right leg, starting at the bottom and slowly moving up to your knees and thighs, all the way to your hips. Notice whether your right leg feels tight or relaxed, warm or cold, light or heavy. Send warm thoughts of gratitude to your entire right leg, like "Thank you for carrying me when I walk" or "Thank you for supporting me."

Copyright © 2026 Debra Burdick, *The Psychotherapy Toolbox for Chronic Illness and Chronic Pain*. All rights reserved.

Now pay attention to both legs, all the way from the tips of your toes up to the tops of your hips. Be still, breathe, and send your legs some more kind and loving thoughts. Breathe gently into your legs.

Now move your attention to your belly, just observing what's there. Notice how your belly feels, and let it be the way it is. Send love and kindness to your belly. For example: "I love how you digest my food" or "You are so good at letting me know when I'm full."

Now shift your focus to your back, starting with your lower back and moving up all the way up to your shoulders. Notice any sensations present in your back, sitting for a moment and just noticing everything about your back. Then send warm thoughts of relaxation to your back, such as "My back is at ease" or "My back is warm and comfortable." Now sit for a moment, just noticing everything about your back.

Now bring your attention to your hands, including your fingers, thumbs, and palms. Notice how they feel. Think about all the things your hands carry, and simply let them relax. Thank them for all their hard work. Now focus on your arms, starting from your wrists and moving up to your forearms, elbows, upper arms, and shoulders. Just notice what's there. Send thoughts of gratitude and compassion to your arms, such as "Thank you for all the things you help me accomplish" or "Thank you for helping me lift things." Remember to breathe.

Now pay attention to your neck and throat. Swallow and notice how your neck and throat feel. Is your neck tense or relaxed? Is your throat sore or comfortable? As you observe your neck and throat, send thoughts of health and healing to this area of your body. For example: "I send you whatever you need to heal" or "I imagine you perfectly healthy."

Now pay attention to your face: your chin, mouth, cheeks, eyes, eyebrows, forehead, and finally ears. Take a moment to observe what's there. Notice everything without attempting to change it. Send thoughts of love and kindness to your face. Allow a smile to emerge.

Now bring your attention to your head, including your hair, your scalp, and your brain. Observe the activity inside your mind. Send thoughts of kindness, healing, and connection to your brain. Take a moment to connect with your inner wisdom.

Finally, take a deep belly breath and fill your whole body with a cushion of healing energy. As you blow the air out gently, let go of anything that needs to go. Slowly open your eyes and bring your attention back to the room.

 Copyright © 2026 Debra Burdick, *The Psychotherapy Toolbox for Chronic Illness and Chronic Pain*. All rights reserved.

Skill 3.12 Relaxation Response

Background: The term *relaxation response* was coined by Dr. Herbert Benson (2000) in describing a series of steps we can take to counter the body's fight-or-flight response. Although there are many different ways to elicit the relaxation response, many of which are described in this book, the meditation included in this skill was developed by Dr. Benson specifically for this purpose. It involves focusing on a single word or phrase, like *calm* or *om*, while closing your eyes and focusing on your breathing. Use this skill to help clients invoke the relaxation response, thereby relaxing their muscles, lowering their blood pressure, and decreasing their pain.

The Skill in Action: *Brendan was in constant pain that started after a car accident and had persisted for nearly a year. When he told his therapist that he was extremely stressed out, which made his muscles tense and increased his pain, she encouraged him to practice a relaxation response meditation. Brendan knew he couldn't sit still for the 10 to 20 minutes that the meditation recommended, but he decided to try it anyway and started with a few minutes. He sat quietly in session and paid attention to each muscle group in his body, starting at his feet. Then he paid attention to his breath and said aloud "calm" every time he exhaled. He eventually stopped saying the word and simply pictured it in his mind. He wondered how long he could do this and was surprised when he glanced at the clock and saw that five minutes had already gone by. He practiced the meditation daily and began to notice a difference. After each time he practiced, he noticed he felt less stressed and his pain had decreased. Over time, he noticed that both his stress and pain levels stayed lower throughout the day as well.*

Skill Building: Explain to the client how the relaxation response is a perfect antidote to the negative effects of stress and it can even lower pain levels as their body relaxes. Use Client Handout 3.12 to walk your client through the process of eliciting this response. Depending on your client's experience with meditation, start with two to four minutes, and slowly increase it to 10 to 20 minutes as the client increases their ability to stay focused for longer periods.

Reflection: What did your client experience during the meditation? Did they notice a feeling of relaxation? Is this a new or a familiar feeling? Did they feel drowsy or fall asleep? Did they notice any particular sensations in their body? Did their body seem to become numb, float, or disappear from awareness? Were they able to maintain their focus the whole time? Could they do the meditation for a longer period of time, or was this already too long?

Relaxation Response

You can find the guided audio for this meditation at **www.thebrainlady.com/pesi-meditations**.

The relaxation response is a simple practice that can significantly improve your mental, emotional, and physical health, especially during chronic illness or pain. It involves two simple steps (1) repeating a word, sound, or phrase to yourself as you exhale, and (2) dismissing everyday thoughts that come to mind and returning your focus to your repetition.

To get the greatest benefits from this skill, it's recommended that you set aside 10 to 20 minutes each day to practice it. However, if that sounds too overwhelming, start with 2 to 4 minutes at a time and increase as you are able.

As you do this practice, you may open your eyes to check the time, but do not use an alarm. Maintain a passive attitude and permit relaxation to occur at its own pace. Do not worry about whether you are successful in achieving a deep state of relaxation. With practice, the response should come with little effort.

When distracting thoughts occur, try to ignore them by not dwelling upon them. Return to repeating the word *calm* or *om* (or whichever word you choose) as you exhale.

If paying attention to your breath makes it difficult to breathe at any time, simply open your eyes, focus on your surroundings, and then return your focus to your breath and say the word *calm* or *om* with each exhale.

When you finish, sit quietly for several minutes, at first with your eyes closed and later with your eyes open. Do not stand up for a few minutes.

Practice the technique once or twice daily, but not within 2 hours of a meal, since the digestive processes seem to interfere with the elicitation of the relaxation response. Work your way up to 20 minutes as you are able.

Use the following process to practice this technique to invoke the relaxation response. You can replace the word *calm* or *om* with whatever resonates with you.

To begin, sit quietly in a comfortable position. Allow your eyes to gently close, or soften your gaze.

Copyright © 2026 Debra Burdick, *The Psychotherapy Toolbox for Chronic Illness and Chronic Pain*. All rights reserved.

Take a deep breath in through your nose and exhale slowly through your mouth with pursed lips like you are blowing a bubble. Now breathe normally through your nose. (If your nose is too stuffy, you can breathe through your mouth.)

Become aware of your breathing. Notice the rhythm of your breath as you gently inhale and exhale. Now, as you breathe out, say the word *calm* or *om* aloud or silently to yourself. Allow yourself to breathe easily and naturally. If you like, you might sing the word as you exhale: "Calm . . . Calm . . ." or "Om . . . Om . . ."

Continue this process for 10 to 20 minutes (or for a shorter length of time if needed).

Copyright © 2026 Debra Burdick, *The Psychotherapy Toolbox for Chronic Illness and Chronic Pain*. All rights reserved.

Skill 3.13 Replace Self-Sabotaging Behaviors

Background: Clients with chronic illness and pain may engage in a variety of self-sabotaging behaviors that make their condition worse. For example, they might ignore their need to rest when they are tired, try to do too much, eat unhealthy food, skip taking medications, or fail to practice good sleep hygiene. This skill helps clients identify behaviors that might be interfering with their progress so they can explore actions that are more supportive of their goals and overall health.

The Skill in Action: *William had a digestive disease that was very sensitive to stress, causing him to frequently land in the hospital when he took on way more that anyone could handle. He rarely asked for help, took on too much responsibility at work, often forgot to take his medications, got no exercise, and didn't get enough sleep. After he identified these problematic behaviors, he worked with his therapist to develop an improvement plan. For example, he set a timer to take his medication and get to bed on time, delegated some of his tasks at work, hired an assistant, and made a commitment to going on a walk most days. By making these seemingly small changes, his stress levels evened out, his digestive disease became better controlled, and he had no further hospitalizations.*

Skill Building: Use Client Worksheet 3.13 to identify any self-sabotaging behaviors the client may be engaging in. Explore how these behaviors might be interfering with their ability to take care of themselves, manage their chronic illness or pain, or improve their health. As part of this discussion, you'll want to explore how these behaviors may have started and why the client continues to engage in them. For example, some clients engage in self-sabotage as a way to avoid what they perceive as a terrible consequence, in which case you can help them shift their behaviors by working to understand why they have this fear and what drives it (e.g., they no-show for a doctor's appointment fearing a terrible diagnosis). In addition, some clients may be in denial about their self-sabotage behaviors, in which case it may be useful to use the motivational interviewing techniques from Skill 2.5 to help them move in the direction of change.

Once the client has completed the worksheet, brainstorm ways in which they can shift their behaviors to be more in alignment with their goals. For example, if they struggle with taking prescribed medications, they can set up an organizational system for their pills and set a timer to remind them to take them each day. Or if they have a tendency to overexert themselves with household tasks, they can ask their spouse to help them with chores that are too difficult or that exacerbate their pain.

Reflection: How did the client react to the concept of self-sabotage? What behaviors were they able to identify and what behaviors did you have to identify for them? How did they feel knowing that these behaviors get in the way of their goals? When did these behaviors start and why have they persisted? Was the client open to making changes in these behaviors? If so, what changes did they suggest? If not, what is getting in the way?

Self-Sabotaging Behaviors

When you engage in self-sabotage, you behave in ways that undermine your progress and that interfere with your ability to achieve your goals. Use this list to check off any self-sabotage behaviors you tend to engage in.

❏ Eating food you know makes you feel ill

❏ Eating food that contributes to your illness

❏ Not drinking enough and becoming dehydrated

❏ Overeating

❏ Forgetting to eat

❏ Not seeking help with disordered eating or exercising behaviors

❏ Sitting at the computer long after your back or neck start hurting

❏ Not taking a break before you are exhausted

❏ Overdoing physical activity, which results in increased pain

❏ Sitting too much

❏ Not exercising enough

❏ Distracting yourself (e.g., with your phone) instead of doing tasks that need to be done

❏ Trying to do too much

❏ Taking on too much responsibility

❏ Not asking for help

❏ Not delegating

❏ Worrying without taking action

❏ Not prioritizing tasks

❏ Expecting yourself to succeed without setting aside time to do so

❏ Not getting help with an addiction

Copyright © 2026 Debra Burdick, *The Psychotherapy Toolbox for Chronic Illness and Chronic Pain*. All rights reserved.

☐ Not following your medical provider's recommendations

☐ Forgetting to take prescribed medications

☐ No-showing for appointments

☐ Putting off making an appointment you know you need

☐ Not seeking help with a medical condition

☐ Procrastinating

☐ Being a perfectionist

☐ Making excuses for not meeting your responsibilities

☐ Blaming others for your problems

☐ Socially isolating yourself

☐ Ignoring self-care

☐ Not taking time for yourself

☐ Taking care of everyone but yourself

☐ Staying up so late you feel awful the next day

☐ Putting yourself down

☐ Staying stuck and not doing things that help you move forward

☐ Giving up on things such as self-care

☐ Other: _____

 Copyright © 2026 Debra Burdick, *The Psychotherapy Toolbox for Chronic Illness and Chronic Pain*. All rights reserved.

Skill 3.14 Ask for Help

Background: Individuals who are dealing with chronic illness or pain often need more help than they ever have before, yet they may be reluctant to ask for it. They may worry about being a burden to their loved ones. They may feel like asking for help is an admission that they're not the person they used to be. They may be determined to do things on their own and be independent. Or they may simply not have anyone they can reach out to. This skill asks clients to identify the reasons they don't ask for help and brainstorm ways they can ask for assistance with specific tasks.

The Skill in Action: *Annette had recently been confined to a wheelchair and needed assistance with many activities of daily living, such as getting out of bed, going to the bathroom, showering, and shopping. However, she hated the idea of asking for help because in her younger years she had been mocked for doing so. At the same time, Annette knew that she couldn't function as independently as she used to—and her husband was beginning to have trouble lifting her in and out of her wheelchair—so she made a list of tasks she needed help with and identified who could help with these. For example, she and her husband decided it was time to get a home health aide to help out with activities of daily living. Her husband was still happy to help her in other ways, such as bringing items to her, carrying things for her around the house, and doing some of the cooking. Annette also asked her daughter to help with getting groceries a few times a month. Her granddaughter agreed to organize her medications once a month. Annette felt so much better now that she had asked for help and things were getting done so much more easily.*

Skill Building: Use Client Worksheet 3.14.1 to explore the reasons it is difficult for your client to reach out for help when needed. Remind them that everyone needs help sometimes, especially when they are experiencing chronic illness or pain. While your client may be afraid of being treated differently if they reach out for support, make sure to emphasize that most people *do* want to help and are glad to lend a hand with specific tasks. Once you've identified the underlying issues that make it challenging for your client to seek support, use Client Worksheet 3.14.2 to identify specific tasks they could use help with and brainstorm specific prompts they can use to be more comfortable and successful when reaching out for help.

Reflection: How did the client feel about asking for help? Have they had any negative experiences asking for help before? Do they have people in their life that they can ask? If not, how can they expand their list of potential helpers? How did they feel when they started asking particular people for help with specific things? How did it feel when they received this needed support? How has their life changed since they improved their ability to reach out for help?

Why Asking for Help Is Hard

There are many reasons people avoid asking for help when they struggle with chronic illness or pain. The following list contains some common reasons people avoid asking for help. Read through the list and check off any that apply to you.

- ❏ I don't want to bother others or be an inconvenience.

- ❏ I feel guilty when I ask for help.

- ❏ I feel embarrassed that I need help.

- ❏ I'm ashamed that I can't do it myself.

- ❏ I'm afraid I will seem weak.

- ❏ I feel like I should be able to do everything myself.

- ❏ I don't want to lose my independence.

- ❏ I'm afraid I'll feel bad if the other person says no.

- ❏ I'm afraid the other person will feel bad if they can't help or don't want to.

- ❏ I'm not sure if others are willing to help.

- ❏ I feel vulnerable when I ask for help.

- ❏ I worry that others will think less of me if I need help.

- ❏ I don't want anyone to see me like this.

- ❏ I don't want to owe anyone a return favor.

- ❏ I don't want to appear needy.

- ❏ I don't want to take advantage of the helper.

- ❏ I don't feel like I have earned the right to ask for help.

- ❏ I don't know anyone to ask for help.

- ❏ I don't know how to ask for help.

- ❏ I would rather be the helper.

 Copyright © 2026 Debra Burdick, *The Psychotherapy Toolbox for Chronic Illness and Chronic Pain*. All rights reserved.

Ask for Help

Everyone needs help sometimes, and chronic illness and pain can make it even more likely that you will need assistance. Use this worksheet to think about what would make your life easier or prevent symptom flare-ups and who you could ask for help.

To begin, make a list of tasks that you need help with. Be as specific as possible! For example:

- I need a ride to my doctor's appointment this coming Monday.

- I need help getting groceries this week.

- I need help carrying my plate to the table.

- I need help standing up to use the restroom.

- I need help taking out the garbage before pickup day.

- I need help getting in and out of the shower tomorrow morning.

- I need help organizing my medications.

_____

_____

_____

_____

_____

_____

_____

_____

_____

Then make a list of who you can ask for help, making sure to be specific about what you need from each helper. For example:

- I can ask my son for a ride to my doctor's appointment.

Copyright © 2026 Debra Burdick, *The Psychotherapy Toolbox for Chronic Illness and Chronic Pain*. All rights reserved.

- I can ask my friend to shop for me this week.

- I can ask my daughter to carry my plate when she visits for lunch.

- I can ask my paid caregiver to help me get to the restroom.

- I can ask my neighbor to put the garbage out at the curb the night before.

- I can ask my spouse to help me get in and out of the shower.

- I can ask my nurse to help me organize my medications.

_____

_____

_____

_____

_____

_____

_____

_____

Here are some additional tips to consider when asking for help:

- Ask the potential helper ahead of time so you give them time to plan.

- Give them an easy way to say no, and thank them no matter what they say. If they can't help, ask them for suggestions of who else might be able to.

- If you are frequently asking the same person for help, check in periodically to make sure they feel okay continuing to help.

- Make your request as specific as possible. Ask for help with the most important tasks on your list first, and try to focus on one thing at a time rather than requesting several things at once.

- Ask the helper in person, as this makes them more likely to say yes to your request.

 Copyright © 2026 Debra Burdick, *The Psychotherapy Toolbox for Chronic Illness and Chronic Pain*. All rights reserved.

Skill 3.15 Social Support

Background: Being chronically ill or having chronic pain can be a very lonely experience. Not only do clients feel isolated and disconnected due to their inability to participate in activities or hobbies they once enjoyed, but they may also suffer with the perceived stigma of being viewed as "lazy" or "weak" due to their symptoms, causing them to isolate themselves further. Not surprisingly, clients who have a good social support system fare better, both emotionally and physically (Gallant, 2003; Reblin & Uchino, 2008), since they are more likely to receive practical help and feel a sense of belonging. This skill guides clients to identify their current social support system and explore options for expanding it if needed.

The Skill in Action: *Gisela was a senior citizen who lived alone. Since her bout with COVID turned into long COVID, she was experiencing a myriad of symptoms, including chest pain, brain fog, and fatigue. Before COVID, she went to the senior center several times per week to play cards, take an art class, and have lunch with friends. But ever since she began struggling with symptoms of COVID, she had stopped going out much. Gisela's therapist helped her realize that she still needed social support—in fact, now more than ever.*

Together, they made a list of activities she felt she could do even with her symptoms, as long as she paced herself. She joined an online group for those with long COVID and found it very helpful to share her experiences with the group. She also contacted a couple of her friends and set up an in-home lunch date once a week where they ordered meals from a local restaurant to be delivered to her home. In addition, she made a list of supportive individuals she could contact when she was feeling isolated, which included her daughter, her grandson, her sister-in-law, her best friend from high school, and a new friend from the senior center. She made it a point to call someone each day and simply say she was thinking about them and wanted to know how they were doing. With time, she gradually felt less lonely and isolated, and she was delighted when friends and family started calling her more often to chat and inviting her to easy outings.

Skill Building: Explore how chronic illness or pain has impacted the client's social support system. What social activities have they withdrawn from due to their physical limitations? What social roles or family dynamics have shifted as a result of their illness or pain? Explain that individuals who have a strong social support system fare better than those without one—even phone contact or online contact helps! Then use Client Worksheet 3.15.1 to explore the four main forms of social support—(1) emotional support, (2) esteem support, (3) informational support, and (4) instrumental support—and identify which supports the client could benefit from. If the client's current support system doesn't meet their needs, use Client Worksheet 3.15.2 to brainstorm options for expanding this system, whether it involves finding others with similar interests or seeking a support group for people with their health issues. Encourage the client to build a social support system that not only meets their needs, but also helps them feel loved and cared about.

Reflection: Did the client already have a sufficient support system? If not, in what areas were they lacking? How has their support system changed since their chronic illness or pain began? What difficulties, if any, did the client encounter when actively seeking out new sources of support? What did it feel like to expand their system to meet their needs? For example, how did improving their system help them combat loneliness or isolation?

Types of Social Support

There are many different types of social support, with the main four types being emotional support, esteem support, informational support, and instrumental support. To begin, read through the following table to learn more about each:

Emotional Support	Esteem Support
Someone who provides a listening ear, reassures you, validates you, comforts you, hugs you, and makes you feel cared for	Someone who points out your strengths, boosts your confidence, encourages you, tells you, "You've got this," and acts as a cheerleader for you

Types of Support

Informational Support	Instrumental Support
Someone who provides you with advice, problem-solves with you, gives guidance, and shares knowledge	Someone who provides you with practical assistance, like chores, meals, errands, transportation, and activities of daily living

After reading through this list, what types of social support do you already have in your life? Describe them here, including who fulfills that role for you.

_____

_____

_____

_____

_____

_____

_____

Copyright © 2026 Debra Burdick, *The Psychotherapy Toolbox for Chronic Illness and Chronic Pain*. All rights reserved.

What types of support do you wish you had more of? In what ways are these forms of support missing from your life?

_____

_____

_____

_____

_____

_____

_____

_____

 Copyright © 2026 Debra Burdick, *The Psychotherapy Toolbox for Chronic Illness and Chronic Pain*. All rights reserved.

Expand Social Support

Chronic illness and pain can be extremely isolating. Since having a strong social support system can contribute to better physical and emotional health, use this worksheet to identify your current social support system and brainstorm options for expanding it to better serve your needs.

Who is currently part of your social support system? This can include family, friends, neighbors, acquaintances, health care professionals, caregivers, support groups, or even a pet. In what ways do these individuals help you?

_____

_____

_____

_____

_____

_____

What would you like to gain from your support system that is currently missing? For example, perhaps you're looking for someone you can talk to on a regular basis, someone to practice a hobby with, someone to help with meals or a ride, or someone who has already dealt with similar health or pain issues.

_____

_____

_____

_____

_____

_____

Copyright © 2026 Debra Burdick, *The Psychotherapy Toolbox for Chronic Illness and Chronic Pain*. All rights reserved.

As you think about what is missing from your support system, as well as what you'd like to gain, what do you need to do differently to make sure you're getting your needs met? For example, what steps can you take to meet more like-minded people? Can you do an online search for groups that share your interests? What options exist in your community, such as art classes, exercise classes, music performances, or book clubs? Where can you find a community of others dealing with the same illness in person or online? Brainstorm some ideas here. Once you've identified some options, pace yourself and get started!

_____

_____

_____

_____

_____

_____

_____

 Copyright © 2026 Debra Burdick, *The Psychotherapy Toolbox for Chronic Illness and Chronic Pain*. All rights reserved.

SECTION 4

Chronic Pain Skills

Skill 4.1 Assess Pain Type

Background: Chronic pain is defined as pain that has been present for at least three months. Often, this follows an acute injury (such as a back injury from a car accident or fall, or following an illness or cancer treatment), but the pain persists after the typical three-month healing time has passed. In fact, many clients with chronic pain experience unremitting symptoms for years or even decades after the initial injury. This skill explains the three types of pain identified by the International Association for the Study of Pain (2024)—nociceptive, neuropathic, and nociplastic pain—and provides resources to assess which type the client is experiencing. This determination will guide the choice of pain management skills in this section.

If the client's pain clearly stems from injury, tissue, or nerve damage, then they primarily have nociceptive or neuropathic pain, in which case you'll want to use the skills in Section 4.A: *Pain Management for Nociceptive or Neuropathic Pain*. If their pain meets the criteria for nociplastic pain, first use the skills in 4.A to help the client manage their pain, and then focus on the skills in Section 4.B: *Pain Management for Nociplastic Pain* to help them reprogram the overly sensitized pain receptors in their brain. Note that if a client's pain is not actually nociplastic, the skills in Section 4.B will likely not eliminate their pain, but they can still be helpful since all types of chronic pain typically have an added layer of suffering and an intensification of physical pain that goes beyond the tissue damage.

The Skill in Action: *Sonya had been in pain for years when she first entered therapy at the recommendation of her primary care doctor. The pain had started out as nociceptive pain—tissue damage after a nasty fall down the stairs—but continued to bother her several years later. She had already done many rounds of physical therapy, visited a pain management specialist for injections to lower inflammation, and taken a variety of pain medication. Although the initial pain level had decreased considerably, Sonya still experienced pain every day, and it often moved around. When her therapist explained the three major types of pain, Sonya began to wonder if perhaps her pain fit the nociplastic category, as her doctors had assured her that healing had occurred and there was no longer any evidence of tissue damage. Indeed, her pain and her history met many of the criteria for nociplastic pain, such as no evidence of current tissue damage, pain that moved around, a traumatic injury causing the initial onset, and being a perfectionist and people-pleaser. Although Sonya had been worrying that it was all in her head, her therapist assured her the pain was real but was most likely stemming from overly sensitized pain receptors in her brain. This was a new concept to Sonya, but it made sense. When Sonya's therapist explained that he would teach her skills designed to normalize these pain receptors, she began to feel a sense of relief and looked forward to trying them.*

Skill Building: Although it can be difficult to accurately assess a client's type of pain, even for pain specialists, it is helpful for you to understand the type of pain that a client is likely experiencing so you can better tailor skills to help them. Use Client Handout 4.1.1 to review the characteristics of the three types of pain with your client. Consider connecting with the client's medical providers (with the client's permission, of course) to get as much information as possible about their relevant history. Then use Client Worksheet 4.1.2 to determine whether the client's symptoms seem to meet the criteria for nociplastic pain. If nociplastic pain is present, your client will likely check off many of the items on the checklist.

Clients with nociplastic pain may also have experienced trauma—including childhood abuse, neglect, loss, and abandonment—and they may have low self-esteem and put a lot of pressure on themselves to fit in and succeed. Although these traits do not, by themselves, predict this type of pain, they are often correlated and are worth exploring with the client to determine whether there is a connection to the onset of their pain and their related emotions (Schubiner, 2022).

If your client has not already done so, encourage them to get a full medical assessment of their pain, which will help determine the type of pain they are experiencing. Keep in mind it may be a combination of types. If their pain has continued long past the typical healing period (and they have the characteristics of nociplastic pain listed on Client Handout 4.1.1), their brain may have become sensitized to experience pain when no source of pain is present. An extreme example of this is phantom limb pain, which occurs when someone experiences pain in a limb that has been amputated and cannot be the source of pain. Regardless, encourage the client to stay engaged with their medical providers and continue relevant treatment as they learn and practice the mind-body pain management skills in this section.

Reflection: Were you and the client able to determine what type of pain they have? What characteristics helped you decide the category their pain fits in? Does their pain fall in more than one category? If the client shows symptoms of nociplastic pain, how did you help them consider the possibility that their pain is not (or is no longer) being generated by tissue damage but, rather, the result of overly sensitized brain receptors? Did they react with relief, or did they think you were telling them their pain is all in their head? If the latter, how did you assure them that their pain is real?

Types of Pain*

Use this handout to identify the category your pain fits in. Keep in mind that pain may overlap categories, as illustrated in the figure here.

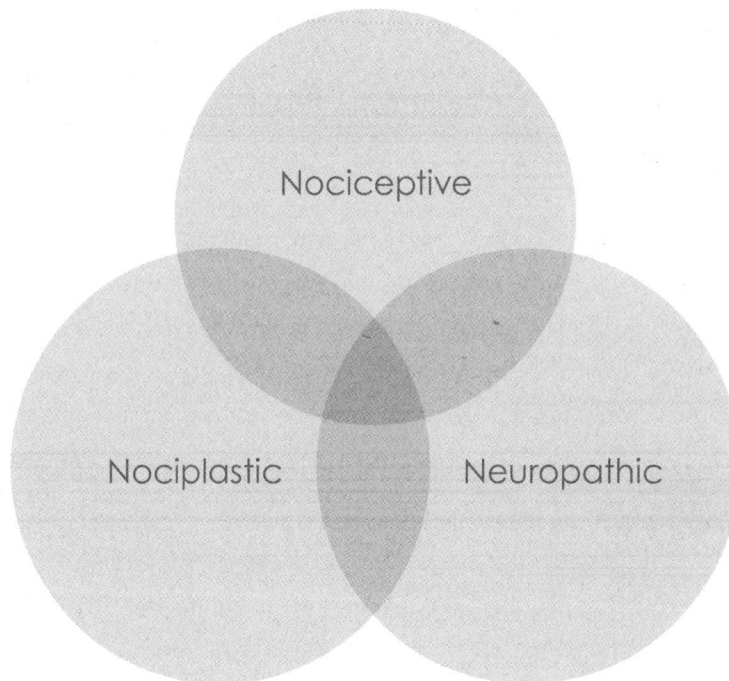

Nociceptive Pain

- **Definition:** Pain that arises from damage to non-neural tissue. Damage is detected by *nociceptors*, which are sensory nerve endings that initiate the sensation of pain.

- **Symptoms:** Sharp, aching, throbbing, stabbing, burning.

- **Common causes:** Injury with tissue damage to bone, joints, ligament, tendons, muscles, organs (e.g., intestines, lungs, heart), or skin. Fractures, tumors, infection, rheumatoid arthritis. Typically involves inflammation.

- **Common diagnoses:** Bone fractures, torn muscles, inflammation from injury or chronic disease, organ injury, bruises, lacerations, burns, infections.

---

* Adapted from Fitzcharles et al. (2021), International Association for the Study of Pain (2024), and Schubiner (2022).

 Copyright © 2026 Debra Burdick, *The Psychotherapy Toolbox for Chronic Illness and Chronic Pain*. All rights reserved.

Neuropathic Pain

- **Definition:** Pain caused by nerve damage.

- **Symptoms**: Shooting or burning pain, neuropathy, tingling, numbness, muscle weakness, insensitivity to heat or cold. May be constant or intermittent.

- **Common causes:** Chronic progressive nerve disease, pinched nerves, surgery, trauma, chemotherapy, infection.

- **Common diagnoses:** Neuropathy, spinal stenosis, carpal tunnel syndrome, lumbar or cervical radiculopathy. Often seen with diabetes, multiple sclerosis, stroke, cancer, cytomegalovirus, or amputation.

Nociplastic Pain

- **Definition:** Pain that arises from altered nociception despite *no clear evidence of actual or threatened* tissue damage or nerve damage (no unhealed fracture, active cancer, heart disease, infection, nerve damage, diabetes, etc.). Also referred to as *neuroplastic pain*.

- **Symptoms:** Various pain symptoms that are often intermittent or may move around.

- **Common causes:** Acute pain that doesn't go away after three months of healing. May stem from an injury that has long since healed. The client often has a history of emotional or physical trauma.

- **Common diagnoses:** Fibromyalgia, low back pain, irritable bowel syndrome (IBS), non-ulcer dyspepsia, migraine and tension headaches, complex regional pain syndrome (CRPS), reflex sympathetic dystrophy (RSD), postural orthostatic tachycardia syndrome (POTS), rheumatoid arthritis, whiplash-associated disorders, osteoarthritis, myofascial pain syndrome, multiple chemical sensitivities, and irritable bladder syndrome (interstitial cystitis).

Characteristics of Nociplastic Pain*

The following characteristics are commonly seen in nociplastic pain. Check off all that apply to you. If you have many of these characteristics, your pain is more likely to be nociplastic, but for some people, only one characteristic is enough to indicate this, as long as there is no structural reason for the pain.

❑ I don't have a clear physical diagnosis that explains my pain.

❑ There is no evidence of structural or tissue damage.

❑ My pain started during a stressful time in my life.

❑ My pain persists after an injury has healed.

❑ My pain came on without any injury.

❑ Symptoms have a quality of tingling, electric sensation, burning, numbness, hot or cold—with no evidence for actual nerve damage.

❑ My symptoms come and go.

❑ My symptoms move or spread to different areas of my body.

❑ I have a lot of symptoms overall.

❑ Stress triggers my symptoms or makes them worse.

❑ Things unrelated to my body (e.g., weather, sounds, smells, time of day) can trigger my symptoms.

❑ My symptoms are symmetrical (same spot on both sides of my body).

❑ My pain starts a while after I've moved or exercised.

❑ I have a history of childhood adversity or trauma.

❑ I am perfectionistic, highly conscientious, a people-pleaser, or very anxious.

---

* Adapted from the Pain Reprocessing Therapy Center (https://www.painreprocessingtherapy .com/faq) and Murphy et al. (2023).

Copyright © 2026 Debra Burdick, *The Psychotherapy Toolbox for Chronic Illness and Chronic Pain*. All rights reserved.

In addition to pain, I experience the following symptoms:

☐ Fatigue

☐ Memory problems

☐ Poor sleep quality

☐ Mood disturbances

☐ Sensitivity to non-painful sensory stimuli (e.g., noises, odors, bright lights)

Copyright © 2026 Debra Burdick, *The Psychotherapy Toolbox for Chronic Illness and Chronic Pain*. All rights reserved.

Pain Management for Nociceptive or Neuropathic Pain

Skill 4.A.1 Awareness of Pain Without Judgment

Background: People with chronic pain often become overly focused on their symptoms, causing them to ruminate about, agonize over, or struggle with their pain. This, understandably, serves to make the experience of pain worse. Practicing mindfulness helps increase awareness of physical sensations without judgment, which can help clients accept their pain without resisting or fighting it and also prevent them from tensing up. Therefore, it can reduce pain perception and improve overall well-being. This skill provides a meditation that incorporates the process of somatic tracking to help clients practice being aware of their pain without judgment, resistance, or labeling. This can help them learn to accept the pain and allow it to be, which is an essential first step in managing pain.

The Skill in Action: *Stephanie had unremitting chronic pain in her back. She tried desperately to reduce the pain with strategies like stretching, pain medication, cortisone injections, and progressive muscle relaxation, but she still seemed to focus on it almost all of the time. In response, her therapist encouraged her to try a meditation practice that involved learning to be aware of pain without judging or fighting it. At first, Stephanie was certain that doing this would make her pain worse, as she worried that if she didn't fight it, the pain would overwhelm her. She nonetheless decided to give it a try, as she was willing to try anything at this point. The first time she practiced the meditation, she had trouble simply noticing her pain and letting it go. But with time, she was soon able to allow the pain to be present, to accept it, and to stop fighting it. She was surprised when she realized that her pain didn't get worse and, in fact, seemed somewhat better when she listened to the meditation.*

Skill Building: Process the client's feelings about their pain, and discuss how they typically respond to their pain. Do they fight it? Try to change it? Judge it? Do they feel like their pain is dangerous? Explain that when they can practice being aware of their pain without judgment, it may reduce pain perception. That's because doing so makes them less likely to tense up, resist, or feel stressed by their pain. Then walk the client through the meditation in Client Handout 4.A.1. You might need to encourage some clients to give this practice a try, as their first reaction might be to worry that focusing on their pain will only make it worse. Explain that by nonjudgmentally accepting their pain, they can decrease their natural tendency to tense their muscles around the pain or their brain's natural tendency to react to the pain as a danger signal. After doing this practice, discuss how it felt for them to just let the pain be. Encourage them to practice this meditation daily or anytime their pain grabs their attention. Remind them that rewiring their brain's response to pain can take practice, just as learning anything new does.

Reflection: Was the client able to just let their pain be? Was this practice a new concept to them? Did they worry that their pain would overwhelm them or worsen if they didn't fight it? Did they notice any change in the pain when they accepted and allowed it to just be? How can they practice this process throughout the day?

Awareness of Pain Without Judgment Meditation

You can find the guided audio for this meditation at **www.thebrainlady.com/pesi-meditations**.

Noticing your pain without trying to change, resist, or judge it can help you avoid tensing up in reaction to pain. This can allow you to better accept the pain and gradually lessen pain perception. Use this meditation to practice being aware of your pain and accepting it without fighting it.

Find a comfortable position, either sitting or lying down, where you won't be disturbed. Close your eyes and take a deep breath in through your nose to the count of four . . . 1, 2, 3, 4 . . . Then breathe out through pursed lips to a count of eight . . . 1, 2, 3, 4, 5, 6, 7, 8.

Now just breathe normally and bring your attention to your body. Simply tune in and take a moment to notice how your body feels.

Now focus on areas of your body that have pain. Just notice the pain without trying to change it. Just let it be.

Accept the pain just as it is. There is nothing you need to do about the pain. Simply surrender to it as it is. Just allow the pain sensations to exist without judging them or resisting them.

Notice the characteristics of the pain. Does it throb, stab, burn, or ache? Is it warm, hot, or perhaps cold? Notice if the pain is steady or if it changes while you pay attention to it.

Spend a moment just sitting with the pain. Notice how you can stop fighting it and make peace with the pain.

Just let it be.

There is no need to judge or fight the pain.

Notice how it feels to simply accept the pain without fighting or resisting it.

Now that you have practiced accepting and allowing the pain without judging it or fighting it, notice if there has been any change in the pain or if it remains the same.

Copyright © 2026 Debra Burdick, *The Psychotherapy Toolbox for Chronic Illness and Chronic Pain*. All rights reserved.

Take a deep breath in and fill the painful areas with a healing cushion of air. Breathe out and let the painful areas empty. Do this again. Take a deep breath in, filling any pockets of discomfort with well-being and ease. Now exhale and allow anything that needs to go to flow out of you.

Now breathe normally again and focus on areas of your body that feel comfortable. Stay focused there for a while and say thank you for the comfort.

Open your eyes and return to your day.

Remember to practice accepting your pain without judgment whenever you notice it throughout the day.

 Copyright © 2026 Debra Burdick, *The Psychotherapy Toolbox for Chronic Illness and Chronic Pain*. All rights reserved.

Skill 4.A.2 Distraction

Background: When clients are in chronic pain, it is not unusual for them to focus on how bad they feel much of the time. After all, it can be very difficult not to when the pain feels constant or overwhelming. However, many clients report that the more they focus on their pain or symptoms, the worse they seem to get. One way clients can achieve symptom relief is to practice distraction techniques, which involve shifting attention away from the physical sensations caused by illness or pain (and the ensuing negative thoughts) to something more positive. This skill provides several distraction techniques clients can use to train themselves to counteract their tendency to overly focus on their pain. Of note, while this skill provides clients with options to distract themselves from pain, remember that there are times when they need to pay attention to pain so they know how to take care of themselves, rest when they are tired, not overdo it, and report to their doctor.

The Skill in Action: *Jody suffered with neuropathy in her feet stemming from diabetes. Her feet burned continuously, making it hard for her to think about anything else. When her therapist suggested using distraction techniques to shift her attention away from pain, Jody was skeptical and pretty sure nothing could distract her. However, she agreed to practice to see if it would make a difference. One technique involved saying "stop" whenever she found herself focusing on her pain and instead thinking about how beautiful the view of the lake was out her sunroom window, observing or visualizing it in her mind. Jody also practiced bringing her attention to her surroundings and using all five senses to notice what was around her in the present moment. After a few weeks, she noticed she wasn't paying as much attention to her pain. She wondered if her pain had actually changed or just her perception of it.*

Skill Building: Begin by asking the client to write down the thoughts that typically arise when they notice pain, especially thoughts that elicit anxiety, fear, anger, resentment, frustration, or sadness. Explore how these thoughts affect their perception of pain and their body's response to pain. Then introduce Client Handout 4.A.2.1, which provides a step-by-step approach they can use to distract themselves from negative thoughts, as well as Client Handout 4.A.2.2, which explains how to draw on the power of the imagination to visualize a pleasant or soothing scene. Finally, use the meditation in Client Handout 4.A.2.3 to teach the client how to shift their attention to their surroundings whenever they notice that they are thinking about their pain. Explain that after they have practiced the full meditation, they can quickly distract themselves from pain by taking a slow, deep breath and bringing their attention to their surroundings without having to do the entire meditation.

Reflection: What type of negative thoughts about pain does the client routinely have? How did you process any resistance to the idea of using distraction techniques? What feelings did this process bring up? How did they feel after practicing distracting themselves from their pain? Did their pain change? What are some times the client should pay attention to their pain and what are some times they should use distraction?

Find a Thought That Feels Better

Whenever you find yourself getting stuck in thoughts about your pain, follow the steps on this handout to find a thought that feels better. Before you begin, you'll need to get into the habit of reflecting inward and noticing any negative or unhelpful thoughts as they arise (see Skill 2.6). Then whenever one of these thoughts pops up, use these four steps.

1. **Verbally interrupt the thought.** Interrupt a negative or unhelpful thought by saying "stop" out loud. This adds an auditory cue that signifies it is time to halt the negative thought process.

2. **Engage in a physical action to reinforce the verbal interruption.** Take some type of physical action, such as tapping your fingers together or on a table, or grasping an object like the arm of the chair. Touching something helps anchor your attention in the present.

3. **Replace the thought.** Replace the negative thought with a more positive one (see Skill 2.6). Make sure it's a thought that you can believe. For example:

   ° Replace the thought "My back hurts so much all the time" with "Even though my back hurts, I will think about my granddaughter's cute face instead."

   ° Replace "I hate feeling so exhausted" with "The garden flowers are beautiful right now."

   ° Replace "I'm so angry that I can't walk right now" with "I remember how good it felt to hike last year."

   ° Replace "My pain will never go away" with "Although I am in pain, I have felt better and will again soon. I will think about how much I love my son."

4. **Say the new thought out loud if possible.** This provides another auditory cue that reinforces the new thought.

 Copyright © 2026 Debra Burdick, *The Psychotherapy Toolbox for Chronic Illness and Chronic Pain*. All rights reserved.

Visual Imagery

Visual imagery is a simple but effective distraction technique that involves imagining a soothing scene or pleasant experience in your mind. This can distract you from pain and illness and promote relaxation.

1. Make a list of five images you would find soothing. For example, this could be a peaceful beach, a pretty flower, a beloved family member's face, a gentle rain, a warm bath, a sunset, or your pet.

2. Choose one of the images from your list to focus on.

3. Close your eyes and take a soothing breath in and out, breathing slowly.

4. Visualize the image you chose in your mind's eye.

5. Bring your attention to the image and tune into the pleasant or soothing feelings it reminds you of.

6. If you have trouble visualizing the image in your mind, you can print out some pleasant or peaceful images and spend some time actually looking at them instead of imagining them. Post these where you can see them regularly.

7. You can also search online for mindfulness videos showing peaceful scenes, particularly of the beauty and healing power of nature.

Copyright © 2026 Debra Burdick, *The Psychotherapy Toolbox for Chronic Illness and Chronic Pain*. All rights reserved.

Mindfulness of Surroundings

You can find the guided audio for this meditation at **www.thebrainlady.com/pesi-meditations**.

Focusing your attention on your surroundings is an effective way to distract yourself from pain and bring your attention to the present moment. Use this meditation to practice noticing everything there is to notice about your surroundings.

Find a comfortable position seated in a chair with your feet flat on the floor, your back resting gently against the chair, and your hands sitting gently on your thighs. Keep your eyes open and focused on your surroundings, whether you are inside a room or outside in nature.

Begin by looking around you. Pay attention to what you see. Are you alone or with others? Are you inside or outside? If you are inside, are there windows in the room? Can you see outside? Can you see the sky? Is there light or sunshine shining in the window? Does it light up an area on the floor or the wall? If you are outside, can you see the sky? Are there clouds? Is the sun shining? What is straight ahead of you? What is beside you? Can you see behind you? Look all the way around you. Observe. When your mind wanders, notice it, accept it, and then bring your attention back to looking around you again.

Notice the temperature around you. Is it warm, cold, or just right? Is the air moving or still? Do you notice any odors or smells? Are they comforting or distasteful? Are they new smells or are they familiar?

What can you hear? Is it quiet? Is there noise? What sounds are there? Where are they coming from? Are they loud, soft, sharp, soothing, or annoying? Do you want to keep listening to the sounds or do you want them to stop?

Is there activity in the space? What is moving? What stays still? Are things moving through the space, coming and going?

Pay attention to your body sitting in the chair. Feel where your bottom is supported by the chair. Is the chair hard, soft, cushiony, or solid? Is the back supporting your back? Does the chair fit you? Do your feet touch the floor or swing above it? Do your knees bend at the edge of the chair? Do you fill the seat side to side?

 Copyright © 2026 Debra Burdick, *The Psychotherapy Toolbox for Chronic Illness and Chronic Pain*. All rights reserved.

Look around and find something that particularly attracts your attention. Notice what shape it is, where it is located, what color it is, its texture, and its purpose. Observe why it draws your attention. Does it remind you of something else? Do you know what it is? Is it common or unusual?

When thoughts arise that are not about this present moment, notice them, accept them, and let them go. Tell them "not now." Then bring your awareness back to your surroundings.

Become aware of yourself in this space. How do you feel? Do you feel safe? Do you want to be here? Does this place feel familiar, or does everything seem new to you? Have you been someplace else that reminds you of this place? Do you feel good, bad, or neutral here?

Notice the energy you feel in this place. Become aware of your inner reaction to being in this place. Is it active or quiet energy? Is it calm, bubbling, hot, or cold energy? Is it positive or negative energy? Is it peaceful or bustling? Is it intense or mild? Is it healing?

Now that you have spent some time completely focused on being in this moment, bring the awareness you have gained back with you as you resume your regular life. Practice this full meditation whenever possible to keep yourself present in the moment. With continued practice, you will be able to quickly distract yourself from your pain by taking slow deep breaths and shifting your attention away from pain and to your immediate surroundings.

Copyright © 2026 Debra Burdick, *The Psychotherapy Toolbox for Chronic Illness and Chronic Pain*. All rights reserved.

Skill 4.A.3 Cognitive Behavioral Therapy for Pain Management

Background: Cognitive behavioral therapy for chronic pain (CBT-CP) is recommended as a first-line treatment for chronic pain. Like regular CBT, this type of therapy involves teaching clients how to change the negative thoughts, feelings, and behaviors that fuel their pain or make it worse. Since the central nervous system (comprising the brain and spinal cord) controls how pain is processed, it's crucial to target the brain along with the body to effectively treat both acute and chronic pain. This skill provides guidance on applying the components of CBT-CP to chronic pain management.

The Skill in Action: *For the last several years, Jaime had suffered from chronic knee pain stemming from a skiing accident. She was constantly thinking about her pain, which was interfering with her concentration at work. She also felt intensely angry that her pain prevented her from doing all the activities she loved, especially skiing. Her therapist introduced her to CBT-CP and taught her a variety of skills to replace negative thoughts, process intense emotions, let go of the past, replace some self-sabotaging behaviors, relax her body, and improve all aspects of her self-care, such as sleep and diet. Using these skills, she gradually became able to limit how often she thought about her pain and also started calming her anger. It took some time to learn and incorporate these skills, but Jaime was amazed when she realized that her knee pain had nearly completely disappeared!*

Skill Building: The essential goals of CBT-CP are to change: (1) unhealthy thought patterns; (2) negative emotions; (3) physical factors, like muscle tension and an overactive nervous system; (4) unhelpful coping behaviors, like avoiding, isolating, or staying inactive; and (5) lifestyle habits like sleep, nutrition, and exercise (Zoffness, 2024). The basic theory of CBT-CP is that:

- Negative thoughts and emotions amplify pain.

- Focusing on pain makes pain worse.

- Positive thoughts and emotions reduce pain.

- Distracting from pain reduces pain.

- Reduction of activity and social isolation make pain worse.

- Movement, exercise, and social support contribute to pain reduction.

Clinician Handout 4.A.3 provides you with a variety of skills from this book that are geared toward managing and reducing chronic pain using the framework of CBT-CP. Choose the skills that your client needs the most, but aim to include skills from each component as treatment progresses.

Reflection: Use the reflection questions provided in each skill.

Treating Chronic Pain with CBT-CP

Use the skills in this book that align with the components of CBT-CP treatment, which are designed to change:

1. Unhealthy thought patterns

    ° Skill 2.3: *Change the Channel*

    ° Skill 2.6: *Reframing Thoughts*

    ° Skill 4.A.2: *Distraction*

2. Negative emotions

    ° Skill 2.7: *Mindfulness of Emotions*

    ° Skill 3.9: *Remembered Wellness*

3. Physical factors like muscle tension and an overactive nervous system

    ° Skill 3.5: *Set Mindful Limits*

    ° Skill 3.10: *Progressive Muscle Relaxation*

    ° Skill 3.11: *Body Scan*

    ° Skill 3.12: *Relaxation Response*

4. Unhelpful coping behaviors like avoiding, isolating, or staying inactive

    ° Skill 2.5: *Identify and Motivate Change*

    ° Skill 3.13: *Replace Self-Sabotaging Behaviors*

    ° Skill 3.15: *Social Support*

    ° Skill 5.4: *Be of Service*

5. Lifestyle habits like sleep, nutrition, and exercise

    ° Skill 3.4: *Manage Fatigue*

    ° Skill 3.6: *Eat to Support Health*

    ° Skill 3.7: *Sleep Hygiene*

    ° Skill 3.8: *Keep Moving*

Copyright © 2026 Debra Burdick, *The Psychotherapy Toolbox for Chronic Illness and Chronic Pain*. All rights reserved.

Skill 4.A.4 Mindfulness for Pain Management

Background: Research has demonstrated that practicing mindfulness can help reduce chronic pain across a wide spectrum of pain disorders (Zeidan & Vago, 2016). Mindfulness can also be used to reduce fear of pain, pain avoidance, and pain-related depression as well as to generally improve the quality of a client's life (Hilton et al., 2017). This skill provides guidance on how to use a variety of mindfulness skills included elsewhere in this book specifically for managing chronic pain.

The Skill in Action: *David had been experiencing intense neuropathic pain for more than six months following chemotherapy treatment for a tumor in his back. He had trouble concentrating, as he thought about his pain almost continuously. He reacted to the pain by tensing his muscles until they hurt, which added to the constant burning pain in his back and legs. In therapy, he learned a variety of mindfulness skills to manage his pain. After practicing the body scan and progressive muscle relaxation skills in particular, he noticed that he felt calmer, his body was way less tense, and his pain decreased along with his body tension. He also learned to quickly shift his attention to his surroundings whenever his pain was high or to "change the channel" when he realized he was watching his pain channel. He noticed that the less he paid attention to his pain, the less he noticed it.*

Skill Building: Use the skills listed in Clinician Handout 4.A.4 to help clients use mindfulness skills included elsewhere in this book to successfully deal with chronic pain. As you use each skill, help the client focus on their pain as well as their pain-related thoughts and emotions.

Reflection: Use the reflection guidance provided with each skill, but tailor it to specifically address the client's chronic pain. Explore how using these mindfulness skills has helped the client manage their pain as well as their pain perception. Which mindfulness skills helped the client decrease their pain the most? How did you help the client focus on the theme of chronic pain as they practiced these skills?

Mindfulness Skills for Managing Pain

Mindfulness skills can be extremely effective for managing chronic pain. This handout provides guidance on using mindfulness skills provided elsewhere in this book specifically to help with chronic pain. Start with the skills listed in step 1 to increase the client's self-awareness of their body and help them relax and remember wellness. Then use the skills in step 2 to help them address any pain-related thoughts and emotions. Finally, use the skills in step 3 to teach clients how to distract themselves from their pain.

Step 1: Increase the client's awareness of body pain and tension while accepting it or, at a minimum, letting it be.

- Skill 3.11: *Body Scan.* Guide the client to check in with each area of the body, notice what's there, acknowledge it, and if possible, release any tension or discomfort.

- Skill 3.10: *Progressive Muscle Relaxation.* Help the client release and relax muscle tension, which will assist in reducing pain.

- Skill 3.9: *Remembered Wellness.* Help the client remember a time when they were pain free and to imagine feeling better.

Step 2: Help the client cope with the uncomfortable thoughts and emotions that often accompany physical pain.

- Skill 2.7: *Mindfulness of Emotions.* Help the client observe and be aware of emotions, without engaging with them, allowing the ebb and flow of emotions that occur with pain without judging the experience.

- Skill 2.6: *Reframing Thoughts.* Help the client become more aware of the thought patterns associated with pain and find thoughts that are more realistic, believable, and helpful.

- Skill 2.3: *Change the Channel.* Help the client watch a "feel-good" channel instead of their pain channel.

Step 3: Increase the client's ability to distract themselves from pain.

- Skill 4.A.2: *Distraction.* Help the client practice techniques to distract themselves from their pain.

Copyright © 2026 Debra Burdick, *The Psychotherapy Toolbox for Chronic Illness and Chronic Pain.* All rights reserved.

Skill 4.A.5 ACT for Managing Pain

Background: Acceptance and commitment therapy (ACT) offers a solid framework for helping clients navigate pain. ACT doesn't try to eliminate pain—instead, it helps clients stop struggling with it since the real cause of suffering isn't the pain itself, but the struggle against it. ACT focuses on improving the client's psychological flexibility when dealing with thoughts, feelings, and behaviors associated with their chronic pain so they can better embrace and accept that uncomfortable emotions and pain are a part of life. It guides them toward taking action that aligns with their goals and values so that they can live a meaningful life despite their pain. This skill provides guidance on applying ACT's core processes to chronic pain management.

The Skill in Action: *Linda often felt stuck since her stroke. Although her cognitive functioning was intact, she lacked control over one side of her body and she had intense post-stroke pain, including headaches, shoulder pain, and muscle spasms. In therapy, she learned several ACT-based techniques that allowed her to accept her current situation, stop engaging with thoughts about her pain, and find ways to participate in activities that aligned with her values that she had discontinued since the stroke. Linda noticed that after using the principles of ACT, she felt calmer and like she wasn't fighting the pain so much. She was also beginning to feel less isolated after she took action and had lunch at a handicap-accessible restaurant with her friend. Although Linda was not always able to disengage from every single unpleasant thought that crossed her mind, she was able to stop struggling against the pain, which left her feeling less stressed and more hopeful.*

Skill Building: Review and explain the three main tenets of ACT as they apply to chronic pain:

1. **A**ccepting experiences instead of avoiding them simply because they may cause chronic pain or emotional discomfort. This helps clients learn to accept their pain and become willing to do things even if they cause pain.

2. **C**hoosing behaviors mindfully and deliberately rather than behaving automatically or as they always have. This helps clients behave in ways that align with their goals and thrive despite their pain.

3. **T**aking action and being in charge of their life rather than being immobilized by uncomfortable thoughts, emotions, or pain. This helps clients find ways to do things they love to do and that are important to them even though they have chronic pain.

Clinician Handout 4.A.5.1 describes the six core ACT processes you can use to help clients strengthen their psychological flexibility (McCracken & Vowles, 2014). An explanation of each component of psychological flexibility is provided first, followed by several examples of skills in this book that teach that process.

The following three client worksheets are referenced in Clinician Handout 4.A.5.2 and included in this skill. Client Worksheet 4.A.5.2 helps clients develop the willingness to try an activity that they would like to do but have been avoiding due to their pain or uncomfortable emotions about doing so. Client Worksheet 4.A.5.3 teaches clients how to notice their thoughts and accept them as just thoughts. With practice, they can learn to observe their thoughts without engaging with them, which allows them to distance themselves from chronic worry or thoughts about their pain.

Finally, Client Handout 4.A.5.4 provides a process for clients to separate from their physical or emotional pain by becoming a neutral observer of their thoughts, surroundings, or pain rather than a participant. It helps them see that they are distinct from whatever they are observing. While they may experience physical or emotional pain, they are not defined by this pain.

Reflection: Was the client able to practice acceptance? In what ways did they resist or struggle with this concept? Was the client able to grasp the concept of being the observer of their thoughts? How did practicing this help them? Were they able to plan activities that aligned with their goals despite their pain? What obstacles did they discover they placed in their way?

ACT Core Processes

In ACT, the concept of psychological flexibility is broken down into six core processes: acceptance, cognitive defusion, present-moment awareness, self-as-context, values, and committed action. Read through each core process below and then use the skills listed to help clients manage their chronic pain.

1. **Acceptance:** Help clients approach their pain and ensuing unpleasant thoughts, emotions, and sensations from a place of acceptance. Explain that their thoughts and feelings are a natural response to dealing with chronic pain and that learning to accept the discomfort they experience will make life worth living and more aligned with their goals.

   ° Use Client Worksheet 4.A.5.2: *Willingness to Try* to help them build willingness to experience pain so they can do things that their pain (and associated emotions) have been holding them back from.

   ° Refer to Skill 2.8: *Accepting What Is* to help them practice radical acceptance.

   ° Refer to Skill 4.A.1: *Awareness of Pain Without Judgment* to help them accept their pain.

2. **Cognitive defusion:** There is a difference between having a thought and engaging with that thought. Defusion is about simply noticing thoughts as they occur without attaching any significance to them. By simply acknowledging their thoughts without any judgment, clients can choose not to allow their thoughts to influence or control their behavior.

   ° Use Client Worksheet 4.A.5.3: *Just a Thought* to help clients observe thoughts without engaging with them. This can help them decrease the negative impact of physical or emotional pain.

   ° Refer to Skill 2.13: *Let Thoughts Go By on a Lazy River* to help clients practice noticing and dismissing thoughts without judging or engaging with them.

 Copyright © 2026 Debra Burdick, *The Psychotherapy Toolbox for Chronic Illness and Chronic Pain*. All rights reserved.

3. **Present-moment awareness:** Explore the benefit of staying present in the moment versus replaying the painful past or worrying about what might happen in the future.

   ° Use Client Handout 4.A.2.3: *Mindfulness of Surroundings* to help clients practice staying in the present moment and dismissing distracting thoughts.

4. **Self-as-context:** Clients can become more self-aware by practicing the concept of "self-as-context" or "the observer self." This means that they understand that their true self is separate from their thoughts, emotions, or even their body. Explore how this concept helps them challenge the identity they've built since their pain became chronic, especially when it's tied to their pain and holding them back from positive change. By practicing this, clients can learn to observe their pain without letting it define who they are.

   ° Use Client Worksheet 4.A.5.4: *Self as Observer* to help clients practice the concept of being the observer.

5. **Values:** Encourage the client to identify and reflect on what is most important to them in life, including how their chronic illness interferes with activities that match their values. Explore areas where they may have let their pain stop them when it didn't really need to, and process how they might refocus on doing things they enjoy instead of their pain.

   ° Use Skill 5.1: *Identify Values* to help clients define their values in major life areas, such as career, family, intimate relationships, friendships, health, and spirituality.

6. **Committed action:** This core ACT process is about helping clients commit to changing their behavior and taking actions that support their values, in spite of their pain. To do so, help clients define goals that align with their values. For example, if a client wants to reconnect socially, they might arrange lunch with a friend. Then problem-solve how to manage situations in which their chronic pain might interfere with their plans. For example, perhaps the client can plan lunch at a handicap-accessible restaurant so they know they can go in their wheelchair if need be. Or perhaps they rest during the morning before the lunch date so they are less exhausted and can enjoy socializing.

Copyright © 2026 Debra Burdick, *The Psychotherapy Toolbox for Chronic Illness and Chronic Pain*. All rights reserved.

Willingness to Try

Willingness is about making a *conscious* choice to accept what is and act in a way that is effective and moves you toward your goals, even when it causes discomfort. When you practice willingness, you can overcome reluctance and resistance to doing things that are important to you despite associated physical or emotional discomfort. This worksheet will help you understand that you do not have to be controlled by your pain or any associated feelings.

Write down an activity that you want to do but don't because of your pain. Perhaps you want to go to the grocery store but fear your chronic pain will make it difficult to walk that far. Or maybe you want to reconnect with friends that you haven't seen since your pain began because you have been afraid of what they will think. Or maybe you miss hiking your favorite trails in the forest and would love to find a way to do so.

_____

_____

_____

_____

_____

Think about what holds you back from doing this activity. Are you physically able to do the activity? Are you worried that it would increase your pain? Have you tried it before? Are you hesitant to use a wheelchair or walker in public, or are you self-conscious? Is your worry immobilizing you?

_____

_____

_____

_____

_____

 Copyright © 2026 Debra Burdick, *The Psychotherapy Toolbox for Chronic Illness and Chronic Pain*. All rights reserved.

Tune into your emotions and body sensations as you think about doing this activity. Do you feel fear, sadness, anger, regret, or loss? What worries you the most? Do you worry that your pain will get in the way? Notice if you feel physical pain when you simply think about doing the activity.

_____

_____

_____

_____

_____

Have there been other times in your life when you felt this way but were able to overcome the emotion or pain for something important? For example, did you fear public speaking but did a great job anyway when you presented your report in class? Or perhaps you were sure that you wouldn't be able to walk far enough to go to the store but discovered that although it hurt, it wasn't as hard as you thought it would be when you went anyway?

_____

_____

_____

_____

_____

Are you willing to do this activity despite your worry, fear, or pain? Remember, willingness is about making a conscious choice. It is not trying, believing, or being forced to do it. Can you choose to do it?

_____

_____

_____

_____

_____

Copyright © 2026 Debra Burdick, *The Psychotherapy Toolbox for Chronic Illness and Chronic Pain*. All rights reserved.

Now that you are willing, how can you do this activity despite your pain? For example, if you want to see your friends, you might ask them to pick up some lunch and bring it to your house to visit rather than going out. Or perhaps you can use a walker to keep your balance at the store. Or maybe you can get a friend to take you out to see your favorite band and drop you off at the door so you don't have to walk far. Or maybe you can find a paved hiking trail through the woods and go there with your scooter. Perhaps you can tolerate the pain more easily when you are willing to.

_____

_____

_____

_____

_____

 Copyright © 2026 Debra Burdick, *The Psychotherapy Toolbox for Chronic Illness and Chronic Pain*. All rights reserved.

Client Worksheet 4.A.5.3

Just a Thought

This following worksheet will teach you how to step back from your thoughts and simply notice whenever you are having a thought. This process reduces the impact of uncomfortable or painful thoughts by helping you observe the thought as separate from you.

Focus on a thought you have been having today about your pain. For example, "My pain is intense today." Really believe that this thought is true. Notice how you feel when you think this thought.

_____

_____

_____

_____

_____

_____

Now, without judging the thought, simply label it by inserting the phrase "I am having the thought . . ." before it. For example: "I am having the thought that my pain is intense today." Notice how you feel.

_____

_____

_____

_____

_____

_____

Now insert the phrase "I am aware that I am having the thought . . ." before your thought. For example: "I am aware that I am having the thought that my pain is

Copyright © 2026 Debra Burdick, *The Psychotherapy Toolbox for Chronic Illness and Chronic Pain.* All rights reserved.

intense today." How do you feel now? Do you still believe the thought? Does it seem less a part of you?

_____

_____

_____

_____

_____

_____

Practice this process with other unpleasant thoughts so you can simply observe them and not engage with every one you have.

 Copyright © 2026 Debra Burdick, *The Psychotherapy Toolbox for Chronic Illness and Chronic Pain*. All rights reserved.

Self as Observer

You can find the guided audio for this meditation at **www.thebrainlady.com/pesi-meditations**.

This exercise is intended to help you develop your "observer" skills so you can release any labels or self-judgments you have created that may not be helpful. This can help you separate yourself from your thoughts, surroundings, illness, and pain and become an observer rather than a participant.

Begin by closing your eyes and taking a deep breath in through your nose . . . and then exhaling slowly through your mouth. Tune into whatever sensations you feel in your body—whether it's a point of distress related to your illness or pain, an itch on your arm, or maybe a sense of relaxation. Simply notice whatever arises.

Now shift your focus to your thoughts. What thoughts are arising? Just notice them and let them go without judgment. Whatever the thoughts are, just observe them and let them go. Imagine you are watching your thoughts on a TV screen. Observe them but don't engage with them or judge them.

Now notice what sounds are around you. What can you hear? Just observe the sounds without judging or labeling them.

Pay attention to the temperature. Is it cool, warm, or just right? Simply tune into how the temperature feels and accept it as it is. Observe how it feels.

Acknowledge that you're simply paying attention to these sensations, thoughts, and sounds. See yourself observing the steady stream of thoughts, sounds, and sensations and let them be as you watch them.

And as you're noticing them, be aware that you're noticing. How does noticing feel?

And as you're observing them, notice who's doing the observing.

Now, recognize that you are separate from all of this—you're just the observer, noticing the difference between the one having the thoughts and the one observing them. Like watching a play versus acting in the play.

Use this process to help you observe your physical or emotional pain without letting it define you. Know that you are not your pain, you are separate from it. Remember you can separate from it by simply becoming the observer.

Copyright © 2026 Debra Burdick, *The Psychotherapy Toolbox for Chronic Illness and Chronic Pain*. All rights reserved.

Skill 4.A.6 Neurofeedback for Chronic Pain

Background: Neurofeedback is a form of biofeedback that teaches clients to change their brainwaves into more normal and functional patterns. It uses operant conditioning and the brain's capacity for neuroplasticity to help reregulate brain function. This type of treatment has been incorporated into numerous private psychotherapy practices, neurofeedback centers, universities, and major health centers around the world. Dr. Bessel van der Kolk (2014) also incorporates it in his work with PTSD. A number of studies show that neurofeedback is effective in decreasing chronic pain, improving quality of life, and reducing the need for pain medications (Diotaiuti et al., 2024; Patel et al., 2020). It is thought to work by normalizing various brainwave patterns linked to pain modulation and pain processing. This skill provides a discussion of what neurofeedback is, how it works, and how to find a neurofeedback practitioner or get trained in it if you are interested in adding it to your practice.

The Skill in Action: *Anna was a scientist who worked at a major pharmaceuticals company. She had a history of migraine headaches that recently had become almost continual. She was out of work on medical disability leave, but her medical workup indicated that there was no tissue damage, nerve damage, or brain-based disease that could account for her symptoms. She had also been cleared of any chemicals or typical migraine-triggering foods, such as aspartame, chocolate, and aged cheeses that could be triggering the migraines. She didn't have any particular stressors or hormonal patterns that seemed to induce the migraines either, as they seemed to come on at random.*

Anna entered therapy at her doctor's suggestion, and after a full assessment, she began receiving neurofeedback treatment twice a week. This involved placing sensors at specific locations on her head, dictated by her assessment, that relayed her brainwaves to a computer display. She played a video game that was controlled by her brainwaves, and via a process of operant conditioning, she was rewarded with points and beeps when the brainwaves changed in the desired direction. The therapist could see her brainwaves changing as she played the game.

Together, Anna and her therapist tracked the frequency and severity of her migraines. After a few weeks of treatment, the migraine intensity decreased significantly. After about six weeks, both the severity and frequency of migraines decreased to the point that Anna was able to return to work part time. Within three months, she was able to work full-time, as the migraines were very infrequent and no longer debilitating. At this point, Anna reduced the treatments to once per week for a few weeks, then every other week, and then once a month until she was assured that the migraines were not coming back. Six months later she reported no migraines.

Skill Building: Neurofeedback is an effective, medication-free treatment for many brain-based disorders, including chronic pain, that can reregulate brain activity and gradually reduce and normalize the pain perception mechanisms in the brain. When introducing this approach to clients, explain that it can be a valuable addition to their existing pain management treatment and that it has been shown to help with all three types of pain as well as sleep, mood, quality of life, and more. It is often added when existing treatment in not effective. Since neurofeedback can be an unfamiliar concept to many clients, use Client Handout 4.A.6.1 to explain the particulars behind this approach. Besides traditional neurofeedback described on the handout, there are numerous types of neurofeedback approaches that employ different techniques, which all aim to help the brain reregulate itself. Some popular ones include z-score neurofeedback, which uses a database of normalized brainwave patterns to guide the training, and Low Energy Neurofeedback System (LENS), which uses weak electromagnetic signals as a carrier for feedback to assist in reorganizing brain physiology.

If you are interested in receiving training to become a neurofeedback practitioner, consult the resources listed on Clinician Handout 4.A.6.2, where you'll find information on the courses, trainings, and equipment necessary to become certified in this approach. Becoming certified is the best way to gain the broad knowledge needed to use neurofeedback when working with clients with chronic pain. Between the courses required, the practical and mentoring hours, and the exam, this could easily take up to a year while you continue to work full-time and gain hands-on experience using neurofeedback to help your clients. By becoming certified, you will add an incredibly powerful and effective tool to your practice.

Reflection: Does it make sense to add neurofeedback to the client's treatment plan? What types of symptoms might it improve? Is the client open to this type of treatment? Do they know anyone who has done neurofeedback treatment? Have they tried neurofeedback previously? If so, in what ways was it helpful? Is there a local neurofeedback provider you can work with? If not, have you found someone who is not local who provides home training? Have you considered becoming a neurofeedback provider yourself?

What Is Neurofeedback?

There are a variety of types of neurofeedback. The most common type is called traditional neurofeedback, which is a non-invasive, medication-free form of treatment that teaches you how to change your brainwaves into more normal patterns. During traditional neurofeedback, you play a simple video game on a computer while you receive information (feedback) about your brainwaves in real time. However, instead of using a hand controller to operate the game, you control it simply with your brainwaves. Your brainwaves need to remain in a certain range for the video game to continue working properly. When you are able to successfully change your brainwaves to be in this range, you get a "reward" that typically consists of beeps, points, game motion, or a movie being displayed on the screen. With repeated practice, your brainwave patterns change and remain closer to normal ranges.

Traditional neurofeedback works via the principles of operant conditioning and neuroplasticity. Operant conditioning is a method of learning that involves rewards and punishments, whereas neuroplasticity refers to your brain's amazing ability to change. Because neurofeedback training is a learning process, you'll gradually see results over time. Most people can see initial progress within about 10 sessions, with some changes as early as the first few sessions, and meet their training goals by 20 sessions. For others, training can require more sessions, especially for complicated issues. No matter the number of sessions you require, once enough neurofeedback sessions have been completed, the improvements you gain will persist after the treatment ends.

Neurofeedback can help with many brain-based conditions, such as chronic pain, migraines, depression, anxiety, sleep disorders, ADHD, learning disabilities, memory, addictions, traumatic brain injury, seizures, autism, anger, trauma, and much more. It is a great treatment option for chronic pain since it rewires the brain to reduce pain perception while also improving sleep, mood, and most of the other conditions that are often comorbid with chronic pain.

 Copyright © 2026 Debra Burdick, *The Psychotherapy Toolbox for Chronic Illness and Chronic Pain*. All rights reserved.

Neurofeedback Providers, Training, Certification, and Equipment

How to Find a Neurofeedback Practitioner

- **Biofeedback Certification International Alliance (BCIA)** (https://www.bcia.org/consumers-find-a-practitioner): BCIA offers a directory of certified practitioners as well as board certification, a blueprint of requirements for certification, and courses that fulfill blueprint requirements.

- **International Society for Neuroregulation and Research (ISNR)** (https://isnr.org/find-a-provider): ISNR is a professional organization that supports excellence in the field of neurofeedback training and provides a directory of neurofeedback providers.

- Search online with keywords such as *neurofeedback provider*.

How to Find Training to Become a Neurofeedback Practitioner

- **Biofeedback Certification International Alliance (BCIA)** (https://www.bcia.org): BCIA offers board certification, a blueprint of requirements for certification, courses that fulfill blueprint requirements, and a directory of providers and mentors. The entry-level requirements for certification can be found at https://www.bcia.org/nf-entry-level.

  ° Certification requires a license/credential issued by the state where you practice, or supervision by someone who has one.

  ° The BCIA-approved health care fields include psychology, social work, marriage and family therapy, counseling, psychiatry, and many other health-related fields.

  ° Also required is a course in neuroanatomy/neurophysiology/physiological psychology, didactic courses to learn the science and theory of neurofeedback, and practical skills training, including practicing neurofeedback on yourself and then with clients under the oversight of a mentor.

- **International Society for Neuroregulation and Research (ISNR):** Besides providing research and education on brain regulation and neurofeedback,

Copyright © 2026 Debra Burdick, *The Psychotherapy Toolbox for Chronic Illness and Chronic Pain*. All rights reserved.

practice guidelines, and a professional journal, ISNR provides a yearly conference that is invaluable for gaining up-to-date knowledge in the field. You can learn about upcoming conferences at https://isnr.org/conference.

- **Neurofeedback equipment manufacturers:** Most equipment manufacturers provide training on their systems that meet some of the certification requirements. Training is typically equipment dependent because although the theories being employed are similar, the systems that actually train the brain vary considerably.

Neurofeedback Equipment

- **Major companies:** There are approximately 10 to 15 companies providing neurofeedback equipment. Here are several:

    ° **BrainMaster Technologies** (http://www.brainmaster.com): Offers neurofeedback equipment and training.

    ° **EEGer Neurofeedback System** (https://www.eeger.com/our-products): Provides equipment and training.

    ° **Ochs Labs** (www.ochslabs.com): Provides equipment and training on LENS, a Low Energy Neurofeedback System.

    ° **Thought Technology** (http://thoughttechnology.com): Provides many types of physiological monitors and biofeedback systems, including training on their use.

    ° **ISNR** (https://isnr.org/neuroregulation-equipment): Provides a list of neurofeedback equipment companies. Many companies have a booth at the ISNR conference so you can get information and try it out.

    ° Search online for *professional neurofeedback equipment*.

- **Equipment cost:** Equipment cost can vary, and many equipment companies use subscription models to keep initial costs lower. Systems can range from $2,500 to $25,000, with the higher end providing more advanced assessment capabilities that can often be obtained without purchasing the high-end equipment. There are also options for home-based versions of the professional systems that clients can use at home under your direction. All the systems pay for themselves many times over when used regularly with clients. Price is less of an issue than learning how to work with neurofeedback and fitting it into your practice in the most effective way.

 Copyright © 2026 Debra Burdick, *The Psychotherapy Toolbox for Chronic Illness and Chronic Pain*. All rights reserved.

Pain Management for Nociplastic Pain

Skill 4.B.1 Understand and Rewire Nociplastic Pain

Background: It can be difficult for clients with nociplastic pain (sometimes called neuroplastic pain) to overcome the fear that something is structurally wrong with their body. Many have been diagnosed with previous physical damage, such as herniated discs, disc degeneration, and broken bones, which makes them believe their pain must be structural. They may also have developed associations with activities that increase their pain. It is essential that clients in this situation understand what nociplastic pain is so they can change their relationship to pain. This skill guides clients to understand that their pain is not a danger signal associated with neural or tissue damage. This, in turn, allows them to rewire their brain to lessen its sensitivity to pain.

The Skill in Action: *Tara had been dealing with symptoms of fibromyalgia for nearly 15 long years. She had pain throughout her body. Everything hurt. And she was exhausted most of the time. She had tried everything the medical and alternative medical community had to offer. When her therapist introduced her to the concept of nociplastic pain, she felt angry and invalidated—"How dare she think my pain is all in my head?" On further discussion, she began to understand how her brain may have been hypersensitized by the numerous traumatic events she had experienced. She realized that her fibromyalgia symptoms first started following a tragic miscarriage and subsequent damage to her gastrointestinal system from antibiotics that were prescribed after her D&C.*

In turn, Tara started to consider the possibility that her brain had been overwhelmed. She changed how she thought about her pain and started telling herself that there was nothing wrong with her. She hoped her brain would get the message quickly because this was hard for her to believe. With time, she noticed that when she said "I am safe" out loud, her body seemed to relax a bit—a new feeling, since her body tended to be tense all the time. She also used a progressive muscle relaxation practice, which further lessened her pain, alongside some other skills that helped her relax, feel safe, and visualize her body as healthy. She got better at telling her brain to back off and stop misinterpreting things as dangerous. She also learned how to accept her pain without judging it and started to replace fearful thoughts with calmer, safer thoughts. Over a few weeks, Tara noticed her fibromyalgia symptoms less and less.

Skill Building: If the client's medical assessment did not find any evidence of neural or tissue damage that would cause pain, explain that they are most likely experiencing nociplastic or neuroplastic pain. This happens when the brain has become oversensitized and experiences pain when the body is no longer generating pain. Share the extreme example of phantom limb pain as an illustration of how the brain continues to feel pain (in a limb that was amputated) even when it is not being generated by an injury to the body. Then use Client Worksheet 4.B.1.1 to help them create their own list of evidence that supports the probability that their pain is not structural but, rather, centralized nociplastic pain. Be sure to emphasize that even with this type of pain, their pain is very real. The brain can cause any symptom imaginable—even theirs. The good news is that they can retrain their brain to respond to their body in ways that don't cause pain.

Use Client Worksheet 4.B.1.2 to help your client reframe their understanding of what's happening with nociplastic pain and to start the process of calming the nociceptors in their brain. This worksheet helps them change their understanding of their pain from "There is something wrong with my body" to "My brain is overreacting." Process the client's feelings as they repeat each statement on the list aloud. Encourage them to read the list aloud daily and to notice how their feelings about their pain begin to change. You can also recommend the book *Unlearn Your Pain Workbook: A 28-Day Process to Reprogram Your Brain* (Schubiner, 2022), which is a great resource for rewiring and unlearning neuroplastic pain.

Reflection: How did the client respond to the possibility that they might have nociplastic pain? Did they feel invalidated or concerned that you thought their pain was all in their head? Were they reassured by your acknowledgment that their pain is very real? Were they willing to try thinking about their pain as brain based? How much evidence did they find that it is nociplastic pain? How did repeating the statements begin to change how they thought and felt about their pain?

Evidence of Nociplastic Pain

The following checklist contains various types of evidence that your pain is likely not structural but a result of nociplastic pain. Check off any items that apply to you:

❑ The scan (e.g., MRI, CT scan, x-ray) of the affected area looks pretty normal.

❑ Many others with test results like mine (such as degenerative disc disease) are pain free.

❑ My bloodwork is normal.

❑ I have a long history of various types of pain (e.g., body aches, headaches, IBS).

❑ My pain started during or right after a stressful event or situation (e.g., getting a new boss at work, a breakup).

❑ My pain started after I experienced trauma (e.g., a miscarriage, violence).

❑ The pain is much worse when I'm at work than over the weekend.

❑ My pain increases when I am worried, lonely, or depressed.

❑ The structural damage from my injury healed long ago.

❑ My pain intensifies when I feel stressed.

❑ My pain started without an injury.

❑ The pain is inconsistent in how it shows up. For example, it varies in pain level or it moves around.

❑ I have a variety of different somatic symptoms (e.g., pain in various parts of my body, fatigue, weakness, shortness of breath).

❑ Pain is often triggered by events in my life (e.g., feeling overwhelmed with too much to do, conflict with a loved one, difficulty getting a timely medical appointment).

❑ My pain is gone sometimes, even when I am in physical positions or activities that generally bring it on.

❑ Other: _____

 Copyright © 2026 Debra Burdick, *The Psychotherapy Toolbox for Chronic Illness and Chronic Pain*. All rights reserved.

Rewiring Nociplastic Pain

Since nociplastic pain is the result of altered pain processing, one way to rewire your brain is to repeat a positive mantra out loud that changes the content of your thoughts. The following are all statements that can help you retrain how your brain thinks. Repeat each statement aloud, and notice what feelings arise as you go down the list. What would it be like to believe each statement?

The pain I feel is very real.

There is no injury causing the pain.

I don't need to run from my pain.

I am safe.

It's just my brain overreacting.

I can let myself cry.

I don't need to worry.

It's not dangerous.

My brain is still trying to alert me but there is no injury.

I know my brain is trying to keep me safe, but I am already safe.

I can rewire my brain and tell my brain I'm safe.

Thanks for keeping me safe, brain, but I'm okay.

I can let the pain go.

Copyright © 2026 Debra Burdick, *The Psychotherapy Toolbox for Chronic Illness and Chronic Pain*. All rights reserved.

Skill 4.B.2 Increase Tolerance for Pain Symptoms

Background: When clients have nociplastic pain, it is important to help them learn to tolerate their pain symptoms as they begin to desensitize their brain. The purpose of increasing pain tolerance for nociplastic pain is to rewire pain signals from danger to safety. A combination of skills from ACT, such as acceptance, cognitive defusion, and self-as-observer, can be useful for this. Pain can become all-consuming, so helping clients separate themselves from it and become the "observer" can help them detach from their pain, thereby increasing their tolerance and turning down the danger signal. In addition, using soothing self-talk and laughter can help clients calm their oversensitized brain. Finally, some clients are reluctant to move their bodies because they fear that doing so will cause pain, even though this can be counterproductive and weaken muscles. Since nociplastic pain is not based on physical tissue damage, gently moving the painful area can slowly help clients decrease their fear and increase pain tolerance. This skill provides guidance to help clients calm their oversensitized pain processing by increasing their tolerance for their pain.

The Skill in Action: *Rafael hurt his knee in a football game in college. Although it had healed, he still felt pain, and the doctors were unable to find any reason for his pain. After he learned that his symptoms were likely the result of nociplastic pain, he agreed to try several exercises to turn down his brain's sensitivity. First, he simply noticed the pain and just let it be. Then he imagined his pain was separate from him and was being displayed on the TV. This visualization exercise felt weird at first, but he noticed that when he was "watching" his pain on TV, it didn't hurt as much. He also used humor to defuse from pain-related thoughts by talking to himself in a Donald Duck voice, which he couldn't help but smile at. Finally, he gradually started to move his knee in ways that usually made it hurt—just a little bit to start and then a little more. He noticed that he could move it more than he realized without pain, so he practiced moving it every day. Even when it did hurt, he kept moving it gently and telling his brain he was fine. He knew his brain was starting to get the message that he was safe and was gradually sending fewer unnecessary pain signals.*

Skill Building: Guide the client to practice increasing their tolerance for pain symptoms using the four exercises in Client Handout 4.B.2. Explain that with nociplastic pain, the goal is to gradually retrain their brain to be less sensitized. These exercises will indirectly increase their pain threshold (i.e., the point where they feel pain) and thereby calm the danger signal to their brain. Using a combination of skills from ACT and CBT, they can practice separating from their pain, become the observer, use calming self-talk, and gently move the pain area. When the client no longer responds with fear, muscle tension, worry, or anger, it sends a signal to the brain that the client is safe, which lessens the brain's sensitivity.

Reflection: How did the client react to being an observer of their pain? Could they see their pain on TV? Ask them to get curious about turning off the TV (and their pain along with it). What was it like for them to talk to themselves in the third person or in a funny voice? Were they able to laugh and how did they feel when they did? What happened to their pain when they tried moving in different ways? What changed with their pain and tolerance for pain as they practiced these techniques?

Increase Tolerance for Pain Symptoms

Practice the following exercises to gradually increase your tolerance for pain symptoms. This will gradually increase your pain threshold (the point where you feel pain) and lessen your brain's hypersensitivity to pain by letting it know you are safe.

- **Be the observer of your pain.** Whenever you notice pain, follow the steps below to practice separating yourself from your pain and learn how to tolerate the pain without reacting as if it's dangerous. This exercise will gradually desensitize your pain perception in your brain.

  ° Take a deep breath in and slowly exhale.

  ° Notice your pain.

  ° Now take a moment to imagine that you are separating yourself from the pain. Imagine that you are stepping back from the pain in your mind so you can observe the pain from afar.

  ° As you do this, remind yourself that you are not your pain. You are separate from your pain, and your pain is separate from you.

  ° Now pretend the pain is on TV and you are watching the show. Spend a moment watching your pain on TV as an observer. Notice how it feels to be separate from your pain.

  ° Just let it be.

  ° Notice how you feel as the observer of your pain.

- **Talk to yourself in the third person.** Whenever you notice your pain, spend a few moments talking calmly to yourself in a reassuring way. This self-talk can turn down your brain's danger signal by letting it know you are safe and okay. It can also help you stand the pain. For example:

  ° "Jill, you are okay. It's just your brain sending an incorrect signal."

  ° "I love you, Jill."

  ° "You can do this."

  ° "You are safe."

 Copyright © 2026 Debra Burdick, *The Psychotherapy Toolbox for Chronic Illness and Chronic Pain*. All rights reserved.

- Imitate your favorite accent. For example, you might try a silky cartoon voice with a southern drawl: "Honey, everything is going to be alright."

- **Laugh out loud.** When you laugh, you can release fear and tension and turn down your brain's danger signal, replacing it with safety.

    - Instead of worrying or tensing up when you notice your pain, take a moment to laugh at the pain or smile at it.

    - Go ahead and laugh right out loud for no reason at all.

    - Do it again.

    - If you have trouble simply laughing, imagine you are talking with the voice of your favorite cartoon character saying, "Okay, I'm laughing, I'm laughing."

    - Notice how you feel after you laugh. What have you released inside you?

    - When you laugh, you are telling your brain you are safe.

- **Move your body with less fear that it will hurt.** Do this exercise when you notice that you are afraid to move because it might hurt. This will give your brain the message that you are safe and gradually increase your pain tolerance.

    - Take a slow, deep breath and exhale slowly.

    - Take a moment to notice your pain.

    - Tune into your reluctance to move what hurts.

    - Now gently move the painful part of your body just a bit.

    - Do it again and notice how it feels.

    - Now perhaps move just a little more.

    - As you practice this, challenge yourself to move a bit more and show your brain you are not afraid to move.

    - Do this gently and often throughout the day, and notice the ways in which your pain or pain tolerance changes or stays the same.

Copyright © 2026 Debra Burdick, *The Psychotherapy Toolbox for Chronic Illness and Chronic Pain*. All rights reserved.

Skill 4.B.3 Change Your Relationship with Pain

Background: With nociplastic pain, the brain's nociceptors have become overly sensitized, leading them to send out danger signals that feel like pain even when there is no tissue or nerve damage generating pain in the body. To reduce nociplastic pain, clients must train their body to feel safe so it no longer reacts to the danger signals the brain is generating. The goal is to rewire the brain and normalize its nociceptors so it stops generating pain that doesn't exist, thereby changing their relationship to pain. This skill provides a visual imagery meditation that helps clients stop reacting to erroneous danger signals sent by the brain.

The Skill in Action: *Gayle still experienced shoulder pain almost two years after she injured it while picking up her granddaughter. Although the X-rays and MRI showed no lingering tissue damage, the pain persisted long after completing physical therapy. Gayle's therapist explained that it sounded like she had nociplastic pain that was being generated by oversensitized nociceptors in her brain. She encouraged Gayle to listen to a meditation designed to help her feel safe, change her relationship to pain, and give her brain the message that it no longer needed to send out danger signals. The first time Gayle listened to it, she felt a sense of calm and peace that she hadn't felt in a long time. She noticed that her shoulder relaxed, although she hadn't realized it was carrying so much tension until now. After listening to the meditation daily for a week, she began to notice the pain in her shoulder less and less. And whenever she did notice it, she reminded herself that she was safe and healthy, and the pain seemed to fade away.*

Skill Building: In session, walk your client through the meditation on Client Handout 4.B.3.1, which begins by asking them to nonjudgmentally notice different areas of pain in their body without trying to change or fix their pain in any way. The goal is to simply observe their pain like they would any other sensations. The meditation then leads them through the process of gently releasing this pain through a series of mantras and visualizations that encourage them to imagine feeling safe and healthy as they turn the dial down on pain. After they are done listening to the meditation, invite them to be curious about how their body and pain sensations reacted to the meditation. Encourage them to regularly practice this meditation on their own.

Reflection: What did the client experience when they listened to the meditation? For example, did they notice they had been holding tension in their body? If so, were they able to release the tension and feel safe? What did it feel like to remember a time when they did not feel pain? How did it feel to talk back to their brain? What, if anything, happened to their pain level after a week or two of listening to the meditation?

Change Your Relationship with Pain Meditation

You can find the guided audio for this meditation at **www.thebrainlady.com/pesi-meditations**.

This meditation will help you change your relationship with pain so your body stops reacting to the danger signal that your brain is generating. With time, you can rewire your brain so it stops generating pain that doesn't exist in your body.

To begin, find yourself a comfortable position where you won't be disturbed. Take a slow, deep breath in through your nose to a count of four . . . 1, 2, 3, 4 . . . and then exhale slowly out of your mouth with pursed lips like you are blowing a huge bubble, to a count of eight . . . 1, 2, 3, 4, 5, 6, 7, 8.

Now set an intention to change your relationship with your pain as you take a moment to tune into your body. Slowly scan every part of your body, starting at your feet and slowly moving up to your legs, bottom, back, chest, arms, hands, neck, face, and head. Notice any areas of pain and gently pay attention to this pain without judging it or trying to change it. Just accept it and let it be. Any thoughts about your pain are just thoughts. Any pain sensations are just sensations. You are observing your pain like you are detached from it and watching it on TV.

As you watch your pain on TV, know that you are safe. Silently say to yourself, "Although I notice this pain, I am safe and I know I am healthy." Pay attention to what changes when you feel safe. For example, perhaps your body relaxes or your mind feels calmer. Notice whether you are holding tension in any areas of your body and let go of that tension as you repeat to yourself "I am safe."

Imagine how it used to feel before there was pain. Perhaps you felt freer, lighter, more at ease, more comfortable, or more energetic. Gently breathe in and out as you remember.

Now gently return your attention to your pain. Is it increasing, decreasing, or staying the same? Take a slow, deep breath and fill the areas of pain with a cushion of healing energy. As you exhale, allow the pain to flow out of you. You don't need it. You are safe and you are healthy. Take another deep breath and again fill the areas of pain with your life force. As you exhale, allow the pain to flow out of you. Repeat silently, "I am safe. I am healthy." Everything is working

Copyright © 2026 Debra Burdick, *The Psychotherapy Toolbox for Chronic Illness and Chronic Pain*. All rights reserved.

exactly as it was designed to work. Blood is flowing freely to all areas of your body, bringing all the oxygen and nutrients you need for perfect health.

Now take a moment to imagine you are inside your brain looking at the control center. Find the display that says "pain." Imagine that you are turning down the level on the pain dial. Turn it to a comfortable level where you will feel the sensation of touch but not pain. Notice how your pain changes when you turn down the dial.

Whenever your brain gives you a pain signal, imagine turning down the pain dial and repeat silently, "Even though my brain thinks there is danger due to pain, there is no danger. I am safe. I love you, brain. Thank you for trying to alert me to danger. But your pain control center is old and out of date. I am safe. The pain you alert me to no longer exists. Relax, brain. Quit working so hard. I am healthy. I am safe."

Breathe in slowly through your nose and gently release your breath through your mouth. Notice what has changed.

As you go through your day, remind yourself that any time you feel pain, it is just a sensation. When you notice you are thinking about your pain, remember it is just a thought and remind yourself that you are safe and healthy.

 Copyright © 2026 Debra Burdick, *The Psychotherapy Toolbox for Chronic Illness and Chronic Pain*. All rights reserved.

Skill 4.B.4 Turn Down Pain-Related Fear

Background: Since living with chronic pain is difficult, clients often develop the habit of avoiding moving their body in certain ways for fear that doing so will cause pain. Indeed, the fear-avoidance model suggests that people dealing with chronic pain often steer clear of activities that could trigger pain because they're afraid of making it worse (George & Zeppieri, 2009). Unfortunately, when a client's pain is nociplastic, and therefore without tissue or nerve damage, this may be counterproductive, and they may actually be able to move more than they realize. This skill helps clients gradually decrease the connection between fear and their brain so they can start moving their bodies in more effective ways.

The Skill in Action: *Jason had developed chronic pain after he fractured his left knee. Although he had completed two rounds of physical therapy and his orthopedist told him the fracture was completely healed, the pain still persisted nine months after his injury. As a result, Jason was still limping and avoiding beloved activities for fear of triggering pain. When his therapist asked him to imagine doing an activity that he feared would cause pain, he imagined bending his knee to pedal his bicycle. Right away, Jason noticed that his leg muscle tightened up and he could feel a sharp pain in his left knee. He was surprised that he had such a strong reaction to simply imagining he was pedaling. This helped him begin to believe that maybe his brain was working overtime to protect him and that perhaps it didn't really need to.*

At his therapist's suggestion, he got on a stationary bicycle and, before pedaling, he took a deep breath and mentally recited some affirmations to remind himself that he was safe. He could feel the tension flowing out of his body with each breath as he recited "I am safe," "My knee is healed," and "I can do this." He then put his feet on the pedals and very slowly pedaled a few times. He noticed some pain, but he kept breathing and reciting his affirmations. He stopped for a minute to rest and regroup. Then he pedaled a few more times, again while breathing slowly and reciting his affirmations. He was amazed and proud that he could pedal at all and that despite experiencing some minimal pain, it wasn't too bad. He practiced this process every day for a week while also while trying some other activities that triggered pain. In turn, he began to notice his pain much less often and started enjoying some of the activities he had been avoiding because of the pain.

Skill Building: Explain to your client that because they have nociplastic pain—which does not stem from actual tissue or nerve damage—they are not likely to make their pain worse by moving. Use Client Worksheet 4.B.4 to explain that by gradually reducing their fear of pain, they can retrain their brain to be less reactive. Encourage them to identify and rank the situations that cause their pain, explaining that these situations serve as triggers. Then guide them to visualize being in these scenarios and doing the actions that usually bring on pain. Ask them to observe any reactions they feel, like fear, worry, muscle tension, or pain. This exercise helps them see that these responses come from their brain's perception, not from real tissue damage, as no physical movement has actually caused pain in that moment.

Next, have them imagine this pain-inducing situation again as they mentally recite some positive affirmations to tell their brain they are okay. Refer to Affirmation 6.14 for some examples of affirming statements specifically for nociplastic pain. Explore what was different this time, and then have them actually engage in an action that usually causes pain while continuing to breathe and recite their affirmations. Coach them to consider it a success if they can move even if they have pain. Encourage them to gradually increase the activity that causes pain as they repeat their affirmations. Ask them to repeat this process with other triggering activities.

Reflection: What happened when the client imagined doing the pain-inducing activity (trigger)? Did they notice any fear, pain, or muscle tightness? If so, did this help them understand that nociplastic pain is generated by an oversensitized brain, not tissue damage? What happened when they tried the actual pain-inducing activity? Were they able to calm their brain and reduce their fear by breathing deeply and reciting affirmations? What happened when they increased the intensity or duration of the triggering activity? Were they able to stick with it and keep repeating the process? If not, what got in the way? What did they notice about their pain after doing this practice daily for a week?

Turn Down Pain-Related Fear

When pain is nociceptive, it stems from an oversensitized brain response rather than physical tissue or nerve damage. Use this worksheet to help retrain your brain by imagining and then actually moving in ways that typically generate pain while calming your fear response.

Begin by writing down some situations or activities that you avoid doing out of fear that they will cause pain—for example, walking, bending, standing, stretching, working out, picking up a grocery bag, rolling over in bed, riding in the car. You can consider these your triggers that "turn on" the neural circuit that causes the pain symptom (this is pain not causing or caused by tissue damage). This is like a dashboard light that indicates the oil is low when the oil level is actually fine.

_____

_____

_____

_____

_____

Now rank your triggers on a scale of 1 to 10 (where 1 = least fear-inducing and 10 = most fear-inducing). This is called a fear hierarchy.

1. _____

2. _____

3. _____

4. _____

5. _____

6. _____

7. _____

8. _____

Copyright © 2026 Debra Burdick, *The Psychotherapy Toolbox for Chronic Illness and Chronic Pain*. All rights reserved.

9. _____

10. _____

Now pick a triggering activity that you rated between 1 and 3 on your fear hierarchy, and imagine that you are engaging in this action (without actually moving your body). Notice if anything arises in your body when you do this. For example, do you feel any pain, fear, anxiety, or muscle tension? Describe whatever you feel here.

_____

_____

_____

_____

_____

Now imagine doing this triggering activity again, but this time, take a deep, calming breath while you repeat any of the following positive affirmations to yourself:

- I am safe.

- I'll be fine.

- I'm strong.

- I'm getting better.

- There is nothing wrong with me.

- I'm healthy.

- I'm in charge.

- I can notice pain and still feel safe.

Smile and imagine how good it feels to do this activity without fear. Tune into what arises in your body now. Do you still feel pain, worry, or tension? What

 Copyright © 2026 Debra Burdick, *The Psychotherapy Toolbox for Chronic Illness and Chronic Pain*. All rights reserved.

differences do you notice? Remind yourself that any reaction was caused by your brain and that you are okay.

_____

_____

_____

_____

_____

Now actually engage in the triggering action while repeating any of the affirmations. What arises when you do this? This step takes courage.

_____

_____

_____

_____

_____

If you feel pain, remember that the pain is not going to hurt you. If you are afraid, take a break and help yourself de-stress with a slow, deep breath, and take a moment to mentally recite the affirmations again. You are helping your brain decrease the connection between fear and pain while building muscle strength that may have been lost from deconditioning.

If pain symptoms increase, reassure yourself that success is being able to do the things that pain has been preventing in your life, regardless of whether you feel pain. When you can stop letting the pain affect your activities, mood, and hope, then you are making progress in disconnecting the fear and danger signal from the pain.

Set small but increasingly difficult goals for yourself, such as walking 10 steps if that typically causes pain, and focus on achieving that goal rather than the pain it causes. As your confidence increases, set a new, more challenging goal, such as walking 20 steps and so on. Keep in mind that this process is helping you train your brain out of danger.

Copyright © 2026 Debra Burdick, *The Psychotherapy Toolbox for Chronic Illness and Chronic Pain*. All rights reserved.

Remember to calm yourself, recite your affirmations, and keep setting more difficult goals until you train your brain out of pain.

Now move on to the next fear-inducing activity on your list and repeat the process.

Copyright © 2026 Debra Burdick, *The Psychotherapy Toolbox for Chronic Illness and Chronic Pain*. All rights reserved.

Skill 4.B.5 Pain Reprocessing Therapy

Background: Pain reprocessing therapy (PRT) is a therapeutic approach that helps mitigate the effects of chronic pain by addressing the brain's role in pain perception. It is grounded in the idea that chronic pain is caused by faulty neural pathways in the brain and that clients can "switch off" their pain by rewiring these pathways (Ashar et al., 2022). Not only can PRT address nociplastic pain, but it can also be used with pain that results from tissue damage. Although a complete primer on PRT is beyond the scope of this book, this skill provides the basic steps involved in this approach.

The Skill in Action: *Jorge had chronic back pain stemming from a car accident. His medical team reassured him that his back was completely healed and that there was no lingering inflammation, tissue damage, or nerve damage, but he still struggled on a daily basis. His therapist explained that he was likely experiencing nociplastic pain and suggested he try PRT. Jorge was intrigued by the idea that his pain could be the result of a brain-based issue and that he could learn skills to "turn it off." He started practicing a variety of PRT skills, such as understanding and rewiring his nociplastic pain, changing his relationship to pain, and turning down his pain-related fear, which felt uncomfortable at first but gradually became second nature. He also processed his feelings about the car accident and the long-term pain it caused, which allowed him to feel lighter as he started to release the hold that his past had on him. He could feel a gradual shift from being in a constant "danger mode" into a "safe mode." After about a month of practicing his new skills, he was delighted to notice that his pain had already decreased considerably.*

Skill Building: Read through Clinician Handout 4.B.5 to learn the basics of PRT. Broadly speaking, PRT involves five main components: (1) educating clients about the origin of pain, (2) gathering evidence about the client's unique pain experience, (3) teaching clients to attend to pain through the lens of safety, (4) reducing the client's overall threat perception level, and (5) increasing the client's overall feelings of wellness and safety. A brief descriptor of each component is provided in the handout, followed by examples of skills in this book that correspond with each component. If you are interested in learning more about PRT, you can refer to the Pain Processing Therapy Center, which offers training and certification (https://www.painreprocessingtherapy.com). Another excellent resource is *The Way Out: A Revolutionary, Scientifically Proven Approach to Healing Chronic Pain*, coauthored by Alan Gordon, the founder of PRT (Gordon & Ziv, 2021).

Reflection: Use the reflection questions provided in each skill.

Pain Reprocessing Therapy

Here are descriptions of the five main components of PRT and the skills in this book that fit in each component.

1. **Educate:** Help clients understand that their pain is nociplastic pain and is not due to structural or physical tissue damage but, rather, a centralized brain-based process that has become hypersensitized. Discuss the pain-fear cycle—how pain causes fear and then fear causes pain. Discuss how this cycle keeps the brain hypersensitized and how by breaking this cycle and calming pain-based fear, this type of pain can be reversed. This step encourages clients to view this type of pain as completely safe.

   a. Client Worksheet 4.1.2: *Characteristics of Nociplastic Pain*

   b. Skill 4.B.1: *Understand and Rewire Nociplastic Pain*

2. **Evidence:** In this step, gather evidence regarding the client's personal experiences with pain that supports the presence of nociplastic pain. Discuss times in the client's life when they had pain that began without injury or that originated during times of stress. Discuss instances where pain should have been present but wasn't, such as when they moved their back but it didn't hurt like it usually does. Share an example of centralized pain, such as phantom limb pain that is felt after an amputation.

   a. Client Worksheet 4.1.2: *Characteristics of Nociplastic Pain*

   b. Client Worksheet 4.B.1.1: *Evidence of Centralized (Nociplastic) Pain*

3. **Safety:** This step involves helping the client attend to their pain through a lens of safety. Help the client shift their perspective on pain—no longer viewing their pain as something harmful but as a false alarm from their brain that can be reprogrammed and retrained. This allows them to interrupt the pain-fear cycle and shift from "danger mode" to "safety mode." They can also use the process of somatic tracking contained in the *Awareness of Pain Without Judgment* skill listed below.

   a. Skill 4.A.1: *Awareness of Pain Without Judgment*

   b. Skill 4.B.1: *Understand and Rewire Nociplastic Pain*

 Copyright © 2026 Debra Burdick, *The Psychotherapy Toolbox for Chronic Illness and Chronic Pain*. All rights reserved.

    c. Skill 4.B.2: *Increase Tolerance for Pain Symptoms*

    d. Skill 4.B.3: *Change Your Relationship with Pain*

    e. Skill 4.B.4: *Turn Down Pain-Related Fear*

    f. Skill 3.11: *Body Scan*

    g. Skill 3.12: *Relaxation Response*

    h. Skill 3.10: *Progressive Muscle Relaxation*

4. **Emotional threats:** Explore and address other emotional threats and decrease the client's overall threat levels by helping them identify past experiences that felt dangerous to them or anything they are currently experiencing that feels unsafe or that puts them in a state of high alert. This may include intense or threatening emotions, a history of trauma, difficult relationships, or sources of fear.

    a. Skill 2.7: *Mindfulness of Emotions*

    b. Skill 2.9: *Release the Past*

    c. Skill 3.9: *Remembered Wellness*

5. **Positive emotions:** Help the client reduce fear and other emotions associated with their pain by encouraging positive sensations and feelings. This will help them shift from a high-threat level "danger mode" to a "safety mode" and help to calm down their oversensitized brain so it can stop overreporting pain. The skills below can help them change the channel and reframe negative or fearful thoughts, de-stress, and tune into their emotions.

    a. Skill 4.A.1: *Awareness of Pain Without Judgment*

    b. Skill 4.A.2: *Distraction*

    c. Skill 4.B.3: *Change Your Relationship with Pain*

    d. Skill 4.B.4: *Turn Down Pain-Related Fear*

    e. Skill 2.3: *Change the Channel*

    f. Skill 2.6: *Reframing Thoughts*

    g. Skill 2.7: *Mindfulness of Emotions*

Copyright © 2026 Debra Burdick, *The Psychotherapy Toolbox for Chronic Illness and Chronic Pain*. All rights reserved.

Copyright © 2026 Debra Burdick, *The Psychotherapy Toolbox for Chronic Illness and Chronic Pain*. All rights reserved.

Mind-Body-Spirit Skills

Skill 5.1 Identify Values

Background: Our core values are the fundamental beliefs we hold that shape our attitudes, actions, and decisions. They influence how we perceive and interact with the world by guiding our choices and behavior. For example, if we value connection, we're more likely to find ways to nurture our relationships and accept help even when illness or pain make it difficult, whereas if we value independence, we're more likely to try to do everything ourselves. By working with clients to identify and understand their values, you can help them make life with chronic illness or pain more intentional, fulfilling, and purpose-driven. That is the purpose of this skill.

The Skill in Action: *Dmitri was dealing with chronic pain stemming from osteoarthritis as well as an old back injury. His knees and hands were often so stiff and swollen that he had difficulty walking, getting out of a chair, or even using his cell phone. When his therapist helped him identify his values, he realized he was a very determined, focused, and courageous man with lots of confidence in his ability to manage whatever life sent his way, including pain. These values helped him be persistent and consistent in trying to complete all the self-care tasks necessary to function despite his pain. He knew these values had been instilled in him by his father, who showed him by example how important these values were.*

Family and forgiveness were also included in Dmitri's most important values. However, he noticed that he had not been in touch with two of his children for many months, ever since they had a disagreement. Since living a values-based life was important to Dmitri, he made a commitment to reach out to them and apologize for his role in the argument. His children also apologized and then offered to help him with some yard-related tasks that he had been struggling with because of his pain. He vowed to make sure his actions aligned with his values going forward so he could stay in touch with his family and keep focused on successfully managing his pain.

Skill Building: Introduce the concept of values to your client, and explain that people are more likely to experience a sense of purpose, meaning, and fulfillment when their life decisions align with their core values. Help your client identify their specific values using Client Worksheet 5.1, and explore how their values impact the ways in which they manage their chronic illness or pain. Discuss which values are most important to them and which values they would like to adopt. As part of this discussion, you might want to explore the roots of their current values and examine how these values are serving them in the present.

Reflection: How many values did the client identify? Could they list actions that were based on and driven by their values? What actions are they currently engaging in that are not aligned with their values? How do they think their values help them deal with their illness or pain? Do they feel that some values don't serve them anymore? If so, why? Are there any new values that the client would like to adopt? If so, why?

Client Worksheet 5.1

What Are Your Values?

Core values are fundamental beliefs that shape your attitudes, actions, and decisions. Look through the list of values here and put a check mark by any that resonate with you.

- ☐ **Accountability:** Owning your actions and decisions, being upfront about mistakes, and making things right when necessary.

- ☐ **Adaptability:** Staying flexible and open to change, taking on new experiences and challenges with a positive mindset.

- ☐ **Appreciation:** Recognizing and showing gratitude for the good in life, including what others contribute.

- ☐ **Authenticity:** Being true to yourself, embracing who you are, and expressing your genuine thoughts, feelings, and beliefs.

- ☐ **Balance:** Keeping a healthy balance between different parts of your life—work, family, social commitments, and personal well-being.

- ☐ **Care:** Putting the well-being of yourself and others first, showing empathy and concern in your relationships.

- ☐ **Challenge:** Welcoming opportunities for growth and pushing past limits to unlock your potential.

- ☐ **Change:** Being open to new ideas and experiences, adapting to life's shifts, and embracing personal growth.

- ☐ **Collaboration:** Working well with others to reach shared goals, valuing their input, and creating a supportive environment.

- ☐ **Commitment:** Showing dedication and responsibility, whether it's in relationships or at work.

- ☐ **Communication:** Prioritizing clear, honest conversations, listening actively, and expressing yourself respectfully.

- ☐ **Compassion:** Understanding and caring for others' experiences and feelings, as well as your own, and offering support when needed.

Copyright © 2026 Debra Burdick, *The Psychotherapy Toolbox for Chronic Illness and Chronic Pain*. All rights reserved.

☐ **Confidence:** Trusting in yourself and your abilities, facing challenges with assurance and determination.

☐ **Connection:** Building meaningful relationships, fostering a sense of belonging, and appreciating others' perspectives.

☐ **Consistency:** Being dependable and reliable, showing up in all areas of life with steady behavior.

☐ **Contentment:** Finding satisfaction and joy in your current circumstances and appreciating the little things.

☐ **Contribution:** Making a positive impact by engaging in meaningful activities that align with your values.

☐ **Cooperation:** Working with others toward common goals, being willing to compromise, and valuing others' views and expertise.

☐ **Courage:** Facing challenges head-on, standing by your beliefs, and taking risks to grow.

☐ **Determination:** Staying focused and motivated even when faced with obstacles, working hard to achieve your goals.

☐ **Diligence:** Putting in persistent effort to meet your goals, complete tasks, and fulfill responsibilities.

☐ **Discipline:** Practicing self-control and focus, managing your time and resources effectively to reach your goals.

☐ **Drive:** Staying motivated and pushing yourself to succeed in both personal and professional pursuits.

☐ **Endurance:** Pushing through adversity with resilience and staying focused despite setbacks.

☐ **Family:** Making your family's happiness and well-being a priority and investing time and care into those relationships.

☐ **Flexibility:** Being adaptable and open to learning and growing when circumstances change.

☐ **Focus:** Staying locked in on your goals and tasks, avoiding distractions, and managing time well.

 Copyright © 2026 Debra Burdick, *The Psychotherapy Toolbox for Chronic Illness and Chronic Pain*. All rights reserved.

☐ **Forgiveness:** Letting go of anger and resentment, understanding that everyone makes mistakes—including yourself.

☐ **Friendship:** Nurturing strong, lasting relationships, investing time and effort in meaningful connections.

☐ **Gratitude:** Recognizing the good in life and expressing thanks for others' contributions.

☐ **Growth:** Constantly seeking self-improvement, embracing change, and learning from your experiences.

☐ **Health:** Making conscious choices to prioritize your physical, mental, and emotional well-being.

☐ **Honesty:** Being truthful and transparent, valuing integrity in all areas of life.

☐ **Hope:** Keeping a positive outlook and believing in a better future, working toward it with optimism.

☐ **Imagination:** Tapping into creativity and innovation, exploring new ideas in both life and work.

☐ **Independence:** Valuing self-reliance and making your own decisions, while also considering others' input.

☐ **Integrity:** Sticking to your principles and staying consistent with your values in every part of your life.

☐ **Intuition:** Trusting your gut instincts and inner guidance to navigate decisions.

☐ **Kindness:** Showing empathy and compassion in how you treat others, both personally and professionally.

☐ **Knowledge:** Seeking wisdom and understanding, always looking to learn and grow.

☐ **Legacy:** Thinking about the long-term impact of your actions and striving to leave a positive mark.

☐ **Love:** Building deep, meaningful connections with others and showing care and understanding in relationships.

Copyright © 2026 Debra Burdick, *The Psychotherapy Toolbox for Chronic Illness and Chronic Pain*. All rights reserved.

- ❏ **Mindfulness:** Staying present and connected to the moment, appreciating life as it happens.

- ❏ **Moderation:** Striving for balance and avoiding excess, making thoughtful choices for well-being.

- ❏ **Motivation:** Staying driven and enthusiastic in the pursuit of your goals, even when challenges arise.

- ❏ **Open-mindedness:** Being open to new ideas and perspectives, appreciating the diversity of thought around you.

- ❏ **Optimism:** Keeping a positive attitude and focusing on possibilities, approaching challenges with hope.

- ❏ **Patience:** Staying calm and understanding when faced with delays or frustration, valuing the journey as much as the outcome.

- ❏ **Peace:** Cultivating inner calm and resolving conflicts through empathy and understanding.

- ❏ **Perseverance:** Pushing through challenges and staying focused on your goals, no matter the obstacles.

- ❏ **Persistence:** Showing tenacity in pursuing your goals, not giving up in the face of difficulty.

- ❏ **Positivity:** Maintaining a positive mindset, focusing on the good, and facing challenges with resilience.

- ❏ **Purpose:** Living with direction and meaning, aligning your actions with your values, goals, and passions.

- ❏ **Self-awareness:** Understanding your own thoughts, feelings, and behaviors, and using that insight for growth.

- ❏ **Self-discipline:** Practicing self-control and dedication to achieve your personal and professional goals.

- ❏ **Self-improvement:** Always looking for ways to grow, learning from challenges and setbacks.

- ❏ **Service:** Making a positive impact by helping others, using your skills and resources to contribute to their well-being.

 Copyright © 2026 Debra Burdick, *The Psychotherapy Toolbox for Chronic Illness and Chronic Pain*. All rights reserved.

- ☐ **Spirituality:** Connecting with something greater than yourself, exploring meaning and purpose beyond material success.

- ☐ **Strength:** Showing resilience and determination, using challenges as opportunities for growth.

- ☐ **Tenacity:** Staying determined and resilient in the face of adversity, refusing to be deterred by setbacks.

- ☐ **Wisdom:** Valuing knowledge and experience, using lessons from the past to guide your decisions.

Once you have identified the values that are important to you, reflect on how these values help you manage life with chronic illness or pain. Which values help you the most? Underline or highlight them. Similarly, are there some values that you want to focus on more? Circle them or highlight them in another color. Then describe how these values improve your life as it relates to your chronic illness or pain. For example:

- Confidence helps me keep a positive attitude and belief in my ability to advocate for myself, do what I need to do to take care of myself, and live a great life despite illness or pain.

- Adaptability helps me go with the flow to make changes required by my illness or pain.

- Discipline helps me stay on top of things I need to do to take care of myself daily.

- Gratitude helps me focus on the positives and lift my mood by reminding myself of the many blessings in my life.

_____

_____

_____

_____

_____

_____

_____

Copyright © 2026 Debra Burdick, *The Psychotherapy Toolbox for Chronic Illness and Chronic Pain*. All rights reserved.

Skill 5.2 Identify Health Beliefs

Background: Health beliefs reflect a client's attitudes, values, and convictions regarding health, illness, and health care practices. These beliefs influence the client's decisions, behaviors, and coping strategies related to their health. For example, a client who believes in traditional Western medicine is more likely to visit a doctor who orders medical tests and prescribes medication, while a client who believes in Chinese medicine is more likely to seek help from a doctor who uses substances that aim to balance the equilibrium between the yin and yang energies of the body. Many different factors can influence a client's health beliefs, including their cultural background, religious affiliations, family history, and community traditions—all of which offer unique perspectives on health and wellness. This skill helps clients identify their health beliefs and explore how these beliefs impact their decisions about health care during chronic illness or pain.

The Skill in Action: *Nita, a Native American, was referred to therapy by her community leader for help dealing with chronic pain following a fall. When her therapist asked her about her pain and what treatment options she had tried, Nita explained she was taking a combination of natural herbs for pain and praying daily. Upon further exploration, the therapist discovered Nita did not use conventional Western medicine and had not had an X-ray or an MRI of her back. The therapist further explored Nita's health beliefs, which helped her understand and stay within Nita's health belief system. This guided her to teach Nita a variety of pain management techniques, such as relaxation, visualization, and thought reframing. Nita was very receptive and embraced these skills quickly.*

Skill Building: Use Client Worksheet 5.2 to help the client explore their health beliefs, including their approaches to health care and their cultural, religious, and family traditions concerning health. Explain that these traditions are the basis from which they conceptualize and approach health, illness, and healing and they guide how they choose from the various options for managing their illness and pain. Discuss how their approach has worked for them and if there is need for change.

Reflection: How does the client's cultural background impact their choices for health care? How does their culture, religion, or family background influence their beliefs about exercise, medicine, or health care more broadly? Does the client prefer conventional Western medical treatments or more natural, holistic options? Do they follow dietary practices based on their culture or religious background? How can they get the most benefits from their health choices? How does knowing their health beliefs guide your choice of therapeutic interventions?

Health Perspectives

Health beliefs are the ideas, attitudes, or perceptions you hold about health, illness, and the health care system more generally. These beliefs can influence how you approach what it means to be "healthy" or "sick," what you believe about the role of doctors and medicine, and what behaviors you believe will help you manage chronic illness or pain. The following prompts will help you explore your beliefs about health.

Exercise. Some cultures and families believe in incorporating exercise into daily life and even promote communal exercise, while others discourage it. What are your beliefs about exercise? How do you incorporate exercise into your life considering the limits of your pain or illness?

_____

_____

_____

_____

_____

Dietary habits. These vary across cultures and influence food choices, preparation methods, and meal rituals—for example, eating typical American fast food versus Chinese or Mediterranean food choices and preparation techniques. What dietary habits do you practice when you plan, cook, or eat? How do your choices support your health?

_____

_____

_____

_____

_____

Copyright © 2026 Debra Burdick, *The Psychotherapy Toolbox for Chronic Illness and Chronic Pain.* All rights reserved.

Approaches to health care. Review the following health care perspectives and consider how you use and perhaps combine aspects of these various approaches.

- **Preventive health care** involves getting regular screenings, vaccinations, and health check-ups considered essential for maintaining well-being.

- **Western conventional medicine** views health and illness through the lens of pathophysiology. It involves identifying and treating specific biological mechanisms underlying diseases. Treatments often involve medications, surgical procedures, and other evidence-based approaches that target the physiological aspects of health.

- **Natural remedies or spiritual practices** involve less engagement with conventional health care providers. These approaches can range from using nutrition supplements to spiritual rituals, prayer, and healing.

- **Naturopathic medicine** uses natural remedies to help the body heal itself. It treats the whole person and aims to heal the root cause of illness.

- **Traditional Chinese medicine** uses natural substances to balance the opposing forces of yin and yang. It views health as a harmonious equilibrium between these two energies.

- **Acupuncture** uses needles on the skin surface to restore qi energy flow to meridians throughout the body in order to influence tissues, gland, organs, and various functions of the body.

- **Indian Ayurveda** restores equilibrium to your unique constitution through lifestyle adjustments, dietary modifications, and herbal remedies.

- **Native American traditional healing** embraces bio-psycho-socio-spiritual approaches and traditions. Stories and legends are used to teach positive behaviors. Herbs, manipulative therapies, ceremonies, and prayer are used in various combinations to prevent and treat illness.

- **Holistic health** considers the interconnectedness of mind, body, and spirit, emphasizing the importance of addressing all aspects of an individual for optimal well-being. The mind-body connection is key.

- **Integrative medicine** combines conventional medical treatments with complementary and alternative therapies, acknowledging the value of various healing modalities.

 Copyright © 2026 Debra Burdick, *The Psychotherapy Toolbox for Chronic Illness and Chronic Pain*. All rights reserved.

Which of those types of health care do you incorporate into your life? In what ways do you follow any particular approach (or combine any of these approaches)? Are there any that you choose not to use and if so, why? Which approaches do you find most helpful for your situation? What types might you consider adding? Be specific in your answer.

> *Example:* "I practice preventive health care and get routine bloodwork and screenings at the recommendation of my doctor. I typically follow the conventional Western medicine approach and seek treatment from doctors who treat my illness or pain with practices such as prescription medication and surgery that are based on medical research. But I also consult an integrative medicine provider who helps to identify and treat underlying issues with a nutritional approach. I have also found acupuncture to be helpful for my pain."

_____

_____

_____

_____

_____

Family and community dynamics. Your family may have followed certain health practices for generations. In some families, health may be perceived as a shared responsibility. Decision-making may be done collectively. Individual health may be interconnected with community and family health. How does your family background influence how you approach your illness or pain? What health practices do you use that your parents or grandparents have used? How involved is your family or community in helping shape how you deal with illness or pain on a daily basis?

_____

_____

_____

_____

_____

Copyright © 2026 Debra Burdick, *The Psychotherapy Toolbox for Chronic Illness and Chronic Pain*. All rights reserved.

Religious doctrines. Some religions prescribe specific health practices, such as dietary restrictions, fasting, or ritualistic behaviors, which are considered integral to spiritual well-being. Others may prohibit conventional medicine and rely on prayer and spirituality. What, if any, health behaviors do you participate in that may be related to your religious background, beliefs, and traditions?

_____

_____

_____

_____

Healing rituals and ceremonies. Rituals and ceremonies play an important role in many people's health beliefs, and they may incorporate symbolic practices to restore balance and promote recovery. For example, many Indigenous cultures engage in ceremonial dances, chants, or the use of sacred herbs to invoke healing energies. What healing rituals or ceremonies do you participate in that are part of your religious or spiritual background? How do they help you?

_____

_____

_____

_____

 Copyright © 2026 Debra Burdick, *The Psychotherapy Toolbox for Chronic Illness and Chronic Pain*. All rights reserved.

Skill 5.3 My Reasons

Background: Studies show that having a compelling reason to get well can contribute to healing (Turner, 2015). When clients focus on their reasons for staying alive, it shifts their mindset from defeatism to hope, which has been found to result in greater healing, fewer symptom recurrences, and fewer treatment side effects. The goal is to help them find a way to live life fully despite their chronic illness or pain. This skill helps clients get in touch with their unique and compelling reasons to get well by answering the questions: "Why do I want to be well and be alive?" "What brings me joy, meaning, and happiness?" and "What will be different when I am well?"

The Skill in Action: *Barry was battling colon cancer. He had undergone surgery, chemotherapy, and radiation, but tests were still showing some cancer cells present. Since he was feeling defeated by these latest results, his therapist encouraged him to write down why he wanted to get well and stay alive. In doing so, he realized that he had been so afraid of dying that he had forgotten why he wanted to live. And there were some important reasons for living! He wanted to finish writing his book on helping teens deal with bullies, he wanted to continue to enjoy his family and the beauty of nature all around him, and he wanted to be there for his wife throughout their retirement years. He also wanted to nurture his spirituality and his love of God.*

Barry posted his reasons for living where he would see it every day and made it a point to read the list aloud. After a few weeks, he noticed that he rarely thought about dying anymore. He felt lighter somehow, and he was remembering to take better care of himself by spending more time outdoors and eating more fruits and vegetables as his nutritionist had recommended many times. His relationship with his wife also started to deepen as he became more present in their relationship. He became aware of a new feeling—that he was going to be just fine no matter the outcome!

Skill Building: Help your client identify their reasons for getting well or staying alive by asking them to answer the questions on Client Worksheet 5.3. Ask them to think about what motivates them to do what they need to do to manage their symptoms and possibly heal. What brings joy, happiness, and meaning to their life? What has their illness restricted them from doing that they love to do and that they want to do again? For example, do they want to dance like they used to? Attend their granddaughter's wedding? Enjoy more quality time with their spouse? Write that book that's been running through their mind? Do they have something they want to share with the world? Do they simply want to feel healthy and vibrant? Process the feelings that arise as they do this work, as it may bring up sadness, regret, and grief. Use this skill in conjunction with Affirmation 6.13.

Reflection: What emotions arose as the client connected with their reasons for getting well? Did they feel sad about the losses their illness has caused them? After the client defined their reasons and read them aloud for a couple of days, what changed? Did they notice any shift in their attitude or mood? Did they see any difference in their motivation to take care of themselves? Did their self-care behavior change? Did they think of additional reasons to get well? Did any of their initial reasons change?

My Reasons

Finding reasons to live can provide you with a sense of purpose and motivation in the face of chronic illness or pain, especially if you are feeling hopeless or like nothing matters. This worksheet will help you make a list of compelling reasons why you want to be well and why you want to live. For example, perhaps you want to:

- Feel comfortable in your own skin

- Enjoy the beauty of the earth and your family

- Live a pain-free life

- Live and enjoy your life

- Love and be loved

- Accomplish your goals

- Have the energy to do your favorite things

- Watch your grandchildren grow up

- Attend your child's wedding

- Do the activities you used to enjoy

- Help other people heal

- Change your job so it aligns with your values

Answer the following questions to identify your reasons for continuing to move forward despite the challenges that your chronic illness or pain may bring. Post your answers where you can see them every day and read them aloud daily.

Why do you want to be well and be alive?

_____

_____

_____

 Copyright © 2026 Debra Burdick, *The Psychotherapy Toolbox for Chronic Illness and Chronic Pain*. All rights reserved.

What brings you joy, meaning, and happiness?

_____

_____

_____

What will be different when you are well?

_____

_____

_____

Copyright © 2026 Debra Burdick, *The Psychotherapy Toolbox for Chronic Illness and Chronic Pain*. All rights reserved.

Skill 5.4 Be of Service

Background: Studies show that helping others can promote a sense of well-being and healing (Oarga et al., 2015). It can also reduce the natural, but unhelpful, tendency to become too focused on illness or pain. Being of service can involve a variety of different activities, whether it's serving a larger cause by volunteering for a charitable organization, doing a small act of kindness for someone, or mentoring someone. All of these can create a positive impact—both for the client and the individuals they are serving. This skill helps clients find options for being of service to others despite their chronic illness or pain.

The Skill in Action: *Esther had been diagnosed with schizophrenia in her late teens. Now in her mid-30s, she was attending an intensive outpatient program at the local hospital every weekday, where in addition to receiving medication and psychotherapy, she was learning mindfulness skills to turn down the voices in her head. Although Esther was too disabled to work, she had become an accomplished knitter over the years. Esther's therapist saw the potential in her and connected her with the infusion center at the hospital. Esther started knitting beautiful shawls and lap blankets and donating them to the center for patients to use while they received chemotherapy infusions. This was a win-win, as the patients appreciated the shawls and lap blankets, and Esther was thrilled that she could be of service. Her confidence increased, and she felt better about herself than she had in years.*

Skill Building: Explain to your client that not only can being of service to others promote a sense of well-being and facilitate healing, but it can also provide a healthy distraction from their illness or pain. Use Client Worksheet 5.4 to brainstorm ways your client can be of service to others—within the limits of their illness and without exhausting themselves. What can they do to help others that draws on their existing expertise? What do they already enjoy doing that they could use to support others in a time of need? Caution them to be careful to avoid situations that feel stressful or that negatively affect their health. The goal is for your client to feel fulfilled and have a sense of purpose—not to put pressure on themselves or exacerbate their symptoms.

Reflection: In what ways was the client already being of service? Were they already helping others without realizing it? What types of service are they capable of doing? What types of activities are they interested in doing to meet the needs of others? Were they surprised to realize they could be of service despite having chronic illness or pain? How did they feel when they helped others?

Be of Service

Being of service involves acting in a way that contributes positively to someone else's life, which can help you restore a sense of well-being and purpose in your own life. This worksheet will help you brainstorm ways you might be of service to others. Put a check mark by any activities you are already doing, and circle any activities you'd be interested in trying. The goal is to find a way, no matter how small, to be of service to someone. Just be careful not to overdo it—you want to find a way to help others that won't lead to exhaustion or worsening your health. Notice how you feel when you have helped someone.

- ❑ Volunteer at a charity, school, or church

- ❑ Provide encouragement to others dealing with illness

- ❑ Share your knowledge and expertise

- ❑ Call a friend or relative

- ❑ Visit an elderly neighbor

- ❑ Volunteer at a library

- ❑ Grocery shop for someone who cannot do so themselves

- ❑ Mentor a teen

- ❑ Volunteer with a suicide hotline or other helpline

- ❑ Cook for a food bank

- ❑ Listen to a friend going through a tough time

- ❑ Care for a pet

- ❑ Tutor a student

- ❑ Knit shawls for a hospital

- ❑ Serve on a committee

- ❑ Bake for a community bake sale

- ❑ Provide guidance to a family member

Copyright © 2026 Debra Burdick, *The Psychotherapy Toolbox for Chronic Illness and Chronic Pain*. All rights reserved.

- ❏ Feed a neighbor's pet

- ❏ Mentor an entry-level employee

- ❏ Pray for people with health challenges

- ❏ Share your experiences with others who have your diagnosis

- ❏ Serve on a community committee

- ❏ Donate clothes, books, or a car

- ❏ Give someone a ride to the doctor

- ❏ Comfort a sick or grieving friend

- ❏ Write a blog about your pain or illness

- ❏ Other: _____

 Copyright © 2026 Debra Burdick, *The Psychotherapy Toolbox for Chronic Illness and Chronic Pain*. All rights reserved.

Skill 5.5 Healing Images

Background: Certain forms of artwork have been found to improve many aspects of physical and mental health. For example, many clients find images of calm water to be particularly soothing. In fact, many hospitals intentionally place images of nature or other nature-inspired elements throughout the facility to create a healing environment. This includes healing gardens and outdoor spaces, as well as large-scale nature murals in waiting rooms that depict serene landscapes. This skill guides clients to create or find art that they find calming, relaxing, and healing.

The Skill in Action: *Cindy was in therapy for ADHD and generalized anxiety disorder. She was so worried about starting classes at a new high school that she couldn't go to sleep. She was afraid she would get lost, be late for class, not know anyone, and not make any friends. In response, Cindy's therapist helped her reframe her negative automatic thoughts and take proactive steps to manage her anxiety. For example, Cindy learned to "change the channel" on her worry thoughts, and her mother set up an appointment to tour the school ahead of time so Cindy would know where her classes were.*

In addition, Cindy and her therapist looked online for a calming, healing image she could use to reduce her anxiety. Cindy chose a photo of a very cute kitten and added text at the bottom of the photo that said, "Everything's going to be alright." Her mother framed the photo and placed it on Cindy's nightstand. Every night, Cindy looked at the kitten and read the affirmation out loud, which allowed her to feel calmer and go to sleep. Whenever she noticed her anxiety ramping up during the day, she stopped, took a breath, and pictured the cute kitten. This helped her keep her anxiety down.

Skill Building: Explain to your client that certain types of images can positively impact health, whether it's by lowering blood pressure, reducing the need for pain medication, or even decreasing the length of hospital stays. Explain, too, that studies have found that the most effective images are those containing positive, caring human faces or certain views of nature, such as still water surrounded by trees (Friedrich, 1999).

Then use Client Handout 5.5 to encourage your client to find or create an image that represents healing to them. Everyone is different, but some examples include a photo of a flower, a calm lake, a peaceful scene from the countryside, a pet, or a loved one. You can get them started by going on the internet and viewing images together that calm them. Once they have found or created their healing image, suggest that they place it where they can see it every day.

Reflection: What type of images did the client find calming? Were they drawn to nature, pets, or people? In what ways was looking at their healing image every day helpful to them? Did they want to have more than one image or swap them out occasionally? Could they have an image at work as well as at home?

Healing Images

Certain art images have been shown to be calming and healing. Find an image that represents healing to you and evokes a calm feeling of well-being. Here are some ideas to get you started:

- Look at the artwork you already have in your home or office and find those that feel restorative to you. Temporarily remove any art that invokes a feeling of stress or unrest.

- Search online for "healing images" or "healing art" and find one that resonates with you.

- Think of symbols or images in your life that may already represent healing to you.

- Look for images of nature, calm bodies of water, trees, flowers, or cute animals.

- Sort through family photos of loved ones.

- Take a photo of something that feels good to you when you view it.

- Sketch or paint an image that creates a peaceful feeling of well-being when you look at it.

Once you identify an image (or series of images) that resonates with you, place it where you can see it every day so you can stay focused on healing instead of illness.

 Copyright © 2026 Debra Burdick, *The Psychotherapy Toolbox for Chronic Illness and Chronic Pain*. All rights reserved.

Skill 5.6 Healing Meditation

Background: Meditation has been shown to be effective for reducing stress, anxiety, depression, pain, and more (Keng et al., 2011). Imagery is often used in meditations to activate the power of the mind to heal. This skill provides a guided meditation that invites clients to visualize a white light that clears and heals. The imagery of a healing white light is often part of spiritual healing techniques but is independent of any specific religious or spiritual beliefs.

The Skill in Action: *Daniel had been struggling with uncontrolled high blood pressure for several years, which prevented him from doing any of his favorite high-intensity exercises that might raise his blood pressure. He had always thought meditation was a bunch of malarkey, so when his therapist suggested he try it, he strongly resisted. His therapist explained that solid research in the field of brain science has confirmed the numerous benefits of meditation, including improving blood pressure and lowering the stress response. Since Daniel felt like he had tried everything else to lower his blood pressure to no avail, he agreed to try. As he focused on the imagery in the guided meditation, he could picture his head filling with light and healing him from the inside out. He could almost feel the warmth of the light as it flowed throughout his body. He was pleased when he noticed his blood pressure was lower after he meditated, and he definitely felt more relaxed when the meditation was finished. In fact, he liked the feeling so much that he decided to keep doing it every day. He also found some other healing meditations online. Although his blood pressure issue didn't magically disappear, he noticed that he felt more relaxed and more hopeful than he had in a long time.*

Skill Building: Explain to your client the wide range of physical, emotional, and mental benefits that meditation offers, including reduced cortisol, greater mental clarity, enhanced immune functioning, greater sleep quality, and improved mood—just to name a few. For clients who are skeptical of these benefits, it can be helpful to point out that meditation has been studied extensively in the field of neuroscience (Tang et al., 2015). In addition, if clients feel like meditation is "too religious" for them, explain that many secular meditations are available as well. Then use Client Handout 5.6 to lead the client through a meditation to set the stage for healing. This meditation uses the imagery of a white, healing light, which is often used in spiritual healing practices and can be thought of as a divine healing light or simply a powerful white light, depending on the client's preferences. If they have trouble imagining or holding a picture in their mind, help them practice by having them look at an object and then closing their eyes to try to visualize it.

Encourage them to notice how they feel before and after doing this meditation, becoming curious about what has changed and what has remained the same. Encourage them to repeat this meditation regularly. After they have practiced it for a while, they can take a deep breath in and quickly remember how they felt at the end of the meditation without having to do the whole thing. Let them know they can also find numerous other guided meditations of varying lengths and styles online by searching for "healing meditation," particularly on YouTube. Encourage them to try a few until they find one that they particularly like.

Reflection: How open was the client to trying a meditation? What worries, if any, did they have about doing the meditation? For example, did they worry that it would be too religious? If so, how did they react when you explained that this meditation is based on neurobiology, not religion? What did it feel like for them to imagine a white, healing light? What did they notice about how they felt before, during, and after the meditation?

Healing Meditation

You can find the guided audio for this meditation at **www.thebrainlady.com/pesi-meditations**.

Meditation can be a powerful tool to calm you and set the stage for healing. Use this meditation to imagine a white light clearing out and healing your illness or pain. You may picture the light as simply a warm light or, if desired, give it meaning such as divine love and healing or a powerful force that erases illness.

To begin, settle into a comfortable position and close your eyes or softly lower your gaze. Then take a deep breath in through your nose to a count of four . . . 1, 2, 3, 4 . . . and breathe out through your mouth with pursed lips, like you are blowing a huge bubble, to a count of eight . . . 1, 2, 3, 4, 5, 6, 7, 8.

Now imagine a bright, healing light is shining down from above you. Picture it illuminating the top of your head. Notice how warm it feels as you allow the light to flow through your scalp and into your head. Imagine it is lighting up and healing all the areas of your brain. Visualize the light resetting everything in your brain to complete wellness.

Now that your brain has been reset, watch as the light gradually fills your whole body, starting from your head, then filling your arms and fingers, slowly moving down your spine, filling your torso, and finally flowing down through your legs and out through the bottoms of your feet. Feel the warmth of the light as it continues to flow, gently replacing any darkness with healing energy. Let it flow.

Allow yourself to let go of anything you simply don't need as the light cleanses and heals your body. Just let it flow.

Now that the light has warmed you and cleansed you from the inside out, sit for a few minutes to allow your body to use that healing energy to heal and rejuvenate. When you are ready, bring your attention back to your surroundings and open your eyes. Notice how you feel.

Copyright © 2026 Debra Burdick, *The Psychotherapy Toolbox for Chronic Illness and Chronic Pain*. All rights reserved.

Skill 5.7 Intuition

Background: Intuition is the ability to understand or know something without conscious reasoning, often referred to as a "gut feeling." When it comes to chronic illness and pain, clients often lean on their intuition to guide their decisions. For example, a client may notice subtle changes in their body that lead them to take action before their symptoms worsen, or they may feel inexplicably pulled toward certain treatments that feel "right" for them, whether conventional or alternative. This skill guides clients to tune into their intuition, often called their inner wisdom, when navigating the diagnosis and treatment of illness.

The Skill in Action: *Sarah, a 35-year-old woman dealing with an autoimmune disease, had been managing her condition for years. One morning, she woke up with an unfamiliar, dull ache in her side. It wasn't unbearable, but she had a gut feeling it was the start of something more. Instead of powering through her day like she normally would, she took a minute to tune in and really listen to what her body was telling her. She felt a strong pull to slow down, even though her schedule was packed. Her intuition told her that if she pushed too hard, she'd probably pay for it later. So, despite the guilt of canceling a few things, she decided to work from home and take the day at a slower pace. She added in extra breaks, meditated a bit, and did some gentle stretching—something her body seemed to really need.*

By the end of the day, that ache was gone. It never turned into a full-blown flare-up like it might have in the past. Sarah realized that if she had ignored that initial feeling and just plowed through her day, she probably would've ended up in a lot more pain. Over time, she learned to trust those early signals. What felt like "just" a hunch was her body's way of giving her a heads-up, and tuning into that intuition ended up being one of her best tools for managing her chronic illness.

Skill Building: Introduce the concept of intuition to clients, explaining that it comes from subconscious, rather than conscious, thought and that it can be amazingly accurate, especially when it comes to personal health. Explore whether the client has ever experienced a gut feeling about something—or a sense of knowing that something was going to happen that proved to be accurate. Explore how they might use their intuition to manage their illness or pain. For example, perhaps they are grappling with a treatment decision and can lean on their intuition to determine which option is the best for them. Or maybe they have not yet received a clear diagnosis and can tap into their inner wisdom to discern what they believe is happening in their body.

Use the meditation provided in Client Handout 5.7 to teach your client how to tap into this gut feeling when seeking guidance. Encourage them to look for the intuitive information to be presented in various ways, including a thought, a sense, a feeling, a knowing, an image, or a symbol. Explain that the more they tune into their intuition, the more information they will get, and the greater the accuracy is likely to be. Practice makes perfect.

Reflection: Did the client embrace the idea of tapping into their intuition or did they resist this process? What type of information did they hope to receive? What information did they actually receive? How accurate was this information? What form did the guidance take—was it a thought, a sense, a memory, a symbol, or an image? Did they notice any intuitive guidance that showed up some time after doing the meditation?

Tapping into Your Intuition

You can find the guided audio for this meditation at **www.thebrainlady.com/pesi-meditations**.

Connecting with your intuition can provide useful information that may help you with your chronic pain or illness. Use this meditation to practice tapping into your intuition to request and receive guidance that you need to make important decisions, to assist you with a difficult issue, or for clarity.

To begin, close your eyes and imagine you are sitting in a beautiful garden. Be still as you breathe in through your nose and then slowly out through your mouth. Repeat this one more time, breathing in through your nose and out through your mouth.

Now set an intention to focus within and connect with your intuition. Your intuition is that place of deep knowing within you—that source of inner wisdom that is sometimes described as a "hunch" or a "gut feeling." Once you've connected with this source of inner wisdom, take some time to ask it for guidance on a recent issue you've been struggling with. You can ask for guidance on a particular issue (perhaps related to your health) or just ask for general guidance.

Look for any signs that help you communicate with your inner wisdom. Intuitive information may be presented in various ways. You may notice a thought popping into your head, seemingly out of nowhere. You might suddenly know or understand something. You might get a feeling such as comfort, peace, acceptance, or love. You might hear a faint voice speaking to you in your head. Or you might see an image or symbol in your mind.

Now relax and just be. Wait, watch, and listen to what is presenting itself to you. Let your mind be free and notice what comes to mind.

If at any point you notice that you are becoming distracted, just remind yourself of your intention to connect with your inner wisdom and reorient your attention back to your intuition.

Stay still and allow yourself to connect with your intuitive guidance. Trust that you are receiving exactly what you need to know right now.

When you are ready, open your eyes and write down the wisdom you received. Practice this process regularly to improve your ability to connect with your intuition.

 Copyright © 2026 Debra Burdick, *The Psychotherapy Toolbox for Chronic Illness and Chronic Pain*. All rights reserved.

Skill 5.8 Connect to Nature

Background: Research has consistently documented the healing power of nature. However, you don't need to go deep into the woods to experience these benefits—simply spending time outside in green urban areas has been found to lower rates of cardiovascular disease, obesity, diabetes, asthma hospitalization, mental distress, and ultimately mortality (White et al., 2019). This skill explains the health benefits of spending time in nature and helps clients incorporate time in nature into their daily routine.

The Skill in Action: *Alejandro was an avid hiker who loved being outside in nature, but after a work-related injury, he struggled with chronic back pain that prevented him from participating in this activity. Now he even struggled to go on short walks. With the help of his therapist, he explored options for spending time outside in his yard. For example, he started sitting on the bench on his front porch, where he could see the grass, flowers, trees, and sky. Even on cold and sometimes snowy days, he bundled up and sat outside for a while. He could feel his body tension relaxing as he breathed in the fresh air. He noticed his mood was brighter and he felt rejuvenated when he came back inside.*

Skill Building: Discuss the health benefits of spending time in nature, reiterating the importance of spending at least 120 minutes per week outside, which has been found to significantly improve health and well-being (White et al., 2019). Help your client explore how they aim to spend this much time outside per week, even if it is in small time chunks. Then use Client Handout 5.8 to walk them through a process they can use while they are outside. This exercise asks them tune into their five senses as they take in the natural world around them. Encourage them to notice any changes that occur in their mind and body as they immerse themselves in nature.

Reflection: Is the client physically able to get outside? If not, how can they overcome any obstacles or resistance to doing so? What options do they have for spending time in nature? Were they able to notice any changes in their health or pain when they did get outside? What types of benefits did they experience with regard to their mood or body?

Connect to Nature

Spending time outside in nature has been shown to improve many aspects of physical and mental health. Use this handout to begin incorporating 120 minutes of weekly outdoor time into your schedule. Notice how you feel before and after doing so.

- Find a place where you can spend time in nature on a regular basis. This might be your yard, a park, a beach, a field, a nature trail, or a forest. It could involve walking on the sidewalk or even looking out an open doorway or window if you can't get outside.

- Aim to be in nature for a total of 120 minutes per week, which you can do in smaller time chunks. If you can't do that much, do what you can. Put it on your calendar.

- While you are outside:

  ° Walk or sit quietly.

  ° Tune in to the natural beauty around you.

  ° Pay attention to all aspects of being in nature.

  ° Breathe in the fresh air.

  ° Detect any fragrance or odor.

  ° Notice the temperature as it surrounds your body.

  ° Tune into the sounds around you.

  ° Look at the sky. Notice the color of the sky, the structure of the clouds if there are any, or how the sun brightens the sky.

  ° Notice the green plants and trees.

  ° Notice how you feel as you immerse yourself in your surroundings.

  ° If your mind wanders, just bring your attention back to what is around you.

  ° Be curious about how this practice changes your mood, illness, or pain.

 Copyright © 2026 Debra Burdick, *The Psychotherapy Toolbox for Chronic Illness and Chronic Pain*. All rights reserved.

Skill 5.9 Tapping into Religious or Spiritual Beliefs

Background: Research supports the idea that religious or spiritual beliefs can provide clients with comfort, hope, emotional strength, and even physical relief in the midst of chronic illness or pain (Koenig, 2012). Not only can the belief in a higher power provide an antidote to the hopelessness and isolation that many of these clients feel, but being part of a faith community provides a form of social support as well. In addition, many religious teachings and spiritual practices incorporate the use of healing prayers or rituals that are meant to alleviate suffering. While these practices cannot necessarily resolve the physical pain that clients are experiencing, they can provide them with a sense of control over their situation that reduces their suffering. This skill guides clients to explore how they can use the power of their own religious or spiritual beliefs as a way to manage their symptoms.

The Skill in Action: *Denise had debilitating neuropathy in her legs and feet. Her symptoms had become so severe that she couldn't sleep and now needed a walker. The neuropathy had disrupted her life and prevented her from participating in many activities she had always enjoyed, such as walking, shopping, dancing, and participating in church activities. Since Denise had been an involved member of a Christian church for most of her life, her therapist helped her explore how her faith supported her during periods of intense chronic pain. Denise believed that God loved her and wanted her to keep contributing to her congregation as best she could. She felt soothed and comforted when she attended church (now with her walker) and particularly when she prayed. She asked God to help her find ways to ease the pain and felt certain that her prayers were being answered, although often in unexpected ways. She thanked God when she found several new neurologists who worked with her to understand the source of her pain and the best options for treating it. Her pastoral care team also kept in touch with her and let her know they were praying for her. Finally, she connected with another parishioner who also had neuropathy, which helped her feel less alone. She felt her faith was keeping her upbeat, hopeful, and connected.*

Skill Building: Explain to clients that their religious or spiritual beliefs can be a powerful force in healing and managing chronic illness and chronic pain. Discuss how their beliefs can promote a positive mindset, hope, happiness, purpose, optimism, and connection to a community with similar beliefs. Use Client Worksheet 5.9 to explore how clients have used, or might use, their religious or spiritual beliefs to support them and their mental health during chronic illness or chronic pain, including how they might increase their connection to like-minded people with similar beliefs.

Reflection: Does the client have strong religious or spiritual beliefs? In what ways do these beliefs help them endure suffering? In what ways do these beliefs improve their resilience and mindset? Do they have a faith community that supports them? If they do not ascribe to any particular religion, did they go through any negative experiences with religious or spiritual leaders or communities that might account for this? How can they connect with others who share similar beliefs? How did it feel to encourage your client to tap into their religious beliefs if their beliefs did not align with your own?

Personal Benefits of Religious or Spiritual Beliefs

Religious or spiritual beliefs can play a significant role in supporting your well-being during chronic illness or pain. The following list contains examples of how these beliefs may have helped you. Put a check mark by any statements that resonate with you.

❏ My faith helps me find meaning and purpose in my life.

❏ I experience spiritual growth through suffering caused by illness or pain.

❏ My trust in a higher power calms my worry and fear.

❏ I use prayer and meditation to center and calm myself.

❏ My faith-based community helps me feel connected to others.

❏ I feel reassured and connected when I participate in shared rituals and traditions.

❏ I believe my mind and body can heal, which gives me hope.

❏ I trust the power of the mind-body connection to promote healing.

❏ My faith supports my endurance to cope with illness or pain.

❏ I use spiritual practices such as meditation, prayer, or connecting with the spirit realm as healing tools.

❏ I practice surrender and acceptance to release control and accept the reality of the present moment. This helps me cope and feel more peaceful during illness or pain.

❏ I am able to detach from the outcome and let go of expectations, which helps me stop worrying about my illness or pain.

❏ I practice gratitude regularly to keep me focused on positive things.

❏ I believe in transformation and am aware of how my illness or pain has transformed me in many ways, such as increasing my faith, teaching me to ask for help, and allowing me to live a good life despite illness or pain.

Copyright © 2026 Debra Burdick, *The Psychotherapy Toolbox for Chronic Illness and Chronic Pain*. All rights reserved.

❏ I feel loved and supported by the universe or God.

❏ I have had experiences of transcendence where I felt connected to a higher realm or power.

❏ Other: _____

 Copyright © 2026 Debra Burdick, *The Psychotherapy Toolbox for Chronic Illness and Chronic Pain*. All rights reserved.

Skill 5.10 Tapping into Spiritual Energy

Background: In her book *Radical Remission*, Dr. Kelly Turner (2015) explored how people who experienced spontaneous and unexpected remission from cancer (what she termed "radical remission") shared nine key factors, one of which was a deep spiritual practice. In particular, these individuals tapped into some form of spiritual energy daily that aligned with their beliefs, and they felt this connection played a key role in their healing. This spiritual energy came in the form of a variety of practices, including yoga, prayer, meditation, Reiki, and more. This skill helps clients explore options for tuning into and connecting with their spiritual energy.

The Skill in Action: *Deana was tired of dealing with a series of chronic health issues she had been struggling with for the past decade. She read extensively as she tried to understand why she was ill, how to heal, and how to find some meaning. In doing so, she learned about people who'd had near-death experiences and who could talk with those in spirit. Although she was very skeptical, she attended classes at a spiritualist church and learned about connecting with those in spirit and took Reiki classes to learn about healing energy. She soon began receiving messages for people from the realm of spirit that were uncannily accurate, which increased her trust and faith in tapping into spiritual energy. She began to meditate every day and found that doing so turned down her pain. She felt a sense of peace and experienced a subtle connection to a spiritual energy she had never known existed. She also noticed that being outside in nature heightened this connection, as did singing or praying. She often listened to guided meditations that reminded her of her innate ability to heal, which allowed her to feel more centered and her mindset to shift drastically. Along with her spiritual developments, she tried other recommended treatments, including major diet tweaks, supplements, massage, exercise, and neurofeedback. She eventually healed from her chronic illness despite being told that she would have it for the rest of her life.*

Skill Building: Explain to your client that a spiritual practice is any type of practice that allows them to connect with something higher than themselves. This typically evokes a deep sensation of calm and peace. Importantly, spiritual practices are based more on personal beliefs and experiences than religious doctrine, although they are not mutually exclusive and many religions have spiritual components. Central to the idea of developing a spiritual practice is the cultivation of inner awareness and mindfulness, which requires that clients find ways to turn off their busy, thinking mind.

Use Client Handout 5.10 to introduce the many types of spiritual practices that can help your client quiet their mind and connect to spiritual energy. Encourage them to try a few practices and see which ones work best for them. Remind them to start small, with short time spans, and to gradually increase the duration as they practice. You can also refer back to Skill 5.6: *Healing Meditation* for a guided meditation that clients might adapt to align with their spiritual beliefs—perhaps visualizing the white light as a spiritual, divine, or healing energy.

Reflection: Was the client open to trying practices to help them tap into spiritual energy? Or did they think the idea was too "woo-woo" for them? What happened when they tried the various practices? Were they able to quiet their busy mind, or did they get frustrated and give up? Were they able to find a few practices that resonated with them? What shifted in their mind and body after they practiced for a few weeks? In what ways did they feel they connected with spiritual energy? Were they able to go further and receive messages from the spiritual realm?

Tapping into Spiritual Energy

The following spiritual practices all help you quiet your busy mind. When your mind is quiet, you can go within—to your own self and your own heart—and listen to that connection with your spirit. You may then sense a gentle flow of spiritual energy, which can be very subtle at first. This feels different for everyone, but some report feeling a subtle vibration, tingling, warmth, peaceful presence, or soothing flow.

Try a few techniques that you can practice on a regular basis. Just tune in and notice what arises. The more you practice, the more you can feel the positive, restorative, and healing effects of spiritual energy.

- **Deep breathing:** Close your eyes and place a hand on your belly, just below your rib cage, so you can feel your belly rise and fall with each breath. Take a deep breath in through your nose to a count of four, and then breathe out through pursed lips to a count of eight. Do this for 8 to 10 breaths. Think about your breath as your life force or, as some languages interpret the word *breath*, as spirit. Notice what changes in how you feel when you open your eyes.

- **Guided meditation:** Use the healing meditation in Skill 5.6 or search online for guided meditations using terms such as "breathing meditation," "healing meditation," or "meditation for spiritual healing." Try a few until you find one you really like. Then listen to it every day.

- **Silent meditation:** Sit comfortably where you will not be disturbed. Set a timer for two minutes and close your eyes. Breathe in slowly though your nose and out even more slowly through your mouth. Now breathe normally. Clear your mind and pay attention to your breath. Every time you find your mind wandering, dismiss the thought and bring your attention back to your breath. Notice how you feel as you breathe—free of thinking. Stay focused on your breath until you hear the timer. Notice what has changed in how you feel. Gradually increase the time of this practice to 10 minutes as you are able to.

- **Prayer:** Pray in whatever way you prefer or use the following format: "Praise [*God/the universe/your higher power*]—I love you. Please help me with _____. Thank you for _____." Then wait silently and notice what arises.

Copyright © 2026 Debra Burdick, *The Psychotherapy Toolbox for Chronic Illness and Chronic Pain*. All rights reserved.

- **Time in nature:** Spend at least 10 minutes walking or sitting outside in nature, paying attention to the beauty, sights, sounds, and smells. When your mind starts thinking about other things, dismiss these thoughts and return your attention to your surroundings.

- **Exercise:** Move your body in your favorite way (such as walking, running, dancing, stretching, bicycling, or weightlifting) within the limits of your illness or pain, for at least five minutes, focusing your attention on your breath and how your body feels as it moves. Work up gradually to 30 minutes.

- **Singing:** Sing or hum out loud. Choose songs that are uplifting and repetitive. Focus on your breathing and the feel of the movement of the air through your body.

- **Yoga:** Practice various poses and keep your mind focused on how each pose makes your body feel. Get into the flow.

- **Chanting a mantra:** Choose a word or short saying and repeat it out loud or in your head for a few minutes. Some examples: *Om. Yam. I am healing. All is well. I accept myself just as I am. I am strong.*

- **Joining a group:** Attend an in-person or online group that focuses on meditation, healing, or prayer. The energy in a group of like-minded people who are all meditating or praying at once can be profound.

- **Practice connecting:** As you practice calming your mind and going within, you may begin to be more aware of spiritual energy. You may get messages from the spiritual realm that help you heal, guide you in making decisions, comfort you, help you understand something, inspire you, or motivate you. These messages may be thoughts or ideas that pop up during your spiritual practice. They may come in the form of a knowing, a feeling, a sensing, a color, a smell, an image, or words. Just tune in after doing some deep breathing and clearing your mind and wait and watch what arises. If you worry about going within, you may surround yourself with the white light of protection and allow only those spirits to connect who are looking out for your highest and best good and send all others away with love.

 Copyright © 2026 Debra Burdick, *The Psychotherapy Toolbox for Chronic Illness and Chronic Pain*. All rights reserved.

Skill 5.11 Preparing to Die

Background: Unfortunately, some clients with chronic illness or pain will be faced with their impending death. They may have a terminal illness with little chance of recovery. Their doctor may have told them they only have a short time to live. They may have stopped medical treatment. This can understandably be a very difficult time for clients as they get their affairs in order and psychologically prepare for the end of their life. This skill focuses on helping clients process their feelings and explore options for taking important steps to prepare for their death.

The Skill in Action: *Bonnie started seeing a therapist when her breast cancer recurred after nearly five years of remission. When she learned that the cancer was metastatic and not responding to treatment, she stopped all further treatments so she could live the rest of her life without the treatment side effects. As she started to get her affairs in order, she made arrangements for ongoing care and rehabilitation for her husband, who had been seriously injured at work. Bonnie was also worried about their 14-year-old daughter, who was going through a difficult time dealing with her father's sudden disability and her mother's recurrence of cancer. Bonnie's siblings agreed to step in and make sure her daughter was taken care of. She confirmed her life insurance policy was up to date and made sure her husband and siblings had the information needed to take care of the finances after her death.*

When Bonnie became homebound, she worked with her therapist to process her anger and deep sadness at her impending death. She reflected on her life and reviewed things she was grateful for and proud of. She explored her fear about death and found comfort in her faith and from accounts by people who had near-death experiences. Gradually, she was able to reach a place of acceptance. She wrote a letter to her daughter that was filled with love and told her daughter how proud she was of her. She wrote her own obituary as well and planned her funeral. She let her family and medical providers know how much pain medication she wanted and whom she wanted with her at her death. She notified her minister and felt loved and comforted by his visit. She began to see family members at the foot of the bed that had already passed and felt their love and a sense of excitement that she would soon be joining them. She passed peacefully surrounded by her husband and daughter.

Skill Building: Use Client Handout 5.11 to help your client accept the reality of their impending death, process their feelings about dying, and make their wishes heard about discontinuing treatment, using pain medication, and so forth. Work with them to reflect on their life as you review their accomplishments and identify what they are proudest of and most grateful for. Explore how they can tap into their religious or spiritual beliefs for support and comfort. In addition to ensuring that the end of their life is the way they want it to be, make sure they talk with their attorney to get all logistical affairs in order.

Reflection: How does the client feel about their impending death? Are they able to accept it? What fears do they have? What obstacles, if any, do they have when it comes to accepting their death? How can their religious or spiritual beliefs help them? What types of wishes did they want to make heard before they die? How did reflecting on their life, relationships, and work affect how they felt about dying? What decisions did they make about treatment, pain medication, and visitors they want with them when they pass? What obstacles did they encounter while getting their affairs in order?

Preparing to Die

Facing death is one of the most difficult and profound experiences that an individual can go through. Use this guidance to help you prepare for your death and develop a peaceful relationship with the idea of dying.

- **Accept what is.**

  ° When you are feeling angry, frustrated, or afraid, notice what thoughts are going through your mind. Are you claiming that reality should be different from what it is? That you should be healthy and everything should be the way you want it? Let go of the struggle and open to reality the way it is.

- **Address your fears.**

  ° Process your feelings with a therapist, friend, or person of faith.

  ° Explore your cultural, religious, and spiritual beliefs about death.

  ° Read some books about near-death experiences, such as *Proof of Heaven* by Dr. Eben Alexander (2012).

- **Keep humor alive.**

  ° Find little things that make you smile or that are so ridiculous they are funny. This can be as simple as noticing the antics of a pet, joking with the nurse about how absurd you look with the oxygen tubes in your nose or without any hair, or kindly teasing the doctor about their bedside manner.

- **Get your affairs in order.**

  ° Work with an attorney to finalize documents such as your will, living will, property transfer, and power of attorney. You'll want to make sure you identify your beneficiaries and make any necessary financial arrangements to care for them after your death. In addition, finalize your funeral arrangements so your loved ones can honor your wishes.

  ° Give necessary permissions and passwords for online accounts to a trusted person.

  ° Sign up to donate your organs if desired.

Copyright © 2026 Debra Burdick, *The Psychotherapy Toolbox for Chronic Illness and Chronic Pain*. All rights reserved.

- **Make your wishes heard about how you want to die.**

  ° List things you want to do before dying. For example: "I want to attend my grandson's wedding before I die" or "I want to go for a ride by my favorite places before I die."

  ° List how you would like to die, including:

    – Where you want to be when you die, such as at home or in the hospital, in bed, or perhaps sitting in nature.

    – Who you want with you, such as family, loved ones, friends, a religious leader, or alone. Do you prefer solitude or being surrounded by friends and family?

    – Who can advocate for you if you can't, such as a family member, loved one, or patient advocate.

    – What cultural practices, rituals, and customs are important to you, such as last rites, prayer, chanting, or meditation.

    – How alert and social you want to be up until you pass. Would you rather be medicated more for pain or be more alert?

- **Process your life's meaning thus far.**

  ° Review relationships you have or have had with those you love and those that love you. Think about each loved one, what they mean to you, and how that relationship has impacted your life.

  ° Review your work and how you've contributed to helping others. This can include jobs, volunteering, caregiving, art, writing, or any other contributions that you consider part of your life's work. Think about the places you have worked, the work you have done, and the impact your work has had.

  ° Review what you love about your life and what you are proud of. Spend some time remembering the parts of your life that were wonderful and what you are most proud of, such as family or accomplishments.

 Copyright © 2026 Debra Burdick, *The Psychotherapy Toolbox for Chronic Illness and Chronic Pain*. All rights reserved.

- **Practice gratitude.**

  - Remind yourself what you are grateful for. Make a list or mentally review those things in your lifetime that you are thankful for and express your gratitude when possible.

- **Practice forgiveness.**

  - Forgive those who have hurt you. Make a list and forgive them one by one in your mind or by writing them a note or email.

  - Ask for forgiveness from those who feel you have hurt them. Contact them via phone, email, or mail to do so.

- **Protect yourself from unwanted medical procedures.**

  - Be clear and strong with the medical providers about what treatments you want.

  - Know when it's time to stop trying not to die and discontinue treatment.

  - Give control to a trusted person who will do what you want, such as a loved one, family member, or doctor.

- **Experience as little pain as possible.**

  - Physical pain: Use pain medication to strike a balance that feels right to you, between managing pain and maintaining alertness.

  - Spiritual pain: Talk with loved ones and a person of your faith about your beliefs and how to find solace.

  - Emotional pain: Talk with a therapist, friends, and loved ones to seek comfort and process the feelings dying is bringing up for you.

- **Say goodbye.**

  - When you are ready, say goodbye to friends, family, loved ones, and life as you know it. Do this in person, by phone, with a video call, or through a mailed or emailed note.

Copyright © 2026 Debra Burdick, *The Psychotherapy Toolbox for Chronic Illness and Chronic Pain*. All rights reserved.

SECTION 6

Positive Affirmations

Affirmation Overview

Background: This section contains 14 affirmations clients can use to reinforce and consolidate the skills in the rest of the book. The affirmations generally fit into the following categories.

Trauma, Worry, Pain, Safety	6.6: *All Is Well* 6.7: *It's Going to be Alright* 6.11: *I Am Safe*
Negative Self-Talk	6.1: *I Am Getting Well* 6.2: *That Feels Better* 6.4: *I Can Feel Better* 6.10: *Things I Say to Myself*
Mood	6.5: *I Am Thankful* 6.8: *I Feel Happy*
Self-Compassion	6.3: *I Do What I Need To* 6.9: *I Am Kind to Myself* 6.12: *I Love Myself*
Motivation to Heal	6.13: *My "Why"*
Nociplastic Pain	6.14: *Rewire Nociplastic Pain*

The Skill in Action: *AJ was referred to a therapist by his cardiologist, who was treating him for coronary artery disease. Before AJ began therapy, he was pretty set in his ways, as he had a steady stream of negative thinking, leading him to always catastrophize and predict the worst. With the help of his therapist, he began learning how to reframe and defuse from his negative automatic thoughts. Since this was a slow process, his therapist also suggested that he try incorporating some positive affirmations into his daily routine. AJ was skeptical at first, but he agreed to choose a few affirmations that he felt could help him, including "It's going to be alright," which was a phrase he used to tell himself but had stopped since becoming ill. He set an alarm on his phone to remind him to repeat this phrase throughout the day, and after a few weeks, he noticed his mood was more positive and his thoughts were more hopeful. He wasn't sure why, but he also noticed it was easier to accept changes to his diet that supported his health.*

Skill Building: Guide the client to choose a few affirmations from this section that particularly resonate with them, and encourage them to print out these affirmations or write them down in the notes section of their phone so they can review them between sessions. The goal is for them to incorporate these affirmations into their daily life, so you might suggest that they set a timer to remind them to practice. There are even affirmation apps available, which the client can use to choose or create affirmations and schedule notifications to remind them of these helpful words or phrases. Once they get into the habit of using these affirmations, explore whether they experience any changes when it comes to their mood, thoughts, or behaviors.

Reflection: Use the reflection question provided in each affirmation.

Affirmation 6.1
I Am Getting Well

Background: This affirmation rewires your brain to facilitate healing. It reminds you that you have everything you need to heal. Through a process called "remembered wellness," you recreate health by encouraging your brain to remember how it feels to feel well.

Affirmation:

....

Repeat the following aloud throughout the day. Do your best to ignore any doubts that pop up:

"I am getting well.

My mind and body have everything they need to heal.

I am feeling better and better.

I love how I feel when I am well.

I am remembering how I feel when I am completely well."

....

Reflection: Notice what changes in your mind and body when you practice this affirmation and when you remember what it feels like to be free of pain or illness.

Affirmation 6.2
That Feels Better

Background: This affirmation reminds you to try to find a more uplifting thought whenever you find yourself feeling defeated, hopeless, or in pain. For example, you can replace the thought "My pain is never going to go away" with "My pain was better last week, and I expect that it will ease again soon." Practice it regularly and soon you will notice that you're having more positive thoughts than negative ones.

Affirmation:

....

Repeat the following:

"When I feel bad,

I will feel better when

I find a thought that feels better."

Practice finding a thought that feels better throughout your day.

....

Reflection: What unhelpful or negative thoughts have you been able to replace with more helpful, realistic, and positive thoughts? Are you noticing fewer negative thoughts?

Affirmation 6.3
I Do What I Need To

Background: This affirmation helps you reprogram your subconscious mind to stay laser-focused on taking the best care of yourself during chronic illness or pain. It helps you remember and motivate yourself to do what needs to be done to support your well-being.

Affirmation:

....

Repeat this out loud several times a day to help you stay focused on creating well-being:

"I do whatever

self-care skills I need to do

to support my well-being."

....

Reflection: What self-care skills are you currently practicing? What more can you do?

Affirmation 6.4
I Can Feel Better

Background: This affirmation helps you focus your mind on feeling better instead of on your illness. By practicing motivating self-talk, you can shift to a more positive mindset. Use it to stay focused on feeling better, especially when your illness or pain is making you feel stuck.

Affirmation:

....

Say the following out loud three times:

"I can do whatever I focus my mind on.

If I can imagine it, then I can do it.

Therefore, I can feel better if I focus my mind on feeling better."

....

Reflection: In what ways has affirming your capabilities allowed you to feel better? Be specific.

Affirmation 6.5
I Am Thankful

Background: This affirmation helps you remember all the things you have to be thankful for. Gratitude can improve both happiness and health by teaching you to shift to a more positive mindset and helping you feel more motivated to take care of yourself.

Affirmation:

....

Repeat the following out loud:

"I am thankful for who I am.

I am thankful for what I have.

I am thankful for my family.

I am thankful for my friends.

I am thankful for my food.

I am thankful for my home.

I am thankful for my work.

I am thankful for my health.

I am thankful for my faith.

I am thankful for ____ [*Add your own*]."

....

Reflection: How does being thankful shift your thoughts and mood?

Affirmation 6.6
All Is Well

Background: This affirmation helps you shift your mind and body into a safe place by breathing in and then slowly exhaling while reciting "All is well." This breathing pattern calms the sympathetic nervous system and helps you feel more relaxed. This breathing and affirmation practice reminds your brain that you are safe.

Affirmation:

....

Inhale through your nose as you slowly count to four . . . 1, 2, 3, 4.

Then exhale through your mouth as you count to eight . . . 1, 2, 3, 4, 5, 6, 7, 8.

Now silently say, "All is well."

Repeat these steps for four breath cycles several times every day.

Notice what shifts in your mind and body when you do this.

....

Reflection: How does doing this breathing technique calm you? How does affirming that all is well change how you feel?

Affirmation 6.7
It's Going to Be Alright

Background: Worry, stress, and pain can make your muscles tense up, which interferes with healing and exacerbates the experience of pain. This affirmation helps you feel calmer and safer by reminding yourself that everything is going to be alright.

Affirmation:

....

Whenever you feel worried, scared, or stressed, repeat this out loud four times:

"Everything is going to be alright."

Notice how you feel before and after doing this.

Print out an image that makes you smile, such as a photo of a kitten, to post alongside this affirmation. Post it where you can see it as a reminder to practice.

....

Reflection: How does affirming that everything is going to be alright help you feel safe? How does it change your stress level or pain?

Affirmation 6.8
I Feel Happy

Background: This affirmation helps you feel better by tuning into the many things that make you feel happy. Notice how you can shift your mood when you deliberately think about things that bring you joy or that have made you happy in the past. Use it whenever you notice you are feeling down or when you become overly focused on your illness or pain.

Affirmation:

....

Read the following out loud:

"I feel happy when . . .

I smile.

I think thoughts that feel good.

I help someone.

I remember a happy time.

I see family that I love.

I do something I enjoy.

I notice this moment.

I complete a task.

I am outside in nature.

I meditate.

I am thankful.

_____ [Add your own]."

....

Reflection: How does remembering these happy times shift your mood?

Affirmation 6.9
I Am Kind to Myself

Background: This affirmation reminds you to be kind to yourself and to treat yourself with self-compassion when you are feeling defeated, hopeless, angry, ashamed, or inadequate as a result of your chronic illness or pain. Saying this out loud every day will remind you to notice and replace any unkind self-talk and encourage you to implement self-compassion instead.

Affirmation:

Say this out loud:

"I am kind to myself.

I treat myself well.

I speak kind words.

I replace unkind thoughts with kind thoughts.

I replace unkind self-talk with kind self-talk."

Then practice treating yourself with self-compassion every day.

Reflection: How does it feel to extend kindness and compassion toward yourself? Are you able to be as kind to yourself as you are to others?

Affirmation 6.10
Things I Say to Myself

Background: This affirmation reminds you that you are good enough, kind, and caring and that you can allow yourself to feel well. This helps you interrupt any negative self-talk that might be getting in your way and replaces it with positive statements that help you feel better

Affirmation:

....

Say this out loud:

"I am good enough.

I believe in myself.

I am kind.

I am caring.

I am brave.

I allow myself to feel well."

....

Reflection: What negative self-talk can you replace with this affirmation?

Affirmation 6.11
I Am Safe

Background: This affirmation encourages you to remember a time or situation when you felt completely safe and to go there in your mind during times of difficulty. This helps your mind and body turn down the stress response. It also replaces your brain's danger signal (caused by pain, trauma, fear, or worry) with a safe signal.

Affirmation:

....

Think of a time when you felt completely safe or imagine a situation where you feel safe.

Use this memory or image to create a safe haven in your mind.

Go there in your mind whenever you need to as you repeat out loud:

"I am safe."

....

Reflection: Notice how your body feels when you feel safe.

Affirmation 6.12
I Love Myself

Background: This affirmation encourages you to practice sending love to yourself. When you can extend unconditional care and love to yourself, it helps to silence your inner critic and reminds you that you are lovable.

Affirmation:

....

Look in the mirror at yourself, focusing on your face.

Smile and then say this out loud three times:

"I love you, [*your name*]."

Notice how you feel after you do this.

Keep doing this until you can really feel the love you have for yourself without judgment.

....

Reflection: How can you remember to love yourself as much as you love others?

Affirmation 6.13
My "Why"

Background: Having a compelling reason to get well can be a powerful motivator in your healing journey. That's because your "why" can motivate you to take care of yourself and keep you focused on getting well. Use this affirmation to get in touch with, and to remind yourself, of your "why." This affirmation operationalizes the work you did in Skill 5.3: *My Reasons*.

Affirmation:

....

Repeat out loud several times daily:

"I want to be alive and well because _____

[*fill in with your list, which may change periodically*]."

Allow yourself to feel and gently accept the emotions that arise while doing this.

....

Reflection: How does reminding yourself of your reasons for living and being well change how you manage illness or pain?

Affirmation 6.14
Rewire Nociplastic Pain

Background: Affirmations are particularly helpful in calming the brain when chronic pain has become nociplastic and the brain is no longer responding appropriately to body sensations. Choose several of the following affirmations that resonate with you to activate a feeling of safety and change any "danger signals" in the brain to "safety signals." Practice saying the affirmations while standing in a powerful pose, such as the yoga warrior pose, or put your hands on your hips, place your feet in a wide stance, and feel strong, powerful, and safe.

Affirmations:

Repeat affirmations like the following out loud several times a day and whenever you notice pain:

"I am safe."

"I'll be fine."

"I'm strong."

"I'm getting better."

"There is nothing wrong with me."

"I'm healthy."

"I'm in charge."

"My brain has simply been overreacting and is calming itself now."

"My brain is learning to respond appropriately to my pain."

"I can notice my pain and still feel safe."

"I laugh to train my brain to know that I am safe."

Reflection: Notice how you feel before and after repeating these affirmations. How does your pain change?

References

You can find a free PDF of the worksheets and handouts from this book, which you can download and print for your use with clients, at www.pesipubs.com/chronicillnesspain. You can also find the audio versions of the guided meditations that accompany some of the skills at www.thebrainlady.com/pesi-meditations.

Al Hamid, A., Beckett, R., Wilson, M., Jalal, Z., Cheema, E., Al-Jumeily Obe, D., Coombs, T., Ralebitso-Senior, K., & Assi, S. (2024). Gender bias in diagnosis, prevention, and treatment of cardiovascular diseases: A systematic review. *Cureus, 16*(2), Article e54264. https://doi.org/10.7759/cureus.54264

Alexander, E. (2012). *Proof of heaven: A neurosurgeon's journey into the afterlife.* Simon & Schuster.

American Psychiatric Association. (2022). *Diagnostic and statistical manual of mental disorders* (5th ed., text rev.). https://doi.org/10.1176/appi.books.9780890425787

Ashar, Y. K., Gordon, A., Schubiner, H., Uipi, C., Knight, K., Anderson, Z., Carlisle, J., Polisky, L., Geuter, S., Flood, T. F., Kragel, P. A., Dimidjian, S., Lumley, M. A., & Wager, T. D. (2022). Effect of pain reprocessing therapy vs placebo and usual care for patients with chronic back pain: A randomized clinical trial. *JAMA Psychiatry, 79*(1), 13–23. https://doi.org/10.1001/jamapsychiatry.2021.2669

Benson, H. (2000). *The relaxation response* (Updated ed.). William Morrow Paperbacks.

Buttorff, C., Ruder, T., & Bauman, M. (2017). *Multiple chronic conditions in the United States.* RAND Corporation. https://www.rand.org/pubs/tools/TL221.html

Cascio, C. N., O'Donnell, M. B., Tinney, F. J., Lieberman, M. D., Taylor, S. E., Strecher, V. J., & Falk, E. B. (2016). Self-affirmation activates brain systems associated with self-related processing and reward and is reinforced by future orientation. *Social Cognitive and Affective Neuroscience, 11*(4), 621–629. https://doi.org/10.1093/scan/nsv136

Cousins, N. (1979). *Anatomy of an illness: As perceived by the patient* (20th anniversary ed.). W. W. Norton.

Diotaiuti, P., Corrado, S., Tosti, B., Spica, G., Di Libero, T., D'Oliveira, A., Zanon, A., Rodio, A., Andrade, A., & Mancone, S. (2024). Evaluating the effectiveness of neurofeedback in chronic pain management: A narrative review. *Frontiers in Psychology, 15*, Article 1369487. https://doi.org/10.3389/fpsyg.2024.1369487

Elma, Ö., Brain, K., & Dong, H.-J. (2022). The importance of nutrition as a lifestyle factor in chronic pain management: A narrative review. *Journal of Clinical Medicine, 11*(19), Article 5950. https://doi.org/10.3390/jcm11195950

Felitti, V. J., Anda, R. F., Nordenberg, D., Williamson, D. F., Spitz, A. M., Edwards, V., Koss, M. P., & Marks, J. S. (1998). Relationship of childhood abuse and household dysfunction to many of the leading causes of death in adults: The Adverse Childhood Experiences (ACE) Study. *American Journal of Preventive Medicine, 14*(4), 245–258. https://doi.org/10.1016/s0749-3797(98)00017-8

Fiorillo, A., de Girolamo, G., Simunovic, I. F., Gureje, O., Isaac, M., Lloyd, C., Mari, J., Patel, V., Reif, A., Starostina, E., Summergrad, P., & Sartorius, N. (2023). The relationship between physical and mental health: An update from the WPA Working Group on Managing Comorbidity of Mental and Physical Health. *World Psychiatry, 22*(1), 169–170. https://doi.org/10.1002/wps.21055

Fitzcharles, M.-A., Cohen, S. P., Clauw, D. J., Littlejohn, G., Usui, C., & Häuser, W. (2021). Nociplastic pain: Towards an understanding of prevalent pain conditions. *The Lancet, 397*(10289), 2098–2110. https://doi.org/10.1016/S0140-6736(21)00392-5

Friedrich, M. J. (1999). The arts of healing. *JAMA, 281*(19), 1779–1781. https://doi.org/10.1001/jama.281.19.1779

Gallant, M. P. (2003). The influence of social support on chronic illness self-management: A review and directions for research. *Health Education & Behavior, 30*(2), 170–195. https://doi.org/10.1177/1090198102251030

George, S. Z., & Zeppieri, G., Jr. (2009). Physical therapy utilization of graded exposure for patients with low back pain. *Journal of Orthopaedic & Sports Physical Therapy, 39*(7), 496–505. https://www.jospt.org/doi/10.2519/jospt.2009.2983

Gordon, A., & Ziv, A. (2021). *The way out: A revolutionary, scientifically proven approach to healing chronic pain.* Avery.

Greenwood, M. (2020, January 15). *Harmful effects of ageism on older persons' health found in 45 countries.* Yale News. https://news.yale.edu/2020/01/15/harmful-effects-ageism-older-persons-health-found-45-countries

Hamed, S., Bradby, H., Ahlberg, B. M., & Thapar-Björkert, S. (2022). Racism in healthcare: A scoping review. *BMC Public Health, 22*(1), Article 988. https://doi.org/10.1186/s12889-022-13122-y

Hilton, L., Hempel, S., Ewing, B. A., Apaydin, E., Xenakis, L., Newberry, S., Colaiaco, B., Maher, A. R., Shanman, R. M., Sorbero, M. E., & Maglione, M. A. (2017). Mindfulness meditation for chronic pain: Systematic review and meta-analysis. *Annals of Behavioral Medicine, 51*(2), 199–213. https://doi.org/10.1007/s12160-016-9844-2

Hoffman, K. M., Trawalter, S., Axt, J. R., & Oliver, M. N. (2016). Racial bias in pain assessment and treatment recommendations, and false beliefs about biological differences between blacks and whites. *Proceedings of the National Academy of Sciences, 113*(16), 4296–4301. https://doi.org/10.1073/pnas.1516047113

International Association for the Study of Pain. (2024). *Pain terminology.* https://www.iasp-pain.org/resources/terminology

Jacobson, E. (1929). *Progressive relaxation.* University of Chicago Press.

Karimov-Zwienenberg, M., Symphor, W., Peraud, W., & Décamps, G. (2024). Childhood trauma, PTSD/CPTSD and chronic pain: A systematic review. *PLOS ONE, 19*(8), Article e0309332. https://doi.org/10.1371/journal.pone.0309332

Keng, S.-L., Smoski, M. J., & Robins, C. J. (2011). Effects of mindfulness on psychological health: A review of empirical studies. *Clinical Psychology Review, 31*(6), 1041–1056. https://doi.org/10.1016/j.cpr.2011.04.006

Koenig, H. G. (2012). Religion, spirituality, and health: The research and clinical implications. *International Scholarly Research Notices, 2012*(1), Article 278730. https://doi.org/10.5402/2012/278730

Linehan, M. M. (2014). *DBT skills training manual* (2nd ed.). Guilford Press.

Liu, Y.-Z., Wang, Y.-X., & Jiang, C.-L. (2017). Inflammation: The common pathway of stress-related diseases. *Frontiers in Human Neuroscience, 11*, Article 316. https://doi.org/10.3389/fnhum.2017.00316

Luo, M. S., Chui, E. W. T., & Li, L. W. (2020). The longitudinal associations between physical health and mental health among older adults. *Aging & Mental Health, 24*(12), 1990–1998. https://doi.org/10.1080/13607863.2019.1655706

Mariotti, A. (2015). The effects of chronic stress on health: New insights into the molecular mechanisms of brain-body communication. *Future Science OA, 1*(3), Article FSO23. https://doi.org/10.4155/fso.15.21

McCracken, L. M., & Vowles, K. E. (2014). Acceptance and commitment therapy and mindfulness for chronic pain: Model, process, and progress. *The American Psychologist, 69*(2), 178–187. https://doi.org/10.1037/a0035623

Miller, W. R., & Rollnick, S. (2023). *Motivational interviewing: helping people change and grow* (4th ed.). Guilford Press.

Mosunic, C. (n.d.). *Compassion fatigue: What it is, symptoms, and 10 ways to cope.* https://blog.calm.com/blog/compassion-fatigue

Murphy, A. E., Minhas, D., Clauw, D. J., & Lee, Y. C. (2023). Identifying and managing nociplastic pain in individuals with rheumatic diseases: A narrative review. *Arthritis Care & Research, 75*(10), 2215–2222. https://doi.org/10.1002/acr.25104

National LGBTQIA+ Health Education Center. (2016, February 17). *Providing inclusive services and care for LGBT people: A guide for health care staff.* https://www.lgbtqiahealtheducation.org/publication/learning-guide

Oarga, C., Stavrova, O., & Fetchenhauer, D. (2015). When and why is helping others good for well-being? The role of belief in reciprocity and conformity to society's expectations. *European Journal of Social Psychology, 45*(2), 242–254. https://doi.org/10.1002/ejsp.2092

Patel, K., Sutherland, H., Henshaw, J., Taylor, J. R., Brown, C. A., Casson, A. J., Trujillo-Barreton, N. J., Jones, A. K. P., & Sivan, M. (2020). Effects of neurofeedback in the management of chronic pain: A systematic review and meta-analysis of clinical trials. *European Journal of Pain, 24*(8), 1440–1457. https://doi.org/10.1002/ejp.1612

Ranganathan, V. K., Siemionow, V., Liu, J. Z., Sahgal, V., & Yue, G. H. (2004). From mental power to muscle power—gaining strength by using the mind. *Neuropsychologia, 42*(7), 944–956. https://doi.org/10.1016/j.neuropsychologia.2003.11.018

Reblin, M., & Uchino, B. N. (2008). Social and emotional support and its implication for health. *Current Opinion in Psychiatry, 21*(2), 201–205. https://doi.org/10.1097/YCO.0b013e3282f3ad89

Rikard, S. M., Strahan, A. E., Schmit, K. M., & Guy, G. P., Jr. (2023, April 14). Chronic pain among adults — United States, 2019–2021. *Morbidity and Mortality Weekly Report, 72,* 379–385. Centers for Disease Control and Prevention. http://dx.doi.org/10.15585/mmwr.mm7215a1

Samulowitz, A., Gremyr, I., Eriksson, E., & Hensing, G. (2018). "Brave men" and "emotional women": A theory-guided literature review on gender bias in health care and gendered norms towards patients with chronic pain. *Pain Research & Management, 2018*(1), Article 6358624. https://doi.org/10.1155/2018/6358624

Schubiner, H. (2022). *Unlearn your pain workbook: A 28-day process to reprogram your brain* (4th ed.). Mind Body Publishing.

Siqveland, J., Hussain, A., Lindstrøm, J. C., Ruud, T., & Hauff, E. (2017). Prevalence of posttraumatic stress disorder in persons with chronic pain: A meta-analysis. *Frontiers in Psychiatry, 8,* Article 164. https://doi.org/10.3389/fpsyt.2017.00164

Tang, Y.-Y., Hölzel, B. K., & Posner, M. I. (2015). The neuroscience of mindfulness meditation. *Nature Reviews Neuroscience, 16*(4), 213–225. https://doi.org/10.1038/nrn3916

Turner, K. A. (2015). *Radical remission: Surviving cancer against all odds.* Harper One.

van der Kolk, B. (2014). *The body keeps the score: Brain, mind, and body in the healing of trauma.* Penguin Books.

White, M. P., Alcock, I., Grellier, J., Wheeler, B. W., Hartig, T., Warber, S. L., Bone, A., Depledge, M. H., & Fleming, L. E. (2019). Spending at least 120 minutes a week in nature is associated with good health and wellbeing. *Scientific Reports, 9*(1), Article 7730. https://doi.org/10.1038/s41598-019-44097-3

Zeidan, F., & Vago, D. R. (2016). Mindfulness meditation-based pain relief: A mechanistic account. *Annals of the New York Academy of Sciences, 1373*(1), 114–127. https://doi.org/10.1111/nyas.13153

Zoffness, R. (2024). *Cognitive behavioral therapy (CBT).* University of California San Francisco, Pain Management at UCSF. https://pain.ucsf.edu/nonpharmacological-pain-management/cognitive-behavioral-therapy-cbt

Acknowledgments

Many amazing people have contributed to the eventual writing of this book. I am deeply grateful for my faith, which supports and inspires me. I am forever thankful to the numerous mental health, medical, and alternative medicine providers who guided me through fifteen years of chronic illness and constant pain associated with fibromyalgia, chronic fatigue syndrome, leaky gut, and more. I treasure what I learned from mindfulness experts encountered along the way who taught me how to develop my own mindfulness practice, which helped me deal with my chronic illness (now thankfully resolved) and which continues to enrich my life in so many ways. I am repeatedly inspired by my former clients who always amazed me and taught me so much about dealing with chronic illness and pain as they used the skills included in this book to accept their condition, manage their symptoms, and thrive despite their illness. Many thanks to Kayla Church, my acquisitions editor at PESI, for supporting, encouraging, guiding, and refining my work. And a world of thanks to Jenessa Jackson for her meticulous, invaluable, and insightful editing. And last but not least, my heartfelt thanks to my husband, Al Zipperle, who encourages and lovingly supports me every day as I endeavor to help others.

About the Author

Debra Burdick, LCSW, BCN, also known as "The Brain Lady," is a national speaker and award-winning, best-selling author who retired from private practice, where she provided outpatient psychotherapy and neurotherapy for over 25 years. Debra specializes in mindfulness, ADHD, depression, anxiety, stress, chronic illness, chronic pain, and sleep. Throughout her career, she has been a pioneer in creating and teaching mindfulness skills to improve mental health. She is often praised for her ability to transform research results into actionable skills.

Debra originally created skills for helping those with medical illness to deal with her own chronic illness (thankfully healed). As a psychotherapist and neurotherapist—and through much study with leading experts in the field—she further developed and taught these skills in her private practice and an intensive outpatient program to adults with physical or mental illness. She also designed and facilitated groups for clients with chronic physical illness and presented a workshop for the National Association of Social Workers (NASW) titled *Psychotherapy for the Physically Ill Client.*

Debra is a seasoned and highly regarded speaker who has taught a variety of professional workshops nationally and online. Her other publications include *Radical Self-Care When You Are Ill* (2024), *Mindfulness Skills Workbook for Clinicians and Clients* (2013), and *Radical Self-Care When You Are Ill Card Deck* (2022), among others.

For more information about Debra's books, card deck, audios, and speaking, visit her website at www.TheBrainLady.com.